Plate 4/5/6 miss'g

" 1-2+3 "

THE HISTORY OF DECORATED
BOOKBINDING IN ENGLAND

THE HISTORY OF
DECORATED
BOOKBINDING
IN
ENGLAND

❧

HOWARD M. NIXON

AND

MIRJAM M. FOOT

CLARENDON PRESS · OXFORD

1992

Oxford University Press, Walton Street, Oxford OX2 6DP
Oxford New York Toronto
Delhi Bombay Calcutta Madras Karachi
Petaling Jaya Singapore Hong Kong Tokyo
Nairobi Dar es Salaam Cape Town
Melbourne Auckland
and associated companies in
Berlin Ibadan

Oxford is a trade mark of Oxford University Press

Published in the United States
by Oxford University Press, New York

British Library Cataloguing in Publication Data
Data available

Library of Congress Cataloging in Publication Data
Nixon, Howard.
The history of decorated bookbinding in England / by Howard Millar
Nixon. —Rev. and edited /by Mirjam Michaela Foot.
Includes index.
1. Bookbinding—England—Ornamental bindings—History. I. Foot,
Mirjam. II. Title.
Z269.3.O75N59 1992
686.3'6—dc20   91–11623
ISBN 0–19–818182–5

Typeset by Cambridge Composing (UK) Ltd
Printed in Great Britain by
Butler & Tanner Ltd
Frome and London

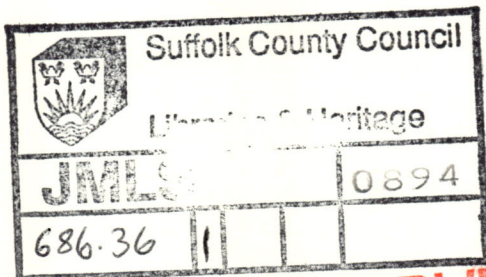

PREFACE

'THERE is one glaring omission among English books about books. No one has ever published a history of English bookbinding.' With these words Howard M. Nixon began the Lyell Lectures at the University of Oxford in 1979. He fully intended to rectify this omission by devoting these lectures to a general survey of the development of binding decoration in England from the earliest surviving example—the binding of the St Cuthbert Gospel, perhaps dating a little before the end of the seventh century AD—up to the beginning of the modern movement in the late nineteen-forties. However, his death on 18 February 1983 prevented him from bringing a lifelong ambition to fruition. Pressure of other work, such as the completion of the catalogue of the bindings in the Pepys Library at Magdalene College, Cambridge (published posthumously in 1984) had pushed the revision of the Lyell Lectures onto the back burner. When I inherited the typescript for these lectures with the request to prepare them for publication, I did not realize the extent of the work that still needed to be done.

I was faced with four main problems. The first was that six lectures were not sufficient to cover the whole history of English bookbinding. Howard Nixon deliberately limited himself to the history of decorated bookbinding. He was mainly concerned with fine binding in leather, with the styles and designs of decoration, and with the tools used to effect these designs. Consequently, the bindings he discussed are those at the top end of the market: presentation copies, collectors' items, grand bindings made by top craftsmen, rather than the run-of-the-mill products of the trade. The latter still await their historian. Binding techniques, their development and change, were not covered either.[1] After much thought, I decided not to tackle here either the history of binding structure or the history of common trade

---

[1] B. C. Middleton, *A History of English Craft Bookbinding Technique*, 2nd edn. (London, 1978) is the only comprehensive work on this subject.

binding. However fascinating these subjects are, and however great
the need is for an extended and comprehensive view of the development of the craft in England, it would have led me too far and
distracted too much from the original purpose of the book as Howard
Nixon envisaged it.

Secondly, the six lectures offered too little scope even to cover the
whole of English binding decoration. It is clear from the original
typescript which gaps Howard Nixon intended to fill and where he
planned to expand the text for publication. I have tried to the best of
my ability to provide the missing portions. As anyone who has ever
attended lectures knows, a really coruscatingly good lecture rarely
provides a readable text. These lectures were no exception, and a fair
amount of rewriting could not be avoided. In addition, during the
time between the delivery of the lectures and the preparation of the
text for publication, some new facts have come to light and amend-
ments and modifications have been made accordingly.

Thirdly, when Howard Nixon gave his lectures he used on average
60 slides for each lecture. Not even the generosity of the Lyell
Electors and the Oxford University Press could run to such a wealth
of illustration, and the total number of plates had to be reduced to
just over a third. The fourth and most time-consuming problem was
the need to provide references. Having received my training in the
history of binding from Howard Nixon, it was, in the majority of
cases, not too difficult to supply references to the literature, although
some quotations proved more elusive.

It was Howard Nixon's decision to discuss only bindings produced
in England. Scottish binding up to 1650 had been covered by Dr W.
S. Mitchell,[2] and Mr J. H. Loudon has meanwhile published a study
of the very interesting and important Scottish bindings of the eighteenth century.[3] The most significant period of Irish binding has been
dealt with by Dr Maurice Craig,[4] and a little had been written about
Welsh bindings.[5] Since the most important Welsh bindery, that of the

[2] W. S. Mitchell, *A History of Scottish Bookbinding 1432 to 1650* (Edinburgh, 1955).

[3] J. H. Loudon, *James Scott and William Scott, Bookbinders* (London, 1980).

[4] M. J. Craig, *Irish Bookbindings, 1600–1800* (London, 1954). Id., *Irish Bookbindings* (The Irish Heritage Series vi) (Dublin, 1976). A recent book on *Gold-Tooled Bookbindings Commissioned by Trinity College Dublin in the Eighteenth Century* by J. McDonnell and P. Healy was published by the Irish Georgian Society, Leixlip, in 1987.

[5] H. M. Vaughan, 'Cardiganshire Book-Binders', *Journal of the Welsh Bibliographical Society*, 2 (1916), 71–2. E. Rees, 'Bookbinding in 18th-Century Wales', ibid. 12 (1983–4), 51–66.

Gregynog Press, was run for most of its life by an Englishman, it will be briefly mentioned in Chapter Six.

Howard Nixon did not want to bring the history of decorated bookbinding in England right up to date, so as to avoid passing judgement inadvertently on living and still-active artists and craftsmen. The book closes, nevertheless, with the work of Edgar Mansfield who, though still alive at the time of writing, was too influential a figure to be left out.

M.M.F.

July 1988

ACKNOWLEDGEMENTS

I gratefully acknowledge the permission of the following owners to repro-
duce bindings from their collections:

Trustees for Roman Catholic Purposes Registered: pl. 1.
Dean and Chapter of Winchester: fig 1.
Pierpont Morgan Library, New York: pl. 3; figs. 60, 61, 74.
Bodleian Library, Oxford: figs. 2, 7, 19, 30.
British Library: pls. 2, 4, 7, 8, 9, 11, 12; figs. 5, 6, 8, 9, 10, 13, 14, 15, 17, 18,
    20, 21, 22, 23, 26, 27, 28, 36, 39, 41, 42, 45, 48, 49, 50, 51, 52, 54, 56, 62,
    63, 64, 65, 66, 68, 69, 70, 71, 72, 73, 75, 77, 79, 80, 81, 82, 83, 84, 85, 86,
    87, 88, 89, 90, 91, 92, 94, 96, 97, 98, 99, 100, 101, 103, 104, 105, 106, 107,
    108, 109, 110, 111, 112, 114, 115, 116, 117, 118, 119, 120, 121, 122, 123,
    124, 125, 126, 127, 128.
Dean and Chapter of Durham: fig. 3.
Master and Fellows of St John's College, Cambridge: fig. 4.
Durham University Library: pl. 5; figs. 35, 37, 53.
National Library of Wales: pl. 6.
Her Majesty the Queen: pl. 10; fig. 44.
Archbishop of Canterbury and the Trustees of Lambeth Palace Library: figs.
    11, 25.
Dean and Chapter of Westminster: figs. 12, 102.
National Museums & Galleries on Merseyside, Liverpool Museum: fig. 16.
Governors of Chetham's Library, Manchester: fig. 24.
Master and Fellows of University College, Oxford: fig. 29.
Governing Body of Christ Church, Oxford: figs. 31, 34.
Master and Fellows of Trinity Hall, Cambridge: fig. 32.
Master and Fellows of Balliol College, Oxford: fig. 33.
Huntington Library, San Marino, California: figs. 38, 55, 57, 95, 113.
Warden and Fellows of Keble College, Oxford: fig. 40.
President and Fellows of St John's College, Oxford: fig. 43.
Syndics of Cambridge University Library: fig. 46.
Spencer Collection, New York Public Library, Astor, Lenox and Tilden
    Foundations: fig. 47.
Controller of Her Majesty's Stationery Office: fig. 58.
Dean of Windsor: fig. 59.

Master and Fellows of Magdalene College, Cambridge: figs. 67, 78.
Provost and Fellows of Eton College: fig. 76.
Mr A. G. Thomas: fig. 93.

I owe a particular debt of gratitude to librarians in the libraries and institutions mentioned above; to my colleagues in the British Library, especially to Ian Willison, Philippa Marks, and Angela Paige; to Mrs Enid Nixon for her generosity in giving me access to Howard Nixon's rubbings, for her help with proofreading and for compiling the index; and to my husband for his forbearance and unfailing support. To Howard Nixon I owe more than I shall ever be able to express.

CONTENTS

———

LIST OF COLOUR PLATES

————

LIST OF FIGURES

———

From the Beginning to 1520

THE history of English bookbinding gets off to an excellent start in that we may lay a well-founded claim to the honour of having produced the earliest surviving decorated European binding, that which covers the St Cuthbert Gospel (Pl. 1). It is a very small book—137 × 95 mm.—and, miraculously, it is still almost in its original condition. It covers a beautifully written copy of the Gospel of St John that was quite probably bound as early as AD 698, when the decorated coffin was made for the elevation of St Cuthbert's remains at Lindisfarne, on the inner lid of which the book was said to have been found.[1] Nothing about the manuscript or the binding suggests that they are not as early as this date. But between the elevation of St Cuthbert's remains at Lindisfarne in 698 and the translation of his body to Durham in 1104, by which time the Gospel was certainly in the tomb, there were several occasions when the outer lid of the tomb was opened and the book could have been added. The year 698 therefore cannot be taken to be firmly proven as the date by which the book was bound, but such a date seems plausible. It is particularly interesting in that the two covers are treated by different techniques, and it is the combination of these techniques that makes it certain that the binding is British. The upper cover's embossed floral design, effected by moulding the leather, possibly over gesso or over cords previously glued to the covers, bears some relationship to Egyptian and Coptic leatherwork of the seventh to the ninth centuries. However, the step design on the lower cover is very close to designs found in the decoration of the

---

[1] T. J. Brown (ed.), *The Stonyhurst Gospel of Saint John* (Oxford (Roxburghe Club), 1969), 13–23, 45–55, frontispiece, pl. 1.

Echternach and Lindisfarne Gospels, both of which may well have
been made at Lindisfarne about the year 698,[2] and designs of that
kind have no counterparts in Egyptian leatherwork or Coptic binding.
Traces of colour are found in the incised lines on the binding.

The binding closest to that of the St Cuthbert Gospel is that which
covers the Cadmug Codex, one of the three bindings at Fulda on
manuscripts believed to have belonged to St Boniface, the English
apostle to the Germans (680–754). Two of these bindings, the
Cadmug Codex (MS Bonifatianus III) and the Victor Codex (MS
Bonifatianus I), are probably English; as St Boniface was aged 38
before he first visited Germany this is quite plausible. The Cadmug
Codex is even smaller than the St Cuthbert Gospel (127 × 100 mm.),
and according to Dr Berthe van Regemorter, these two small books
have much in common.[3] She instances the similarity of the leather and
the boards, of the sewing and of the decoration, and continues 'Ces
deux volumes sont frères'. Its decoration is in fact much simpler than
that of the St Cuthbert volume. It consists of a St Andrew's cross of
lines dividing the covers into four triangles, each containing a
triquetra. The impressed or incised lines on the covers appear to have
been coloured with gold. An inscription in a late ninth-century
minuscule shows that the tradition that the book belonged to St
Boniface can at least be traced back to that date. This is mentioned in
an article by Dr D. M. (now Sir David) Wilson in the *Antiquaries
Journal*, which deals mainly with the second of the St Boniface
manuscripts, the Victor Codex.[4] This is a sixth-century manuscript
twice as tall as it is wide (285 × 143 mm.), whose shape suggests that
it may perhaps have had an ivory diptych as its original covers. Its
present binding differs considerably from the other two bindings
suggested as English. Being notably smaller, they do not need clasps
or catches nor the metal work used on the Victor Codex. Sir David
believes that the metal mounts were made in Northumbria at the end
of the seventh or the beginning of the eighth century. He shows the
pastedowns to be contemporary with or earlier than the leather
binding, and points out that the heavy vellum with a suede-like finish

---

[2] Brown, op. cit. 22. See also G. D. Hobson, *English Binding before 1500* (Cambridge, 1929), pl. I (where both covers are illustrated).

[3] B. van Regemorter, 'La Reliure des manuscrits de S. Cuthbert et de S. Boniface', *Scriptorium*, 3: I (1949), 45–51. H. Loubier, *Der Bucheinband* (Leipzig, 1926), 67, fig. 65.

[4] D. M. Wilson, 'An Anglo-Saxon Bookbinding at Fulda', *Antiquaries Journal*, 41 (1961), 199–217, pls. XXXV–XXXVII.

to the surface used for the pastedowns is characteristic of manuscripts written in the British Isles. He concludes that the whole binding is English, probably Northumbrian, and that it is likely to date from the first half of the eighth century. There seems no reason to connect the third of the Boniface codices at Fulda, the Codex Ragyndrudis, with England. Paul Needham[5] has pointed out that this early eighth-century manuscript has been attributed to the scriptorium of Luxeuil, in Franche-Comté, and the binding was presumably made on the Continent. From the eighth century we have to wait until the middle of the twelfth century before we next find decorated leather bindings being produced in England, for there is no reason to believe that any of the ninth- and tenth-century bindings discussed by Karl Christ[6] and G. D. Hobson[7] are English. Bindings made of other materials will be discussed at the end of this chapter.

At one time it was considered that all the so-called 'Romanesque' bindings of the twelfth and thirteenth centuries were English. The reason for this assumption was that the English examples were the first to be published. Weale[8] first drew attention to the group in 1894, by describing or mentioning twenty-two examples, of which eighteen were in English libraries. He not unnaturally assumed that this was an English style, possibly copied to some extent in France. But in 1929, when G. D. Hobson published *English Binding before 1500*, he recorded forty-seven examples, of which only twenty-one were in English libraries. 'The old English preponderance of ownership has gone', he wrote, 'and with it have gone the assumptions to which it gave rise'. In his 'Further Notes on Romanesque Bindings', published in *The Library* for September 1934, he brought the number of bindings up to a total of ninety, and considered that only eleven of these had been bound in the British Isles. In 1938 he increased this number to 106, adding two more English examples.[9] Of the 138

[5] P. Needham, *Twelve Centuries of Bookbindings: 400–1600* (New York, London, 1979), 58. See also H. Loubier, op. cit. 67, fig. 64.

[6] K. Christ, 'Karolingische Bibliothekseinbände', *Festschrift Georg Leyh* (Leipzig, 1937), 82–104.

[7] G. D. Hobson, 'Some Early Bindings and Binders' Tools', *The Library*, 4th ser., 19 (1938–9), 214–33.

[8] W. H. J. Weale, *Bookbindings and Rubbings of Bindings in the National Art Library, South Kensington*, ii (London, 1894).

[9] G. D. Hobson, 'Further Notes on Romanesque Bindings', *The Library*, 4th ser., 15 (1934–5), 161–211, pl. VIII. Id., 'Some Early Bindings and Binders' Tools', *The Library*, 4th ser., 19 (1938–9), 233–49, pls. III–VI.

Romanesque bindings now known, the majority were made in France and a few have been attributed to Germany and Austria.[10] The ten twelfth-century Romanesque bindings that really can be considered English can be allocated with reasonable certainty to their place of origin. Three seem to have been produced in Winchester and date from around 1150.[11] They are Hegesippus, *Historia de excidio Judaeorum*, from the Phillipps, William Morris, Yates Thompson, and Dyson Perrins collections, which is now MS XVII in the library of Winchester Cathedral (Hobson XXII), and which has not been rebound (Fig. 1); the Winton Domesday, now Society of Antiquaries MS 154 (Hobson V), which has been rebound, but appears to have the covers correctly replaced; and the Cartulary of St Swithin's, Winchester (Hobson XXI), the covers of which were probably reversed when it was first rebound in the fourteenth century; this book is Add. MS 15350 in the British Library and the binding is now preserved separately from the manuscript.

It should be pointed out that, while the second and third books are very closely connected with Winchester, a careful examination of the Hegesippus shows no sign that it was ever in the library of the cathedral priory, or Hyde Abbey, or St Mary's Abbey, Winchester during the Middle Ages. It has been attributed to Winchester because it shares seven of the ten tools used on the Winton Domesday and probably five that occur on the St Swithin's Cartulary. The Hegesippus and the Winton Domesday are bound in similar brown tanned leather with a smooth surface; the St Swithin's Cartulary is in tanned leather originally stained pink with a rough surface and with very worn impressions of the tools, so that it is not possible to identify any of these with complete certainty. Hobson originally believed that these Winchester bindings, two of which were most probably bound sometime during the years from 1148 to 1150, were the earliest of the whole series of Romanesque stamped bindings, but they are preceded by a number of glossed books of the Bible which were almost certainly bound in Paris for Henri, son of Louis

[10] C. F. R. de Hamel, *Glossed Books of the Bible and the Origins of the Paris Booktrade* (Woodbridge, 1984), 64–86. F. A. Schmidt-Künsemüller, *Die Abendländischen romanischen Blindstempeleinbände* (Stuttgart, 1985).

[11] H. M. Nixon, 'The Binding of the Winton Domesday' in M. Biddle (ed.), *Winchester Studies. 1. Winchester in the Early Middle Ages* (Oxford, 1976), 526–40. M. M. Foot, 'Bindings' in *English Romanesque Art, 1066–1200*, Arts Council exhibition (London, 1984), 342–9.

VI and brother of Louis VII of France, before he entered the monastery of Clairvaux c.1146. Dr Rosy Schilling suggested that four Paris bindings from the same shop may have been in the monastic library at Engelberg, Switzerland, by 1143.[12] Dr Christopher de Hamel has slightly reorganized Hobson's classification, and has established that the main groups of French Romanesque bindings were produced in Parisian monasteries and that the majority covered glossed books of the Bible. Their production ceased c.1200 with the establishment of the lay book trade in Paris.[13]

The nineteen tools used on the three Winchester bindings are mostly similar to those found on Paris Romanesque bindings, but the circular dragon tool, the segment of a circle with an acanthus scroll, and the cock have not been found elsewhere.[14] If the suggestion that the covers of the St Swithin's Cartulary have been reversed is correct, all three bindings had a design with two or three large circles on the upper cover and a rectangular pattern on the lower cover.

The three London bindings cover late twelfth-century manuscripts. Peter Lombard's *Sententiae* (Hobson XXIV), a manuscript that could be as early as 1185, belonged to Llanthony Priory and is now in the Bodleian Library (Fig. 2).[15] The *Inquisitio terrarum* of the Knights Templar in the Public Record Office (E. 164/16; Hobson XVII) must date from 1185 or very shortly thereafter.[16] A twelfth-century manuscript of Petrus Comestor, from the library of the Augustinian priory of St Mary Overy, Southwark, is now Egerton MS 272 in the British Library (Hobson XVIII).[17] This manuscript could also possibly be as early as 1185, so we may take that as the approximate date of this group of bindings.

The Bodleian Library's Peter Lombard is the largest of these three

[12] R. Schilling, 'Neue romanische Bucheinbände. 2. Engelberg', *Jahrbuch der Einbandkunst*, 3, 4 (1929–30), 15–31, esp. 21–2. This suggestion has been disputed by Prof. Dr F. A. Schmidt-Künsemüller, op. cit. 21.

[13] de Hamel, op. cit. The latest published work on the subject by Schmidt-Künsemüller (op. cit.) consists of a census of all known Romanesque bindings with a summary of the literature.

[14] These tools are respectively nos. 1, 4, and 11 on pl. x in H. M. Nixon, 'The Binding of the Winton Domesday' (see n. 11).

[15] S. Gibson, *Some Notable Bodleian Bindings* (Oxford, 1901–4), pls. 1, 2. Hobson, *English Binding before 1500* (Cambridge, 1929), pl. 8.

[16] Hobson, *English Binding before 1500*, pls. 6, 7. *English Romanesque Art*, no. 471.

[17] W. Y. Fletcher, *English Bookbindings in the British Museum* (London, 1895), pl. 11. *English Romanesque Art*, no. 473 and p. 346, where the London tools are illustrated.

books and has on one cover a circular disposition of the tools, similar to that found on the Winchester bindings of thirty-five years earlier, but now we find the circle on the lower cover. The other two bindings of the group are smaller and quite similar to one another. The Public Record Office Knights Templar Inquisition is practically unrestored. The semicircular tab at the head and traces of one at the tail, typical of these twelfth-century bindings when they have not been 'restored' away, are visible. Its decoration closely resembles that of the Egerton manuscript from Southwark, both having the same five vertical rows of tools, with rampant lions down the centre and horizontal rows of palmettes at head and tail on the upper cover. Altogether thirty-five tools have been used on these three bindings, thirty of them being found on the Peter Lombard. They form a closely knit group which is likely to have been bound within a period of a few years.

Durham Cathedral Library owns a four-volume manuscript Bible, written on vellum, c.1170–80 (Hobson VI–IX), that is now generally assumed to have been written in Durham Cathedral Priory. The volumes were rebound in 1845, but the original brown hide covers have been onlaid onto the new bindings (Fig. 3). They are tooled in blind to rectangular designs on one cover and circular designs on the other cover, but it is of course possible that in rebinding some of the covers were reversed. The Bible was bequeathed to Durham by Bishop Hugh de Puiset, also named Hugh Pudsey.[18] It is by no means certain that bindings of this sort were produced in Oxford. In 1929 G. D. Hobson mentioned an early thirteenth-century Romanesque binding on a manuscript, *Summa super Gratiani decretum*—now Add. MS 24659 in the British Library (Hobson XVI)—which he attributed to Oxford with the qualification 'the evidence in favour of . . . Oxford, is, I regret to say, particularly weak'.[19] Although he commented in 1934 'I remain convinced that one binding comes from Oxford',[20] the grounds for this conviction are none too firm and the origin of this binding should be treated as unknown rather than as Oxford.

Two other late-ish Romanesque bindings have been attributed to England: Hobson's 1938 additions to his list, numbers C and CVI. The

[18] Hobson, *English Binding before 1500*, pl. 9. *English Romanesque Art*, no. 474 and p. 348, where the Durham tools are illustrated.
[19] Hobson, *English Binding before 1500*, 5.
[20] Hobson, 'Further Notes on Romanesque Bindings', 164.

first of these is a thirteenth-century manuscript of medical tracts at St John's College, Cambridge, with the boards of the binding composed of leather instead of the usual wood (Fig. 4). The book appears to come from Mersea Priory, Essex. The second is a thirteenth-century manuscript collection of Latin sermons, now at Durham (Cosin MS v. II. 8). The manuscript has an inscription dated 1278 and the volume is listed in the Durham monastic catalogue of 1395. Also at Durham is what may be the only fourteenth-century English stamped binding, but as the original sides have been inlaid in a nineteenth-century binding these covers are particularly difficult to date.[21]

There are a number of books known from at least two workshops— one probably at Oxford, the other in London—which are tooled in close imitation of twelfth-century bindings, although the tools used on these are close copies and not survivors from the twelfth century. Egerton MS 2892 in the British Library is an example of the first group and is not likely to be much later than 1460.[22] Thirty-four bindings are now known to have been made in this shop. They cover books and manuscripts dated between c.1450 and 1489.[23] From the second shop comes an example in Westminster Abbey Library.[24] It is a copy of the *Epistolae familiares* of Marsilio Ficino printed in Venice in 1495, with as endleaves at each end, a pair of conjugate leaves of a *Prognostication* for 1502 by William Parron, printed by Pynson in [1501]; the binding of the Ficino cannot therefore be earlier than that date. The same three tools based on Romanesque Winchester models, with two additional ones, were used on the binding of a Terence, *Vulgaria*, printed by Machlinia c.1483, which was sold at one of the Phillipps sales at Sotheby's on 25 November 1974[25] and is now in the British Library (Fig. 5). The book had been rebound and was

[21] A. I. Doyle, 'Medieval Blind-Stamped Bindings Associated with Durham Cathedral Priory' in G. Colin (ed.), *De libris compactis miscellanea: Studia Bibliotheca Wittockiana*, i (Brussels, 1984), 31–42. The (?) 14th-century binding has been illustrated in Hobson, *English Binding before 1500*, app. C, 34–5, pl. 31.

[22] G. D. Hobson, *Bindings in Cambridge Libraries* (Cambridge, 1929), 10, no. VIII. Id., *English Binding before 1500*, pl. 35. G. Pollard, 'The Names of some English Fifteenth-Century Binders', *The Library*, 5th ser., 25 (1970), pl. III.

[23] M. M. Foot, 'English Decorated Bookbindings' in J. Griffiths and D. Pearsall (eds.), *Book Production and Publishing in Britain, 1375–1475* (Cambridge, 1989).

[24] CC. 24. Hobson, *English Binding before 1500*, pl. 54. Foot, 'English Decorated Bookbindings'.

[25] Lot 3205; the binding is illustrated in the catalogue. See also Foot, 'English Decorated Bookbindings'.

described in the catalogue as having the sides of a twelfth-century Winchester binding mounted on the sides of a nineteenth-century rebinding. But comparison with the Westminster Abbey book made it clear that this was the original early sixteenth-century binding of the Terence, preserved when the book was rebound.

J. B. Oldham carried out the main spadework on the history of blind-tooled binding in England, from its revival shortly after 1450 until large blind-tooled panels and rolls ceased to be generally used soon after the beginning of the seventeenth century.[26] He built on the work of W. H. J. Weale, whose rubbings are to be found in the Victoria and Albert Museum, and the excellent studies of blind-tooled binding at Oxford and Cambridge by Strickland Gibson[27] and G. J. Gray,[28] respectively. Oldham also expanded G. D. Hobson's pioneer study of English panel stamps,[29] in which with characteristic modesty Hobson claimed to have gained much of his knowledge from Oldham. Hobson had also written about the fifteenth-century English bindings decorated with single tools in *English Binding before 1500*, and Oldham expanded this in his contribution to the *Festschrift* for Ernst Kyriss, published in 1961.[30] Graham Pollard took this work a stage further in his important article on 'The Names of some English Fifteenth-Century Binders' in *The Library*, 5th ser., 25 (1970). Mirjam Foot's article on English decorated bookbindings between 1450 and 1500 was published in J. Griffiths and D. Pearsall (eds.), *Book Production and Publishing in Britain, 1375–1475*, Cambridge, 1989.

Nicolas Barker has made out quite a good case for London as the place of origin of the earliest fifteenth-century English bindings to exhibit blind tooling. In the second of his articles on 'A Register of Writs and the Scales Binder',[31] he brought to nineteen the number of bindings by this craftsman, first noticed by M. R. James and more

---

[26] J. B. Oldham, *Shrewsbury School Library Bindings* (Oxford, 1943). Id., *English Blind-Stamped Bindings* (Cambridge, 1952). Id., *Blind Panels of English Binders* (Cambridge, 1958).

[27] S. Gibson, *Early Oxford Bindings* (Oxford, 1903).

[28] G. J. Gray, *The Earlier Cambridge Stationers and Bookbinders* (Oxford, 1904).

[29] Hobson, *Blind-Stamped Panels in the English Book-Trade, c. 1485–1555* (London, 1944).

[30] J. B. Oldham, 'English Fifteenth-Century Binding' in *Festschrift Ernst Kyriss* (Stuttgart, 1961), 159–74.

[31] *Book Collector*, 21 (1972), 356–79.

fully discussed by Hobson.[32] Barker suggested that a manuscript in his own possession is likely to date from the 1450s and that twelve of the bindings may all be before 1465. A recently discovered example on a legal manuscript, now in the British Library (Fig. 6), may have been made c.1456–65. One of the bindings of this group first discovered by Albert Ehrman in the Guildhall Library (MS 208), bears the name of its original owner, Thomas Segden, and was probably bound as soon as the manuscript was written in 1457. The most notable feature of this binder's work is that he is the only known English binder to make use of the cuir-ciselé or cut-leather technique not uncommon on German and Austrian bindings of the fifteenth century.[33] Another binding from this shop, now in the library of St John's College, Cambridge (MS 98), covers an English manuscript of Orosius. It has no cut-leather work, but is decorated with a large tool bearing the inscription 'en dieu/ma fye' and with a very small leopard's face tool. A second group of tools occurs on seven later bindings—the last not before 1481—which makes it possible that a second binder was at work. The continuation of the cut-leather work caused Mr Barker eventually to decide that all nineteen (now twenty) bindings were probably the work of one man. But the complete break between the two groups of tools at least suggests that the one binder in England who did cut-leather work may have been an employee and not the head of the shop, and that around 1465 he changed shops. The scales tool (Barker's c on his plate XII), after which Hobson named the whole bindery, unfortunately only occurs on bindings from the second group.

Another group of four bindings has been attributed to a bindery at Salisbury, active for a few years up to 1463.[34] Two of these cover manuscripts written for Gilbert Kymer, Dean of Salisbury, by Herman Zurke, an Oxford scribe whom he took into his service and who went with him to Salisbury. Another, now BL Add. MS 28870, covers the Register of Vallis Scholarium at Salisbury, which certainly strengthens the attribution of the bindery to that city. But the owner

[32] G. D. Hobson, *Bindings in Cambridge Libraries*, 14–24, pls. IV–VIII. Id., *English Binding before 1500*, 17–18, pl. 39.
[33] F. A. Schmidt–Künsemüller, *Corpus der gotischen Lederschnitteinbände aus dem deutschen Sprachgebiet* (Stuttgart, 1980).
[34] G. Pollard, 'The Names of Some English Fifteenth-Century Binders', *The Library*, 5th ser., 25 (1970), 204, 212. (cited below as Pollard, 'Names').

of the fourth, William Witham, Dean of the Arches and Canon of Wells, seems to have no Salisbury connection; he was an Oxford DCL,[35] although the majority of the numerous posts he held were not in Oxford. Bearing in mind that Gilbert Kymer was twice Chancellor of that university, it may be as likely that the whole group was bound in Oxford as at Salisbury, for a manuscript is not necessarily bound in the place where it is written if the owner knows of a suitable binder elsewhere who is better than local talent.

There is, however, incontrovertible evidence for the existence of a fifteenth-century binder using blind tooling in Canterbury (Fig. 7). In 1929 Hobson called attention to six bindings by him,[36] and Oldham recorded five more twenty-three years later.[37] Yet it was not until Graham Pollard visited Canterbury after another thirteen years[38] that anyone interested in bookbinding noticed that Charles Cotton had published in *Archaeologia Cantiana* (London, 1917) a description of the tools used on the binding of the churchwardens' accounts of St Andrew's Church, Canterbury. It was the work of the same binder, and Cotton had also quoted the note 'Item paidd to John Kemsyn for byndyng of this boke for the Inventorie of the chirche goods to be wreten therin. xvjs.' Pollard pointed out that these Canterbury bindings are probably not as early as their rather archaic appearance suggests, as Kemsyn was still at work for the churchwardens of St Andrew's in 1496.

In 1962 Neil Ker drew attention to a possible Winchester binder whom he called the Virgin and Child Binder. Graham Pollard added four to Ker's seven known examples, and about ten years later the British Library acquired an Anthology of Middle-English verse, a Winchester manuscript bound in the same shop (Fig. 8).[39]

The next bindery to be discussed was unquestionably located in Westminster, where a considerable number of books were bound for William Caxton, England's first printer, and for his assistant and successor, Wynkyn de Worde. This bindery might actually have

[35] A. B. Emden, *A Biographical Register of the University of Oxford to AD 1500*, 3 vols. (Oxford, 1957–9), iii. 2065–6.
[36] Hobson, *English Binding before 1500*, 15, pl. 33.
[37] Oldham, *English Blind-Stamped Bindings*, 24.
[38] Pollard, 'Names', 204–5, 212.
[39] N. R. Ker, 'The Virgin and Child Binder, LVL, and William Horman', *The Library*, 5th ser., 17 (1962), 77–85. Pollard, 'Names', 208–9, 213. See also E. Wilson, *The Winchester Anthology: A Fascimile of B. L. Add. MS. 60577* (Cambridge, 1981), 7–8.

belonged in turn to Caxton and to de Worde, since out of thirty-nine
recorded examples now known from this shop thirteen are on books
printed by Caxton and four are on books printed by de Worde.[40] If
they did not in turn own this binder's shop it was certainly near their
premises; all the printed waste found in its bindings comes from
Caxton's press, and the shop also bound manuscripts for Westminster
Abbey. But although one or two of the shop's kit of tools turn up
alone considerably later, 1511 appears to be the latest date of printing
of any book in the group. If the shop was de Worde's, it must have
acquired a new set of tools about that time. De Worde continued in
business until his death in 1535. He remembered in his will two
bookbinders: Alard, 'my servant', who presumably worked on his
premises, and Nowell [Havy], the binder in Shoe Lane, who clearly
did not. Graham Pollard suggested[41] that the original Caxton Binder
was the Jacobus Bokebynder who leased from the Abbey the shop
next to Caxton's old one and who disappeared after 1510. But this
man, whose name turns out to have been James Griffith, left his shop
early in 1508, but was still paying rent to the churchwardens of St
Margaret's, Westminster in 1513/14 for a 'litel pece of voide grounde'
in Abingdon Rents.[42] There were other binders living in Westminster
as tenants of the Abbey during this period, but none of their dates fit.

   Ten examples in the first group (A) of Caxton bindings (Fig. 9),
show fleurs-de-lis in lozenge-shaped panels in a style highly reminiscent of Bruges—indeed Pollard averred that these were Bruges tools.
But if one compares the tools used in Bruges with those used by
Caxton's binder, it is clear that neither the fleur-de-lis nor the dragon
in the triangle is the same.[43] Some of the bindings of group C seem to
be earlier than any of the bindings of group A and we are—as usual—

   [40] H. M. Nixon, 'William Caxton and Bookbinding', *Journal of the Printing Historical
Society*, 11 (1976–7), 92–113. Id., 'Caxton, His Contemporaries and Successors in the Book
Trade from Westminster Documents', *The Library*, 5th ser., 31 (1976), 305–26. Since these
articles were published, two more Caxton bindings have been acquired by the British
Library (IB. 37262 A: *BMC* III, 746 and IA. 3941: *BMC* I, 241). Another is at Queens'
College Cambridge, MS James 18 (Horne 31) and covers a 15th-century MS Formula
Novitiorum in English.
   [41] Pollard, 'Names', 205–6.
   [42] Nixon, 'William Caxton and Bookbinding', 105, Id., 'Caxton, His Contemporaries
and Successors'.
   [43] Pollard, 'Names', 205, pls. VI, VII, but note the 'armpits' of the fleur-de-lis and the
neck and feet of the dragon. See also M. M. Foot, 'Influences from the Netherlands on
Bookbinding in England during the late 15th and early 16th Centuries', *XIᵉ Congres
International de Bibliophile, Communications* (Brussels, 1979), 39–64.

misled if we try to give designs of bindings priority over tools used as a method of distinguishing craftsmen. Group *B* is probably the latest of the three styles and all the bindings in this group may date from Wynkyn de Worde's period as manager of the printing shop.

The ingenious argument that the Indulgence Binder was in some way connected with the London printer, John Lettou, was first advanced by Bradshaw, then taken up by G. D. Hobson, and strengthened and confirmed by Graham Pollard.[44] This has, however, crashed with William Ward's and Christopher de Hamel's discovery that strips of indulgences, printed by Lettou and by Caxton, were used to strengthen the spines of bindings by the Oxford Rood and Hunt Binder. All that can be said at present is that the unfortunately named Indulgence Binder worked from c.1475 to c.1480 or possibly c.1482, that nineteen bindings from this shop are now known, and that its location is still uncertain.[45]

Cambridge was late, apparently, in adopting the practice of decorating bindings with blind tooling, but once a start had been made it produced a number of craftsmen who were highly prolific. One of the earliest known of these is the Demon Binder, who worked between c.1473 and c.1497.[46] A bindery that started slightly later is that of the Unicorn Binder, from whose workshop Hobson and Oldham recorded seventy-three bindings, ranging in date from 1478 to 1507. Graham Pollard brought the number to nearly one hundred.[47] Only two of these cover books printed later than 1500, and Oldham produced plausible reasons for regarding these two as having been bound by a later owner of some of this bindery's tools. Hobson first suggested that the Unicorn Binder was Walter Hatley and Oldham agreed. Hatley bound books at Cambridge from 1484/5 and was parish clerk of St Mary's Church, Cambridge, in 1501 and 1504. But Pollard pointed out that the Cambridge Heavy Binder also seems to

[44] Pollard, 'Names', 195 (with further references), 207, 214–15.

[45] M. M. Foot, 'English Decorated Bookbindings'. For a binding from this shop see Hobson, *English Binding before 1500*, pl. 45.

[46] Hobson, *Bindings in Cambridge Libraries*, pl. xiii. Id., *English Binding before 1500*, pl. 46. Oldham, *English Blind-Stamped Bindings*, 18, pl. xiv. Foot, 'English Decorated Bookbindings'.

[47] Hobson, *Bindings in Cambridge Libraries*, pls. xiv, xv. Id., *English Binding before 1500*, 21–2, pls. 47–9. Oldham, *English Blind-Stamped Bindings*, 18–9, pl. xi. Id., *Shrewsbury School Library Bindings*, 52–5. Id., 'Note on some New Tools Used by the "Unicorn Binder"', *The Library*, 5th ser., 2 (1948), 283–4. Id., 'English Fifteenth-Century Binding', 169–72. Pollard, 'Names', 208, 212, 213. Foot, 'English Decorated Bookbindings'.

have stopped working between 1504 and 1509, and his dates seem to fit in equally well with Hatley's as do those of the Unicorn Binder.

The Oxford binders of the fifteenth century are better documented than those of Cambridge, and here Graham Pollard has been able to suggest some possible identifications. The products of the Rood and Hunt Binder, which form a closely knit group, he would attribute to one Nicholas Bokebynder.[48] The bindings all seem to have been produced between 1478 and 1486 (Fig. 10). In September 1478 Nicholas was paid for binding books for Oriel College; in 1483 he bound a copy on vellum of the 1482 Oxford Lathbury for Magdalen. But by 1484 he had left Oxford, leaving rents for his house and store-rooms unpaid. However, the copy of Peter Lombard's *Sententiae* (now at Stonyhurst College), which was bound in this shop, was printed in Basel in 1486 and cannot have reached Oxford and received its binding until over two years after Nicholas Bokebynder appears to have left. [49] Thomas Uffyngton, bookbinder, had a shop next door to Thomas Hunt, who was University Stationer from 1479 to 1496. He seems a possible candidate for Oldham's Floral Binder, who bound some thirty books dating from 1476 to 1496.[50] For the Fishtail Binder Pollard suggested Christopher Coke, of Oxford, as a likely candidate. Nineteen or twenty examples from this shop are now known, covering manuscripts and books printed between 1473 and 1498.[51] Thomas Bedford was binding books for Magdalen College in 1487, and his successor as University Stationer was appointed in November 1507. Pollard's identifying him with the Dragon Binder seems plausible; forty-six bindings from this workshop are known and cover books with imprint dates ranging from 1486 to 1506.[52] Finally, George Chastellaine, who had a shop on the present site of Oriel College, is known to have been in Oxford from 1502; administration of his will was granted in October 1513. Again Pollard would seem to have strong grounds for identifying him with Oldham's Fruit

[48] Pollard, 'Names', 209, 212.
[49] Foot, 'English Decorated Bookbindings'.
[50] Pollard, 'Names', 210, 213. Oldham, *English Blind-Stamped Bindings*, pl. XVIII.
[51] Oldham, *English Blind-Stamped Bindings*, 22; pls. XVI, XVIII. Pollard, 'Names', 210, 213. Foot, 'English Decorated Bookbindings'.
[52] Pollard, 'Names', 210–11. See also Hobson, *English Binding before 1500*, pl. 52 and Oldham, *English Blind-Stamped Bindings*, pl, xv.

and Flower Binder, whose work is found on books dating from 1491 to 1512.[53]

In a university town there is quite a good chance of identifying the binders of groups of books linked by the tools used to decorate them. But in London, with no university archives for this period to help, it is a considerable feat to connect groups of bindings with known binders. In 'English Fifteenth Century Binding'[54] J. B. Oldham mentions the Antwerp and the Athos Binders (whom he attributes to Cambridge) together with the Lattice Binder and the Heavy Binder. He also notes as likely Londoners the Crucifer Binder (who may have been employed by Richard Pynson),[55] the Huntsman Binder, Lily Binder, Octagonal Rose Binder, and Foliage Staff Binder.

Unfortunately it does not look as if it is going to be very easy to follow up the lead Pollard gave with Oxford binders elsewhere in the country, and the position is particularly difficult with London for the first century and a half after the introduction of printing. Oldham has done great work in identifying the groups of bindings, but there is much work to be done in the linking of these groups with individual members of the book trade, even if the tools or panels used on them bear initials. Oldham was convinced that initials on a roll or panel were those of a binder or of a bookseller who owned a binder's shop. It seems much more likely that these initials on English bindings originally denoted booksellers, and that an independent binder might have had a number of signed rolls and panels which he originally kept separate for the booksellers to whom they belonged, but after a time used indiscriminately for different booksellers or individual owners for whom he was working.

The date of the introduction of the panel stamp into England has been most recently discussed by Graham Pollard.[56] G. D. Hobson[57] had tentatively suggested that the first volume of a six-volume set of Vincent of Beauvais's works at Corpus Christi College, Oxford, was

[53] Pollard, 'Names', 211. Oldham, *English Blind-Stamped Bindings*, pls. XVII–XVIII. Foot, 'English Decorated Bookbindings'.

[54] *Festschrift Ernst Kyriss* (Stuttgart, 1961), 159–74. See also Oldham, *English Blind-Stamped Bindings*, pls XI–XIV.

[55] M. M. Foot, 'A Binding by the Crucifer Binder, *c.*1500', *Book Collector*, 28 (1979), 554–5. Id., 'English Decorated Bookbindings'. See also Oldham, *English Blind-Stamped Bindings*, pls. XXI, XXIII, XXV, XXVI.

[56] Pollard, 'Names', 214–18.

[57] Hobson, *Blind-Stamped Panels in the English Book-Trade* (London, 1944), 19–29.

bound in England by William de Machlinia between 1482 and 1487. This volume has three unconnected signed panels of Netherlandish origin, including one (ascribed to the thirteenth century) that has the name Woter van Duffle. Pollard suggested that Pynson took over Machlinia's business; that this is a made-up set, four of the volumes having been bound probably in Lübeck and one perhaps in or near Cologne; that one of the other two panels found on the remaining volume (Oldham's AN 6[58] with the name Martinus de Predio) was almost certainly used on a Pynson book printed in 1499; and that Pynson probably acted as the agent of Bishop Richard Foxe, who presented the book to Corpus. Pollard considered that the evidence suggested that volume 1 might have been bound by Pynson in a consciously antiquated style, so that it would agree with the much earlier bindings of the other volumes. Pollard therefore thought that it might be as late as c.1515, not long before the first consignment of books was sent by Foxe to Corpus.

Whether we accept this suggestion or not, it seems likely that the earliest use of a panel in London dates from about 1494. Undated, but firmly attributed to that year, is a vellum copy of a Sarum *Horae* at Lambeth Palace.[59] It is traditionally said to have been bound for the Lady Margaret Beaufort, mother of Henry VII, and blocked with a panel showing animals in foliage (Fig. 11). It bears no evidence of her ownership, but it is likely to have been produced with an important owner in view and also to have been bound as soon as it was printed. When Pollard was writing in 1970 this was the only example known of the use of this panel, but in 1976, in a paper read to the Caxton International Congress, two further examples were recorded. These were reported respectively by Mr H. S. Herbrüggen (the first to note that this panel had been used by the Caxton Binder), and by Dr A. I. Doyle.[60] The second of these items was a manuscript dating from the middle of the fifteenth century, but the first is on a printed Book of Hours of 1506. However, there is nothing at all extraordinary in the use of a panel over a period of twelve years.

Oldham's panel ST 10,[61] a small and not very impressive depiction

[58] Oldham, *Blind Panels of English Binders* (Cambridge, 1958).
[59] E. G. Duff, *Fifteenth-Century English Books* (Oxford, 1917), no. 182. See also Nixon, 'William Caxton and Bookbinding', 95, no. 20.
[60] Nixon, 'William Caxton and Bookbinding', 110–11, nos. 25 and 30 in the list.
[61] Oldham, *Blind Panels of English Binders*.

of St George belonging to WG at Cambridge, is only found on three small books with the impressively early imprint dates of 1490, 1491, and 1494. It is therefore quite probable that this panel was used before the Caxton Binder's panel, and is indeed the first to have been used in England.[62] The other member of the book trade who certainly seems to have used panels before 1500 is Richard Pynson. He owned two rose panels, two signed panels (one of which bears his device), and a panel depicting John the Baptist. They are found either alone or in various combinations on eleven bindings; the rose panels occur in combination with one of the tools used by the Crucifer Binder.[63] From the beginning of the sixteenth century until about 1550 panels (or blocks) were used mainly on small books. Probably something like half the panels used in England were imported from the Continent, as were the three already mentioned which were used on the Corpus Vincent of Beauvais.[64] Oldham recorded a total of 262 panels that he believed had been used in England in this period. His group of panels with acorn cresting and that of animals and birds entwined in foliage probably found their inspiration abroad and, like the fairly large heads-in-medallions group, are not particularly interesting in design. The heraldic class, when taken together with the Tudor roses, forms one of the largest groups. This group, with Oldham's biblical, religious, and saints classes (which may be considered together), contains most of the more decorative and interesting examples.

One clearly English type bears the English royal arms: several of these—rather primitive in style—have had early dates suggested for them. One example in the Westminster Abbey Library (Fig. 12) has two lions assisting two angels to support the royal arms. It was at one time claimed for the reign of Edward IV, which would bring it back to 1483 at the latest.[65] But there is no reason to believe that it is earlier than 1495, for Oldham has shown the binding to be the work of the Half-Stamp Binder, who was active between about 1489 and 1511.[66]

---

[62] Pollard, 'Names', 216–18.

[63] Oldham, *Blind Panels of English Binders*, RO 1–2, MISC 4, 14, ST 18. Foot, 'A Binding by the Crucifer Binder, c.1500'. Foot, 'English Decorated Bookbindings'.

[64] S. Fogelmark's *Flemish and Related Panel-Stamped Bindings* (New York, 1990) throws new light on the manufacture and use of panels.

[65] It now contains some MS prayers of Erasmus, written probably sometime after the book was bound. Oldham, *Blind Panels of English Binders*, HE 5.

[66] Oldham, *English Blind-Stamped Bindings*, 29–30, pls. XXIV, XXV. Pollard, 'Names', 196, 213.

Another very similar royal arms panel (which Oldham thought was by the same die cutter) is also known from a single example, now in the British Library (IA. 55550).[67] The majority of these royal arms panels seems to have been in use only between 1512 and 1535, although they were very popular for a short period from about 1525 to 1530. They were frequently used combined with Tudor rose panels, and two or probably three panels exist (Oldham HE 9; HE 21–2),[68] with the initials E. G. and those of John Reynes, respectively, that show the royal arms and the rose placed above one another on the same panel.

Among the most handsome of these royal arms panels are two showing the arms of Henry VIII dimidiating those of Catherine of Aragon. One of these appears to have been used at least once on a book of 1533; in January of that year Henry VIII married Anne Boleyn. The binder evidently eventually woke to his danger, as the British Library has a copy of grammatical tracts by Robert Whittinton, London, [? 1522]–34, decorated with an example of what is to all appearances the same block, with the arms of Catherine replaced by those of Anne (Fig. 13). On the other cover are the plain arms of the king. This type of binding does not indicate royal ownership.

One of the most interesting of the panels in Oldham's 'religious' group is John Reynes's 'Redemptoris mundi arma' panel (REL 5), with a shield bearing the Cross and other emblems of the Passion. It is derived from a cut used by the Paris printer, Thielman Kerver, who as a printer of Sarum service books had considerable connections with the English book trade. The two unicorns used as supporters also appear on Kerver's printer's mark. The commonest scene in the 'biblical' group is the Annunciation; the panels of this scene, of which Oldham knew twenty-two Netherlandish, French, and English examples, show a marked similarity of treatment. Of these, twelve were used in England and eight closely resemble one (BIB 2) which has the initials of Nicholas Spierinck, the Cambridge bookseller. It is always used together with a panel of St Nicholas bringing to life the three children whom a frugal innkeeper had slaughtered and pickled to provide food for his guests (ST 37).[69] Panels were normally used on fairly small books. On the comparatively rare occasions when folios

---

[67] Oldham, *Blind Panels of English Binders*, HE 7.
[68] J. B. Oldham believed that HE 21 and HE 22 are two states of the same panel.
[69] G. J. Gray, op. cit. 43–53.

were decorated with them, either four casts of the same panel or four different panels had to be employed. Yet a St Bernard panel (ST 7), probably used between c.1525 and 1534, was clearly designed for a folio. At a height of 7¼ inches it is the largest panel that was used in England.

This discussion of panel-stamped bindings has been deliberately curtailed. The topic has been covered extensively by Oldham in his *Blind Panels of English Binders* (Cambridge, 1958); Hobson's *Blind-Stamped Panels in the English Book-Trade* (London, 1944) is also still well worth reading. The whole subject of the manufacture and use of panels needs extensive revision in the light of the research recently carried out by Dr S. Fogelmark in Sweden.

When we turn to sixteenth- and early seventeenth-century bindings decorated in blind with rolls, we find that Oldham's Sandars Lectures (published in 1952 as *English Blind-Stamped Bindings*) are almost our only authority. Consequently even less is said here about these roll-tooled bindings.[70] Probably comparatively few of these rolls were designed in England, but those with Tudor emblems almost certainly were. An anonymous roll (Oldham AN. g. (1)) shows a crowned portcullis among foliage and animals. It was probably used by the Octagonal Rose Binder at the very end of the fifteenth century, although it may later have belonged to another binder who worked in the 1520s and early 1530s. A Cambridge binding by Garrett Godfrey, bearing his initials (Fig. 14), shows a signed animal roll and a small Tudor emblem roll with towers, fleur-de-lis, crowned pomegranate, and crowned rose, together with a shield containing three horseshoes and Godfrey's initials.[71]

Not all medieval bindings were made of blind-tooled or plain leather. Bindings of other materials have survived, though very few English examples are known. Bindings made of ivory or metal—with or without precious stones—are not bindings in a structural sense: the covers do not form an integral part of the book, nor were they made by bookbinders. They were produced by metal workers, ivory carvers, and jewellers, and were considered objects of art rather than a means to protect a text. They were the grandest bindings of the Middle Ages, and as their use was largely confined to the service

[70] See also N. R. Ker, *Pastedowns in Oxford Bindings* (Oxford, 1954).
[71] Oldham, *English Blind-Stamped Bindings*, AN. *f* (1) and HE. *b* (1). Gray, op. cit. 28–42.

books of the pre-Reformation Church, English silver-gilt and silver bindings disappeared almost entirely into the rapacious hands of Henry VIII. The majority were melted down and no binding of this type has survived which can be called English with absolute certainty. Many of the more elaborate fabric bindings were also destroyed.

The only more or less complete metal binding that has been claimed as English with some confidence is now in the Pierpont Morgan Library. It covers an illuminated manuscript Gospels on vellum written in England in the mid-eleventh century. The book originally belonged to Judith of Flanders (c.1028–94), who gave it to the Swabian Abbey of Weingarten (Pl. 3). It has wooden boards to which a gold and silver-gilt cover has been attached.[72] Treasure bindings often have only one decorated cover or, if they have two metal or ivory plaques, one is normally more elaborate. In England and France from about 1300 until 1600 at least, the second cover would normally be the more elaborate: it was customary to close the book on its lectern or stand with the last leaf, rather than the beginning of the book, uppermost. However, the upper cover of the binding of Judith of Flanders's Gospels is the one that has been elaborately decorated. It has an engraved silver-gilt frame, gold filigree and jewels, as well as figures that were cast in silver, then gilt and attached to the background. The spine and lower cover are covered in pink leather. The silver–gilt figures represent Christ in majesty sitting within a mandorla between two six-winged angels. Below him is the Crucifixion with the Virgin Mary and St John. English experts do not seem to be quite so sure about the English origin of this binding as are their American colleagues. Indeed, there seems to be such a lack of comparable clearly localized metal work of this period, that it would be rash to take a firm decision on the binding's nationality.

Another manuscript Gospels in the Pierpont Morgan Library (M. 709), with an identical pedigree (perhaps written in Canterbury, possibly in the second quarter of the eleventh century) is bound in wooden boards with a gold repoussé cover attached to the upper board. It has a gold filigree border encrusted with jewels and shows, in a central mandorla surrounded by the symbols of the four Evangelists, the full-length figure of Christ in majesty. This cover has been assigned both to England and Flanders, but no conclusive case

[72] P. Needham, *Twelve Centuries of Bookbindings: 400–1600*, 33–5, 37–8, pl. p. xxi.

has been made for either attribution.[73] Judith of Flanders, an important patron of the arts, was only in England from 1051—when she
married Tostig, the younger brother of Harold—until 1064 or 1066.
During this period she also paid a visit to Rome and was elsewhere
on the Continent. After Tostig's death late in 1066 Judith spent her
widowhood in Flanders. In 1070 she married Welf IV, Duke of
Bavaria, in whose duchy she spent the rest of her life.[74]

That most of the English cathedrals and abbeys did possess bindings
of this type in the Middle Ages is clear from the various surviving
inventories of the plate, vestments, and service books with covers of
precious metal. The earlier inventories tend not to describe the
bindings in much detail, but we do learn something from the 1388
Inventory of the Vestry of Westminster Abbey, now in the library of
Canterbury Cathedral.[75] Chapters viij and ix of the third section of
this inventory list the more elaborate service books; in chapter ix
something is said about nearly all the bindings of the *Textus* books
preserved in the vestry. The term *Textus* seems usually to have been
applied to elaborately decorated and bound copies of one or more
Gospels for use at Mass, but it also included the equally elaborately
bound volumes from which the Epistles were read. In 1388 Westminster Abbey owned six of these books. The best of these had an
image of the Trinity flanked by two angels on the upper part of the
silver–gilt cover; a Crucifixion with the Virgin and St John occupied
the lower half. The second and third of these books at Westminster
were decorated respectively with a Crucifix supported by the Virgin
Mary and St John, and with a representation of the Trinity. The
fourth and fifth were smaller, each with a Crucifix on a silver–gilt
cover, while the sixth had been despoiled of all ornament by a thief.
A later hand has added to the inventory three more large Gospel
books with silver–gilt covers, one decorated with the Assumption of
the Virgin, the other two with the Crucifixion. These are followed by
three small silver-plated examples, the first bearing a Crucifixion with
Mary and John; the second, Christ in majesty with the symbols of
the four Evangelists; and the third, an ivory crucifix. A Benedictional
covered in red silk is also mentioned.

[73] P. Needham, op. cit. 35–8.
[74] F. Barlow, *Edward the Confessor* (London, 1970), 195.
[75] J. Wickham Legg, 'On an Inventory of the Vestry in Westminster Abbey, taken in
1388', *Archaeologia*, 52 (1890), 195–279, esp. 233–6, 276.

The Dissolution Inventory of Westminster Abbey, taken in 1540,[76] mentions only four books in bindings of this type—a 'Pystyll Boke', a 'Gospell Boke', the 'best Text', and 'an other Texte Book'. These are, however, described rather more fully, such as 'the best Text close coveryd on the one syde wyth plait of sylver gyltyd garnyshed with an ymage of sylver and gylt in the mydds and with vij ymages enamyled vj counterfett turkes [turquoises] and iij other gret counterfett stonys and with iiij plates of latyn [latten] at the iiij corners of the same text at the baksyde, cxlvij [o]unces'. We also learn that the famous late fourteenth-century 'Masse Booke of Abbott Nicholas Lytlyngton gyffte', was described at that time 'with claspys of copper and the booke ys covered with clothe of gold'. (This manuscript is happily still preserved at Westminster Abbey, presumably because it contained the Coronation service and was therefore Royal and not Popish.) There was also a Pontifical described as 'with a coveryng of clothe of golde and a claspe of sylver', which had appeared previously in the 1388 inventory.[77]

The 1846 edition of Dugdale's *Monasticon Anglicanum* prints a number of cathedral inventories, mostly dating from the sixteenth century; two or three of these give details of treasure bindings. Most bear resemblance to the Westminster holdings. In the sixteenth century, for example, York had three Gospel texts with silver–gilt covers ornamented with precious stones: two bore the Virgin Mary and St John standing at the foot of the Cross; the third had the figure of Christ in majesty. An Epistle volume, also in a silver–gilt binding, bore an image of the Trinity and the four evangelists at the corners; another *Textus* volume had an image of the coronation of the Virgin Mary.[78]

Dugdale also gives the 1536 Inventory of Lincoln Cathedral,[79] but a more accurate old-spelling version is quoted in Christopher Wordsworth's article in *Archaeologia*.[80] Elaborate gold- and silversmith's work is again found on the Gospels: a 'Text after Mathew' is covered

[76] PRO, L. R. Misc. Books III. Printed by M. E. C. Walcott in *Transactions of the London and Middlesex Archaeological Society*, 4 (1873), 313–64, esp. 320, 323.

[77] Walcott, op. cit. 343–4. The Missal was rebound in two volumes by John Bohn in 1806. See Nixon, *Five Centuries of English Bookbinding* (London, 1978), no. 82.

[78] Sir William Dugdale, *Monasticon Anglicanum*, 6 vols. (London 1846), VI: iii. 1205, 6.

[79] W. Dugdale, op. cit. VI: iii. 1278 ff.

[80] C. Wordsworth, 'Inventories of Plate, Vestments, etc., belonging to the Cathedral Church of the Blessed Mary at Lincoln', *Archaeologia*, 53 (1892), 1–82, esp. 22.

with a silver-gilt plate 'havyng a Image of the Maieste w^t the iiij evangelistes and iiij angelles'; a second St Matthew's Gospel, and those of St Mark and St John, have images of the Crucifixion with Mary and John. One of the most interesting and complete series of inventories is that for St George's Chapel, Windsor, published by M. F. Bond.[81] There one finds in the Inventory for 1501, 'A book of the Gospels having on one side a cover of red velvet, and on the other, one of silver-gilt, containing the figures of the Crucified and the Evangelists enamelled, with two silver–gilt clasps bearing the arms of Saint George'.

The most important parish churches would also have had elaborate Epistle and Gospel books, and in the 1511 inventory of St Margaret's, Westminster, we find among the service books listed: 'Item a gospeler garnysshed wt. a crucyfyx mary & John wt. iiij cristall stones quadrant sette', followed by: 'Item a pisteler garnysshed wt. the fadir of heven of coper'.[82]

However, as has been mentioned, hardly any examples of this type of binding made in England have survived. Among the Royal Manuscripts in the British Library are an Epistolar and a Gospel Book,[83] which were given to the church of St Mary Aldermanbury, London, in 1508. The present front cover of each volume now consists of an oak board deeply recessed for the reception of a crucifix or other metal ornament, while the present back board of each is covered in velvet. The sunken holes in the plain wooden boards for the attachment of the metal would be equally suitable if the two boards had originally been on the opposite sides, and the four holes on the Epistolar's wooden cover would be in the natural places to attach a crucifix, at top and bottom, and above and below the cross bar. A reversal of the covers also makes sense of the only medieval English binding which retains any trace of original enamel. This is the Sherborne Chartulary in the British Library, which has an inverted Limoges enamel angel nailed on the upper cover (Fig. 15). The illustration of the binding in T. Hearne's edition of *The Itinerary of John Leland* (Oxford, 1744, ii. 58) shows the cover as if it was the lower cover of the book, with the Limoges enamel figure of an angel

---

[81] M. F. Bond, *The Inventories of St. George's Chapel, Windsor Castle* (Windsor, 1947), 148–9 (editor's translation from the Latin original).
[82] H. F. Westlake, *St. Margaret's Westminster* (London, 1914), 235.
[83] MSS Royal 2.B. XII, XIII.

the correct way up. Viewed like this there would be comfortable space in the sunken wooden compartment above the angel to take a crucifix.

Ivory bookcovers made in England are now equally scarce. Throughout the Middle Ages the supply of elephant tusks from Africa and India was erratic. It is clear that in Britain and in the rest of northern Europe elephant ivory was in very short supply during the twelfth century, because virtually all surviving pieces have been made of whalebone or walrus tusk. This has a yellower, more buttery colour and a coarser grain than the almost white, fine-grained elephant ivory. A twelfth-century English ivory, depicting the deposition from the cross, was reused on an early sixteenth-century German binding of brown calf over wooden boards, decorated with rolls on the lower cover. It covers an Evangelarium in Latin, written on vellum in Germany in the late eleventh century, and is now in the Pierpont Morgan Library.[84] The ivory has been attributed to St Albans or Bury St Edmunds and to the second quarter of the twelfth century. Another English panel of the last quarter of the twelfth century, made of whalebone (Fig. 16), now in the Merseyside County Museums in Liverpool, was almost certainly used to decorate a binding. The holes around the edge were for the ivory pins used to fasten it down; the cut-out compartments on the right-hand side might have been made to accommodate clasps.[85] Four scenes from the Old Testament, showing Moses receiving the tables of the law, the sacrifice of Isaac, the offering of the Paschal Lamb, and the priest Melchisedech offering bread and wine, surround the central scene from the New Testament: the Presentation of Christ in the Temple.

The only surviving English medieval embroidered binding is that on the Felbrigge Psalter in the British Library. The fourteenth-century embroidered panels are now inlaid in eighteenth-century calf. The upper cover shows the Annunciation, while the lower cover has a much worn representation of the Crucifixion (Fig. 17).[86] Most fabric-covered English bindings of the Middle Ages, however, were either of patterned silk, cloth of gold, or velvet, often provided with

[84] Needham, op. cit. 52–4.
[85] P. Lasko (and others), 'Ivory Carvings' in *English Romanesque Art, 1066–1200*, Arts Council exhibition (London, 1984), 230, no. 219.
[86] M. M. Foot, *Pictorial Bookbindings* (London, 1986), 53–5. P. Wallis, 'The Embroidered Binding of the Felbrigge Psalter', *British Library Journal*, 13: i (1987), 71–8.

bosses and with finely decorated clasps of precious metal. These
bindings are now best visualized from published wills, such as that of
Cecily, widow of Richard, Duke of York, proved in 1495. It includes
the following:

I geve and bequ[e]ath to the Quene . . . a sawter [psalter] with claspes of
silver and guilte enamelled covered with grene clothe also I bequeith to my
lady the Kinges moder [Lady Margaret Beaufort] a portuos [breviary] with
claspes of gold covered with blacke cloth of gold . . . Also I geve to my
doughter Cecill a portuous with clasps silver and gilt covered with purple
velvet . . . also I geve to Sir William Grave . . . a prymour with claspes silver
and gilt covered with blewe velvett, and a sawter that servith for the closett
covered with white ledder.[87]

But the great majority of English bindings of this type have also
now vanished, not only because most of them covered service books,
which were destroyed at the Reformation, but because all of them
were especially prone to insect attacks as well as to ordinary wear and
tear, which affected bindings in fabric far more severely than those in
leather. A few velvet bindings made in pre-Reformation England have
survived, in particular two very splendid copies of the Indentures
between Henry VII and John Islip, Abbot of Westminster, concerning
the foundation of Henry VII's Chapel, dated 16 July 1504. The King's
copy is now in the Public Record Office; the Abbot's copy, presented
to the Harleian Library by Sir Thomas Bisham, Bart., is now in the
British Library (Fig. 18).

It is in magnificent condition with a binding of red velvet lined
with pink damask, surmounted on both covers with gold and silver
enamelled bosses showing portcullises in the corners and the royal
arms in the centre. A deep velvet chemise hides the five examples of
the Great Seal in their gilt metal boxes.

[87] H. R. Plomer, 'Books Mentioned in Wills', *Transactions of the Bibliographical Society*,
7 (1904), 99–121, esp. 109–10.

TWO

Gold-Tooled Sixteenth-Century Bindings

WHILE gold tooling had been practised in Italy early in the fifteenth century and in Spain during the second half of the fifteenth century, it took a long time to cross the Alps and the Pyrenees. The earliest English example probably dates from 1519 and can be found on a binding in the Bodleian Library which covers manuscript *Epigrams* by Robert Whittinton presented to Cardinal Wolsey. The design appears to have been carried out by using two blocks, one showing three Tudor emblems (rose, portcullis, and pomegranate), and the other depicting St George.[1] This was essentially an experimental effort and the blocks fit the binding but clumsily (Fig. 19).

The next two English gilt bindings are also of an experimental nature. The first, discovered by Louis-Marie Michon in the Bibliothèque Sainte-Geneviève in Paris, covers a presentation binding for Henry VIII from Thomas Linacre, his physician, dating from the early 1520s.[2] The royal arms block used here in combination with a roll signed by John Reynes, was designed for use in blind and the idea of using it with gold leaf no doubt came from Linacre, who had already had gold-tooled bindings prepared for Henry VIII in Paris. The edges of the leaves are gilt and gauffered with the monogram HR. The other gilt binding is in Archbishop Marsh's Library in Dublin, and again comes from Henry VIII's library. It has the well-

---

[1] Though referred to in the literature as Thomas and Richard, Whittinton signs the dedication of his *Epigrams* as Robert. W. S. Brassington, *Historic Bindings in the Bodleian Library, Oxford* (London, 1891), pl. VII. H. M. Nixon, 'The Gilt Binding of the Whittinton Epigrams', *The Library*, 5th ser., 7 (1952), 120–1, *Fine Bindings 1500–1700 from Oxford Libraries: Catalogue of an Exhibition* (Oxford, 1968), no. 63.

[2] H. M. Nixon, *Five Centuries of English Bookbinding* (London, 1978), no. 5 (cited below as Nixon, *Five Centuries*).

known roll with a bird and a wivern signed WG and IG (Oldham, AN. *e* (1)) as a border and a strip of impressions of a pineapple tool (Oldham (E1)) down the centre, but both roll and tools are again used in gold, instead of being in blind.[3] It can be dated only approximately, but was probably made between 1520 and 1525.

Until *c.*1529 gold tooling in England was essentially an experimental technique and no one in this country had any tools specially cut for the purpose. The distinction is that in blind tooling the pattern stands out in relief, while in gold tooling the previously heated tool is impressed through gold leaf into the leather and the pattern shows in intaglio.

Hardly any English gold-tooled bindings of the sixteenth century are signed and hardly any can be attributed to known binders on other grounds. Therefore, when G. D. Hobson first started to sort out the different London binderies in his *Bindings in Cambridge Libraries* (Cambridge, 1929), it was necessary for him to invent names for the groups he was able to identify. Cyril Davenport had published in 1901 a book called *Thomas Berthelet, Royal Printer and Bookbinder to Henry VIII . . . with Special Reference to his Bookbindings.* There he quoted the one known document on the supply of bindings to Henry VIII, which is a bill from Berthelet. Unfortunately, except on rare occasions, a bill for supplying bindings is seldom evidence that the man who presented the bill bound the books. Gold-tooled royal library bindings between 1530 and 1558 show a considerable variety of tools, including a number of similar tools of the same basic design which fall into easily recognisable groups. It is clear that there were a number of different binderies working in London at the same time, and presentation copies of books printed by Berthelet appear to have been bound in at least three different shops. It is not possible to identify any of these shops as his own, and it seems very probable that he did not own one at all or he would surely have saved himself money by patronizing it on every occasion.

The first shop in England to have produced gilt bindings with tools specially designed for the purpose belonged to the man G. D. Hobson named King Henry's Binder. In 1929 Hobson recorded twenty-three bindings by him; only two have turned up since (Fig. 20).[4] One of

---

[3] Nixon, *Five Centuries*, no. 6. It has the royal library mark no. 484 on the title-page.
[4] G. D. Hobson, *Bindings in Cambridge Libraries* (Cambridge, 1929), pl. XXII. For one additional example see H. M. Nixon, 'Early English Gold-Tooled Bookbindings' in *Studi*

the bindings from this shop, a Yates Thompson manuscript now in the British Library (Yates Thompson MS 18), shows the use of a well-engraved panel stamp of the royal arms. Yet the majority of the bindings have rather uninspired tools probably copied from French gold-tooled bindings of the 1520s, which in turn were copied from Italian models. New College, Oxford, owns four examples from this shop, all covering Greek manuscripts written in England and presented to the College by Cardinal Reginald Pole.[5] The Bodleian Library has a number of examples, which probably were all given by Charles Howard, Earl of Nottingham (better known as Lord Howard of Effingham, who brought about the defeat of the Spanish Armada). But the best of them is an example sold at Christie's in 1978, which covers one of the documents concerned with Henry VIII's divorce and which can be dated 1530.[6]

It is possible that there was an actual break in the production of gold-tooled bindings in London between about 1534 and 1544. In 'Early English Gold-Tooled Bookbindings'[7] it was suggested that this ten-year gap between the known products of the shop of King Henry's Binder and that of the man whom Hobson christened the Medallion Binder might be bridged by some of the undated manuscripts bound by either craftsman. The Medallion Binder, who was active from at least as early as 1544 (the date when MS Royal 13. B. xx was completed) until 1559, gets his name from the medallions of Plato and Dido used on this and on two others of his bindings. There is no doubt that the Medallion Binder owned one roll and a number of tools that had belonged to King Henry's Binder. But as more bindings from the Medallion Binder's shop continue to appear (Hobson listed six, and a further ten with the royal arms and/or initials (Fig. 21), as well as another twelve, have been found since that seem to come from the same shop)[8] there is an obstinate refusal to fill

di Bibliografia e di Storia in onore di Tammaro de Marinis, 4 vols. (Verona, 1964), iii. 289. This was sold at Christie's on 8 Nov. 1978 as lot 107, and is now in private hands. Another example is BL MS Harl. 1338, illustrated here (Fig. 20).

[5] Hobson, Bindings in Cambridge Libraries, 66, nos. I–IV.

[6] 8 Nov. 1978, lot 107.

[7] Nixon, 'Early English Gold-Tooled Bookbindings', Studi di Bibliografia e di Storia in onore di Tammaro de Marinis (Verona, 1964), iii. 283–308.

[8] Hobson, Bindings in Cambridge Libraries, 79. Nixon, 'Early English Gold-Tooled Bookbindings', 292–4 lists 11 more. Id., Sixteenth-Century Gold-Tooled Bookbindings in the Pierpont Morgan Library (New York, 1971), 89–91 lists 2 more. See also Nixon, Five

the 1534–44 gap. It now seems likely that the Medallion Binder succeeded King Henry's Binder after an interval of several years, having
acquired at least some of his tools. One of the most typical products
of the Medallion Binder's shop, formerly in the Hely-Hutchinson
collection, now forms part of the Henry Davis Gift to the British
Library.[9] It looks as if quite a number of folios received this type of
binding as a standard royal library style in the reign of Edward VI.

A slightly less elaborate design on Eusebius Pamphili, *Evangelicae
praeparationes* (Paris, 1544), discovered by Paul Morgan in the library
of St John's College, Oxford, was also probably bound for the young
King's library,[10] although it reached the college from Henry Cole,
while he was Dean of St Paul's in Queen Mary's reign. A binding in
the Pepys Library at Magdalene College, Cambridge[11] is perhaps the
earliest surviving English binding to have been bound in turkey
leather rather than the customary calf. It may be safely attributed to
this shop, thanks to the existence of an English Book of Hours at
Lambeth Palace which has the same unusual centre-piece with the
characteristic linked-circle border and corner tools of this binder.[12]
The Pepys Library copy has a presentation inscription from Clement
Adams, schoolmaster to the king's pages, dedicated to Philip II of
Spain, here addressed as Queen Mary's husband and 'Rex Angliae'.
Pepys no doubt acquired this book as part of what appears to have
been a policy of acquiring single examples of bindings from different
periods and countries. Another binding from the Medallion Binder's
shop, now in the British Library (C. 54. k. 1), is decorated with the
arms of Henry Fitzalan, Earl of Arundel (c.1511–c.1580). This is the
earliest known non-royal English armorial bookstamp.[13] It covers a
Venice Aristotle of 1513, but the binding probably dates from c.1555.

Centuries, nos. 12, 15. M. M. Foot, *The Henry Davis Gift*, ii (London, 1983), no. 35 lists 4
more. The additional five examples are BL C. 25. m. 7, C. 37. a. 6, C. 83. a. 20, C. 11. a.
27, and Bodley o. 2. 7. Th.

[9] H. M. Nixon, *Twelve Books in Fine Bindings from the Library of J. W. Hely-
Hutchinson* (London, 1953), pl. 1. M. M. Foot, *The Henry Davis Gift*, ii, no. 35.
[10] *Fine Bindings . . . from Oxford Libraries*, no. 65.
[11] Pepys Library, 1663. H. M. Nixon, *Catalogue of the Pepys Library at Magdalene
College Cambridge: Vol. VI Bindings* (Cambridge, 1984), pl. 29, p. xxv.
[12] H. M. Nixon, 'Early English Gold-Tooled Bookbindings', pl. 11, opp. p. 290.
[13] Nixon, *Five Centuries*, no. 15. For British armorial bookstamps see J. P. Harthan,
'Armorial Bookbindings from the Clements Collection', *Apollo*, Dec. 1960, June 1961,
Dec. 1961.

The next binder to be considered is the King Edward and Queen Mary Binder. Hobson attributed twelve bindings to his King Edward Binder and nine to his Queen Mary Binder; he considered the latter to be the better workman of the two, using simple designs and well-cut tools.[14] Since Hobson wrote at least sixty-four bindings—including twenty-three dating from the reign of Henry VIII—have come to light, and it is clear that we are dealing with the products of only one shop, which must have been active from about 1545 until at least 1558.[15] R. Morison, *Rerum ac muniorum Clientelarium liber*, a manuscript c.1545 (BL MS Royal 11. A. xvi) bound in turkey leather and not in the usual calf, is one of those that can certainly be attributed to the reign of Henry VIII, since both it and its companion in the Royal MSS in the British Library (Fig. 22) bear his initials on either side of the royal arms.[16] An example from Trinity College, Oxford, that covers an Oecumenius of 1532 does not have the royal initials flanking the coat of arms, but REX HENRICUS is painted on the upper and fore-edges.

It came from the Royal Library at Greenwich and reached Trinity with a number of other royal bindings given to the college in 1555 by Sir Thomas Pope, who was the executor of Henry VIII's estate.[17] Three bindings also known from this shop were made for Edward VI before he became king. The binding on a Xenophon of 1547, now in the British Library, is typical of those produced by this shop during Edward VI's reign (Fig. 23). It shows an interlacing ribbon painted black, a design clearly copied from French patterns. The royal arms are not blocked but have been built up with separate tools.

Equally characteristic and very attractive is a book formerly in Major J. R. Abbey's collection, covering *The Forme and maner of makyng and consecratyng of Archebishoppes, Bishoppes, Priestes and Deacons* (London, 1549).[18] Unless the binding is very elaborate, Bibles and Service Books with the royal arms are normally likely to have been made for use in royal chapels rather than for the sovereign

[14] Hobson, *Bindings in Cambridge Libraries*, pls. XXVI, XXVII.
[15] Nixon, 'Early English Gold-Tooled Bookbindings', 294–8. M. M. Foot, *The Henry Davis Gift*, i (London, 1978), 18–26.
[16] MS Royal 11. A. xvi is pl. III in Nixon, 'Early English Gold-Tooled Bookbindings'.
[17] *Fine Bindings . . . from Oxford Libraries*, no. 67.
[18] *Le livre anglais: Trésors des collections anglaises. Exposition* (held at the Bibliothèque Nationale) (Paris, 1951), no. 392. G. D. Hobson, *English Bindings 1490–1940 in the Library of J. R. Abbey* (London, 1940), no. 6 (sold at Sotheby's, 23 June 1965, lot 525).

personally. But this is not the type of liturgical work that would be needed in a royal chapel, and as the first post-Reformation book of its kind it is likely to have been specially bound for presentation to the king. Indeed, on this book the crowned royal initials appear in the circles above and below the royal arms. Another example with a more elaborate black-painted ribbon, also bound for Edward VI, covers a Bembo of 1551.[19] This binding has the king's initials, the motto DIEV ET MON DROYT, and the date of presentation, 1552, but the most obvious feature—doubtless intended to delight the boy king—is that the book appears to have no spine. The leaves are stabbed, and the backs of the sections have been cut off, covered with fabric, and painted with gold paint, so that the book appears to have four gilt edges. A copy of Bishop Bonner's *Profitable and necessarye Doctryne* of 1555, now in the British Library (C. 27. e. 13), was bound in this same shop during the reign of Queen Mary. Several bindings produced in the King Edward and Queen Mary bindery were made of white leather, possibly tawed buckskin. One of these is a 1546 Arnobius at Merton College, Oxford. The single M on the covers suggests that it may have been bound for Queen Mary before her accession in 1553.[20] *A Prognostication of right good effect* (London, 1555) by Leonard Digges, now in the Huntington Library (59155), shows that this shop bound for other people as well as for members of the royal family. It is decorated rather in the style of the bindings for Edward VI, but the interlacing ribbon has not been painted black.

Other bindings in white leather come from the shop of the Greenwich Binder. This shop got its name from the fact that the first three bindings from it to be identified were folios in Trinity College, Oxford, which, like the Oecumenius bound by the King Edward and Queen Mary Binder, came from the royal palace at Greenwich, via Sir Thomas Pope.[21] One of them covers A. Broickwy, *In quatuor Evangelia enarrationes* (Cologne, 1539). All the tools used by this

[19] BL C. 24. c. 20. Illus. in H. B. Wheatley, *Remarkable Bindings in the British Museum* (London, Paris, 1889), pl. XLI; W. Y. Fletcher, *English Bookbindings in the British Museum* (London, 1895), pl. XV; and C. J. H. Davenport, *Thomas Berthelet* (Chicago, 1901), pl. I.

[20] Arnobius, *Disputationes adversus gentes* (Basle, 1546). *Fine Bindings . . . from Oxford Libraries*, no. 68.

[21] They are reproduced in H. M. Nixon, 'Early English Gold-Tooled Bookbindings', pl. v, opp. p. 294; Nixon, *Five Centuries*, no. 10; and as the covers of the *Anglo-Saxon Review*, 9 (June, 1901).

shop are very like those used by the King Edward and Queen Mary Binder, but they are definitely different. Graham Pollard discovered another folio at Chetham's Library, Manchester, in a closely similar binding, again with the royal arms, but without the word 'Grenwiche' on the title-page (Fig. 24). The same tools occur on two bindings in the British Library: one covers a copy of Sir Thomas Elyot's *Image of Governance* (London, 1541),[22] the other is on an anonymous geometrical manuscript that has a most unusual design based on a geometric diagram in the text.[23] All six are in white goatskin and were bound for Henry VIII; all have REX IN AETERNVM VIVE painted on the edges of the leaves. One other book without this inscription on the edges also comes from this shop. It is a 1536 Smaragdus in the library of York Minster,[24] and it seems also to have been a royal library book for it bears the inscription, 'This booke was founde by me in the Juell house amongst K. Henries the 8: his bookes the 22th of November 1600 in the Tower:' It is not known who 'me', the finder, was.[25]

The next binder to be mentioned again used similar tools to those already discussed, but he disposed them with an abandon that has earned him the name of the Flamboyant Binder. The first binding by him to be published appeared on plate v in Cyril Davenport's *Thomas Berthelet* (Chicago, 1901). It covered the *Libellus de tribus hierarchiis* of Galterus Deloenus (otherwise Wouter Deleen or Deelen), who was a Dutch Protestant pastor resident in London.[26] Davenport attributed this manuscript to (?) 1528–30, and suggested that it was 'probably the earliest example of gold-tooling on an English leather binding'. It was in all likelihood bound about fifteen years later, and it has many tools in common with the binding of Hermann, Archbishop of Cologne, *Ein Christliche in dem Wort Gottes gegrünte Reformation*

---

[22] C. 21. b. 7. W. Y. Fletcher, *English Bookbindings in the British Museum* (London, 1895), pl. x.

[23] Add. MS 34809. Davenport, *Thomas Berthelet* (Chicago, 1901), pl. vii.

[24] viii. 1. 32. Smaragdus, *Summaria in Evangelia et epistolas . . . dominicales et festivas* ([? Hagenau], 1536).

[25] It has also been suggested that a folio volume containing six tracts dated between 1526 and 1536 in the BL (C. 21. f. 14) may have been sewn and forwarded in the same shop before receiving its embroidered satin binding, since it is the only other known binding of Henry VIII's reign to have REX IN AETERNVM VIVE on the edges. See Davenport, *English Embroidered Bookbindings* (London, 1899), pl. 34.

[26] BL MS Royal 12. B. XIII.

(Bonn, 1543).[27] This binding also has the royal arms on the covers, together with a long inscription and the date 1545. It also has a lengthy letter to Henry VIII by the same Wouter Deleen; both books were probably his New Year's gifts to the king. A third royal binding from this shop, now in the library of Lambeth Palace, covers yet another production of Deleen, the Latin *New Testament* of 1540, edited by him and published in London by J. Mayler. This is a simpler binding with only a roll-tooled frame, corner ornaments, the royal arms, and the initials HR (Fig. 25). Another binding from this shop is, however, not connected with Deleen. It covers Martin Luther's *Enarratio Psalmorum LI & CXXX* (Strasburg, 1538), and again has the royal arms and a long Latin inscription on both covers addressed to the king, which may be rendered:

The wealthy, Sire, give their friends golden gifts, but this book contains something better than gold. Your Adam, who is your devoted servant, hopes that you will be as pleased to receive this as he is to give it.[28]

'Your Adam' ('Tuus Adamus') may possibly be the Clement Adams, schoolmaster to the king's pages, who presented the Pepys Library manuscript bound in the Medallion bindery to King Philip.

Another bindery seems to have been responsible for the binding of a book about which there has been considerable debate. This is the copy of Gesner's *Historiae animalium* (Zurich, 1551) at Trinity College, Cambridge,[29] which Hobson hesitantly described as French when he discussed it as plate xxv in *Bindings in Cambridge Libraries*. It was clearly a presentation copy bound for Edward VI, with the royal arms on the covers and ER on three panels of the spine. The gauffered edges of the leaves, as well as the covers, bear the inscription DIEV ET MON DROYT. By the time Hobson published his invaluable *English Bindings in the Library of J. R. Abbey* in 1940, he had changed his mind and listed it in appendix IV among 'English bindings, 1550–60, with elaborate interlacing ribbon'. That this was the correct decision is shown by the fact that this binding has a number of tools in common with a binding in the Pierpont Morgan Library, which has an inscription in Greek stating 'This book belongs to Anne

---

[27] I. G. Philip, *Gold-Tooled Bookbindings* (Oxford, 1951), pl. v. *Fine Bindings . . . from Oxford Libraries*, no. 66.

[28] Nixon, *Five Centuries*, no. 11.

[29] S. 18. 36.

Bacon, the gift of her husband Nicholas Bacon 1553'.[30] 'Anne Bacon' was clearly Lady Bacon, wife of Sir Nicholas (Lord Keeper of the Great Seal) and mother of Francis Bacon. She was a formidable scholar, said to read Latin, Greek, Italian, and French 'as her native tongue'. This explains what might otherwise appear to be a rather unusual present from a Tudor husband to his wife, the Works of Saint Basil in Greek, printed at Basel in 1551. Two other bindings that Wouter Deleen presented to Edward VI may have come from this shop. One is MS Royal 7. D. xx in the British Library,[31] the other is illustrated on plate 8 in R. R. Holmes's *Specimens of Bookbinding from the Royal Library, Windsor Castle* (London, 1893). Deleen, already mentioned when the Flamboyant Binder was discussed, was born in Brabant, became a denizen in 1539, and was appointed minister of the Dutch Church in London in 1550.[32]

It may be useful here to mention some of the more important bindings which have in the past been considered as English or possibly English, and which can now, with a greater knowledge of the tools used to decorate the covers of the books of this period, be firmly attributed elsewhere. One is the binding on the Wingfield *Horae* in the Spencer Collection of the New York Public Library. In the catalogue of the Baltimore Exhibition of 1957[33] it was described as English, but it was subsequently identified as French and as the work of one of Grolier's first binders, Pierre Roffet.[34] A binding with painted medallions, probably made for Cuthbert Tunstall, Bishop of Durham, was originally described as English in both the *Livre anglais* catalogue of 1951 (no. 391) and in H. M. Nixon, *The Broxbourne Library* (London, 1956, no. 22). This is certainly French, as is another binding with similar painted medallions (including one with Tunstall's arms), which is now in the Walters Art Gallery in Baltimore.[35] When discussing the latter book in *Bindings in Cambridge Libraries* (Cam-

---

[30] Nixon, *Sixteenth-Century Gold-Tooled Bookbindings in the Pierpont Morgan Library*, no. 28.

[31] Nixon, *Five Centuries*, no. 14.

[32] For other English bindings from this period see Nixon, 'Early English Gold-Tooled Bookbindings', 302–6.

[33] D. Miner, *The History of Bookbinding 525–1950 A.D. : An Exhibition Held in the Baltimore Museum of Art* (Baltimore, 1957), no. 345.

[34] H. M. Nixon, 'French Bookbindings for Sir Richard Wingfield and Jean Grolier' in *Gatherings in Honor of Dorothy E. Miner* (Baltimore, 1974), 301–15.

[35] B. Quaritch Ltd., *Catalogue of English and Foreign Bookbindings* (London, 1921), no. 3, pl. 1.

bridge, 1929, p. 67) Hobson considered that it and two other bindings of c.1530 were English. One of these, decorated with the arms of Henry Fitzroy, Duke of Richmond and natural son of Henry VIII, is fairly certainly French. The other, about which Hobson followed Colonel Moss's absurd suggestion that 'Tho. Roul. Abb.' must mean that it belonged to Thomas Pentecost, alias Rowlands, last Abbot of Abingdon, is quite clearly an Italian binding.[36]

Colonel Moss's ingenious brain also produced the theory that the bindings executed for Thomas Wotton were produced in Canterbury. (Wotton was the son of Sir Edward Wotton, Treasurer of Calais, and father of Sir Henry Wotton, Provost of Eton, diplomat, and poet.) All Thomas Wotton's more elaborate bindings, in fact, are French and were made for him in Paris in three different binderies, probably during the five or six years up to 1552.[37] Moss was interested in another English sixteenth-century collector, on whom (as on Wotton) he produced one of his privately printed books.[38] This was Robert Dudley, Earl of Leicester, from whose library Moss located seventy-seven volumes—and these were certainly bound in England. Another seventeen have come to light since Moss wrote.[39] As in his book on Wotton, Moss gave evidence of a great deal of very careful study of the bindings, but once again he failed to keep his imagination under full control. The distinguishing mark of these Dudley bindings is a bear and ragged staff in the centre of the covers, which has on its shoulder a crescent, the mark of cadency of the second son. Robert was born the fifth son of John Dudley, Duke of Northumberland, and did not become the second surviving son until 1557. Moss therefore suggested that Ambrose Dudley (afterwards Earl of Warwick), who was the original second son, first owned the books, and then passed them on to Robert after the death of their eldest brother. The simpler solution seems to be that, although many of the books bear imprint dates earlier than 1557, they were all bound subsequent

[36] W. E. Moss sale, Sotheby's, 5 Mar. 1937, lot 937 (illus.), now part of the Henry Davis Gift to the BL.

[37] Nixon, *Sixteenth-Century Gold-Tooled Bookbindings in the Pierpont Morgan Library*, nos. 15, 27. Foot, *The Henry Davis Gift*, i. 139–55.

[38] W. E. Moss, *The English Grolier: A Catalogue of Books ... from the Library of Thomas Wotton* (Worth (Sussex), 1941–44). Id., *Bindings from the Library of Robt. Dudley, Earl of Leicester, K. G., 1533–1588* (Sonning (Berks), 1934).

[39] H. M. Nixon, 'Elizabethan Gold-Tooled Bindings' in *Essays in Honour of Victor Scholderer* (Mainz, 1970), 219–70. Foot, *The Henry Davis Gift*, i. 27–34.

to that date and do not come from any of the binding shops active in the reigns of Edward VI and Mary. This seems to be now generally accepted.

Dudley seems to have patronized a number of different binding shops, although some of the later bindings may well be presentation bindings for him made at a shop chosen by the donor. The first group, the Cartouche group, consists of four bindings, all at Lambeth Palace. The second group, the Frame group, comprises twenty bindings of a simple type, decorated to a panel design with corner fleurons and Dudley's large badge in the centre (Fig. 26). Probably all the books in these two groups were bound to his orders within a year or two of 1560 as standard library bindings.[40] The binder of the next group bound ten books for Dudley, but he also worked for other collectors. One of the more interesting bindings covers a 1563 Basel St Cyril of Alexandria, *Commentarii in Hesaiam*, translated by Laurence Humphrey and presented by him as the dedication copy to Queen Elizabeth I in 1563, now in the British Library (C. 82. f. 11). It has two large initials ER; a close relative at Harvard, with the initials WB instead of those of Queen Elizabeth, covers William Bullein's own copy of his *Bulwarke of Defence* (London, 1562).[41] The binder has been named the Initial Binder, and both the W and B on the Harvard binding and the E and R on the British Library binding came from a set of printer's initials used by John Kingston. Kingston was also the printer of Bullein's book. Unfortunately Kingston's will does not appear to have survived and it has not been possible to establish whether he had a binding shop attached to his printing office.[42] Another binding from this shop bears the initials (though not from Kingston's set) of Nils Gyllenstierna, the Swedish Ambassador to London, and is in the Royal Library at Stockholm.[43]

The best-known example of the next small group of Dudley bindings is the Clemens Alexandrinus of 1550 in the British Library, from which the group takes its name (Fig. 28). Again there are only four bindings in this group, but although two of the tools at first

[40]   Ibid. See also Nixon, *Five Centuries*, no. 16.

[41]   Nixon, *Five Centuries*, nos. 19, 20.

[42]   Dr K. Pantzer has kindly confirmed that these initials seem to show virtually no wear over the years. This may suggest that they were made of engraved brass rather than of type metal.

[43]   Nixon, 'Elizabethan Gold-Tooled Bindings', pl. 2.

sight seem to link this group with that of the Initial Binder and—as Colonel Moss stated—with one of the Wotton binders, on close examination they turn out to be different. Three books were certainly and the fourth was probably bound for Dudley. They were all bound during Queen Elizabeth's reign, although the latest imprint is 1554. One group of twelve bindings shows a strong Parisian influence in their designs, since nearly all the hatched tools used to decorate them are fairly close copies of those used by Grolier's last binder. As nine of the twelve books in this group were bound for Robert Dudley, its binder was consequently christened the Dudley Binder (Fig. 27). Two others were bound for Henry Fitzalan, twelfth Earl of Arundel, and Edward Seymour, Earl of Hertford, the son of Protector Somerset. The last of this group is a charming little Venetian book of 1558 that came to the British Library as part of the Old Royal Library, but there is no indication for whom it was bound.[44] The latest imprint of the books in the Dudley Binder group is 1558, but the whole group was probably bound a year or two later than that.

The successor of the Dudley Binder was unfortunately named the Morocco Binder. Not only was this binder not the only one to use tanned goatskin, but the goatskin that was (distinctly rarely) used in Elizabethan England came not from Morocco but from Turkey. The Morocco Binder group now contains thirty-one books, two of which are bound in five volumes. The bindery was active until at least 1576.[45] A fine binding on a 1558 volume of *Statutes* in the British Library (C. 54. f. 5), probably bound c.1562, has the same admirable kind of freehand tooling as occurs on the Dudley Binder's Aristotle at Lambeth Palace.[46] The Morocco Binder bound a five-volume set of the 1569 Bible for Archbishop Matthew Parker, which has now been dispersed.[47] A similar five-volume set of the 1573 Bible, bound by the same binder for John Whitgift, Parker's successor as Archbishop of Canterbury, is still at Lambeth Palace.[48] Although this bindery continued to do some work for Robert Dudley, it also worked for

[44] Felipe de la Torre, *Institutione d'un Re Christiano* (Venice, 1558), BL C. 20. a. 24. Nixon, *Five Centuries*, no. 17.
[45] Nixon, 'Elizabethan Gold-Tooled Bindings', 237–43. Foot, *The Henry Davis Gift*, ii, no. 45.
[46] Nixon, 'Elizabethan Gold-Tooled Bindings', pls. 3, 4.
[47] Nixon, 'Elizabethan Gold-Tooled Bindings', 238, no. 19. Id., *Sixteenth-Century Gold-Tooled Bookbindings in the Pierpont Morgan Library*, no. 47.
[48] Burlington Fine Arts Club, *Exhibition of Bookbindings* (London, 1891), pl. LXXVII.

other collectors including Elizabeth I, Dudley's elder brother
Ambrose, Earl of Warwick, and Sir Roland Heywarde, who was
Lord Mayor of London in 1571. The latter's Bible, now in the
Grenville Library at the British Library, was no doubt bound for him
in that year (Pl. 2).

It is possible to produce both a name and some bindings for two
London binders of Queen Elizabeth's reign. The first of these was
John (or Jean) de Planche, and it is reasonably certain that he was a
member of a Protestant binders' family in Dijon; he was probably the
second of the three Jean de Planches who were in business there from
1548 until well into the seventeenth century. Although they were
continually in trouble with the authorities during this period, they all
apparently managed to die in their beds, because the only other
important member of the book trade in Dijon had similar religious
leanings, and the authorities did not wish to find themselves without
any booksellers or printers. Jean de Planche the elder was several
times placed under house arrest and his son may have come to
London as a refugee. He was admitted a Brother of the Stationers'
Company in October 1567, took out letters of denization in May
1570, and in 1571 lived with three servants in the parish of St Martin's
Outwich, Broad Street Ward. In May of the following year he
married the daughter of a shoemaker at Temple Bar; three weeks later
he was accused of bigamy. Evidence was produced that before coming
to London he had been married in Rouen, but the ecclesiastical
authorities were unimpressed with his defence that his French wife
was a prostitute and therefore had no claim. He was excluded from
the Eucharist, but continued to bind for his distinguished clients.
When exactly he left London is not known, but he was still at work
there in the late 1570s.[49] De Planche introduced to London the 'sunk
panel' style also found in France and Geneva—a heavily restored
large folio Bible in the British Library bearing the royal arms and the
date 1568 must have been magnificent in its prime.[50] The sunk panels,
now covered with gold-tooled leather, were no doubt originally

[49] Nixon, 'Elizabethan Gold-Tooled Bindings', 243–53. M. M. Foot, 'A Binding by Jean
de Planche', *Book Collector*, 27 (1978), 230. H. M. Nixon, 'Some Huguenot Bookbinders',
Proceedings of the Huguenot Society, 23, no. 5 (1981), 324.

[50] *La Sainte Bible* (Lyons, 1566), BL C. 23. e. 10. C. J. H. Davenport, *Royal English
Bookbindings* (London, New York, 1896), fig. 12. One example is at St John's College,
Oxford (MS 4) and is illus. in *Fine Bindings . . . from Oxford Libraries*, no. 126, and
another was sold at Christie's, 9 Dec. 1981, lot 202.

covered with velvet. Another binding, also from the Old Royal Library, has a sunk panel with painted royal arms in the centre of the covers and gilt white onlays in the corners. It covers a copy of Nicolay's *Navigations et pérégrinations orientales*, printed in Lyons in 1568.[51] His third first-class binding in the British Library covers the presentation copy to Elizabeth I of Archbishop Parker's edition of Matthew of Westminster;[52] it has onlaid L-shaped cornerpieces with the initials IDP, which enable us to identify these bindings as the work of Jean de Planche. The same signed cornerpieces occur on the presentation copy to the queen from John Foxe, the martyrologist, of his 1571 edition of the Gospels in Anglo-Saxon.[53] Both these books, like many other presentation copies, strayed from royal ownership and reached the British Museum with the Cracherode Library in 1799. Another example with these signed corners covers a copy of the *Harmonia ex Evangelistis* (Geneva, 1572) at Lambeth Palace.[54] A binding at University College, Oxford, also bound c.1570 by de Planche, covers the first part of W. Forrest's *History of Joseph: a poem*.[55] This is a de Planche binding without sunk panels or onlays, but with attractive metal corners (Fig. 29). A binding from this shop made for William Alyn in 1571, formerly in the possession of Major J. R. Abbey, is now in the British Library.[56] Jean de Planche was next heard of back in Dijon in 1593. He must have left his finishing tools behind in London, for fifteen bindings are known on which some of his tools were used, covering books printed between 1577 and 1645.[57]

The MacDurnan Gospels Binder gets his name from the most famous book he bound, the little ninth-century Gospels of Maelbright MacDurnan in Lambeth Palace Library.[58] The design, like that on much of this binder's work, shows blocked corner- and centre-pieces,

[51] BL C. 18. c. 8. W. Y. Fletcher, *English Bookbindings in the British Museum*, pl. xviii. Nixon, 'Elizabethan Gold-Tooled Bindings', pl. 5.

[52] BL C. 18. b. 11. Fletcher, op cit., pl. xx. Nixon, 'Elizabethan Gold-Tooled Bindings', pl. 6.

[53] BL 675. f. 16. Fletcher, op. cit., pl. xxi.

[54] Nixon, *Five Centuries*, no. 22.

[55] *Fine Bindings . . . from Oxford Libraries*, no. 70.

[56] BL C. 108. aaa. 3. Hobson, *English Bindings . . . in the Library of J. R. Abbey*, no. 15.

[57] Foot, 'A Binding by Jean de Planche', *Book Collector*, 27 (1978), 230. Id., 'A London Binding, c. 1638', *Book Collector*, 31 (1982), 482. Id., *The Henry Davis Gift*, ii, no. 46.

[58] Nixon, *Five Centuries*, no. 21. Nixon, 'Elizabethan Gold-Tooled Bindings', 254, no. 1.

here heightened with green and white paint. Above and below the centre block is one of this binder's most characteristic tools—an obliquely hatched opening bud. From its appearance on a Paris Book of Hours in the Bodleian Library bound by one of Wotton's binders, this tool appears to have been used in Paris before coming to England.[59] Notwithstanding the MacDurnan Gospels Binder's customary reliance on large centre and corner blocks, his bindings vary considerably in appearance. The result is very different on the 1570 edition of Matthew of Westminster's *De rebus Britannicis*, a sizeable folio that, like the Gospels of Maelbright MacDurnan, was bound for Matthew Parker.[60] In the early 1570s Parker was his most consistent patron. He also made quite a number of bindings for other well-known persons, but the majority of these appear to have been presentation copies from authors. Thus nine bindings from this shop are now known on presentation copies to Queen Elizabeth, and six are known for Robert Dudley, Earl of Leicester. In the later part of his life Dudley seems to have acquired most of his fine bindings as gifts; an example in the Bodleian Library[61]—again looking quite unlike the other two bindings from this shop that have been mentioned above—was probably a gift to him. It covers Aelfric's *Testimonie of Antiquitie* printed by John Day in [1566] (Fig. 30).

It seems that the MacDurnan Gospels Binder started work in the 1560s, and tools that link with this shop are found well into the seventeenth century. John Bateman, the Royal Bookbinder, made a group of bindings for James I; Henry, Prince of Wales; and Charles, Prince of Wales, as well as for various non-royal owners, and these are decorated with tools and blocks that link with those used by the MacDurnan Gospels Binder. As John Bateman did not become free of the Stationers' Company until January 1580 he cannot have been responsible for the earliest output of the MacDurnan Gospels Binder's shop. There is a slight shift in the tools in the late 1580s and it is possible that John Bateman took over at that time.[62]

Though Matthew Parker patronized the MacDurnan Gospels Binder's shop in its early days, the latest imprint of any book bound there

[59] Nixon, 'Elizabethan Gold-Tooled Bindings', 254, 269–70 n. 38. *Fine Bindings . . . from Oxford Libraries*, no. 35. See also Foot, *The Henry Davis Gift*, i. 145.
[60] *Fine Bindings . . . from Oxford Libraries*, no. 120.
[61] Ibid. no. 75.
[62] Foot, *The Henry Davis Gift*, i. 36–49.

for him personally is 1571.[63] The bindings that he commissioned during the last three years of his life appear to come from his private bindery at Lambeth. The evidence for this comes in a well-known letter written by Parker to Lord Burghley in 1572, which is preserved at the British Library in Lansdowne MS 17 (f. 63).[64] In it he says 'I have within my house in wagis, drawers & cutters, paynters, lymmers, wryters, and boke bynders'. Earlier in the letter, he talks of 'some of my small travels [travails], whereof I send youe one bound by my man', it therefore seems as if he had in his employ a binder capable of doing a special binding suitable for presentation to Burghley. Further-more, there is a very reasonable chance that the copy of Parker's own *De antiquitate Britannicae Ecclesiae* (London, 1572), now in the University Library in Cambridge, is the very book 'bound by my man'.[65] Indeed, tipped into it is a note in the hand of Henry Bradshaw which reads 'This is the author's presentation copy to the Lord Treasurer Burleigh'. Possibly there was some evidence of its original provenance which has now disappeared. All that one can say now for certain is that it was bought by Bishop John Moore at a time when other books were on the market which appeared to come from Burghley's library. But, like some of the others, it does not occur in the catalogue of the Burghley sale by T. Bentley and B. Walford on 21 November 1687. Only eight elaborate bindings are known that have been made in this shop (Fig. 31),[66] but the University Library in Cambridge has a considerable number of books (which formed part of the Archbishop's gift in 1574 of seventy-five books), which are in standard bindings and show some of the tools found on the grander bindings. More standard bindings are scattered throughout various Cambridge colleges: Trinity Hall has a copy of Matthew of West-minster's *Flores historiarum* (London, 1570) in such a binding, which has at the end a manuscript list of ninety-eight books given by Parker to the university in 1574 (Fig. 32). After Parker's death in May 1575, the binders evidently returned from Lambeth to the City; some of their tools are found in use later.[67]

[63] Nixon, 'Elizabethan Gold-Tooled Bindings', 256–7, list nos. 22 and 26 may have been presentation copies. See also ibid. 262.

[64] Printed in E. Almack, *Fine Old Bindings* (London, 1913), 21–2.

[65] Cambridge University Library, Sel. 3. 229. Nixon, 'Elizabethan Gold-Tooled Bind-ings', pl. 8, p. 264.

[66] Nixon, 'Elizabethan Gold-Tooled Bindings', 265.

[67] Foot, *The Henry Davis Gift*, i. 32.

Jean de Planche and John Bateman are the only two London binders active during Elizabeth's reign whose name and work are both known to us. But we do know the names of quite a number of binders, and many of those appear to be of French origin. Indeed, the designs and the finishing tools that were used to decorate many of the bindings of this period show close similarities to French designs and tools. In 1578 we find the native-born binders demanding—among other things—that no work should be given to 'forens or strangers', and that the 'ffrenchmen and straungers beinge Denizens maie not haue excessiue nomber of app[re]ntic[es]'.[68] Quite a number of fine bindings of the period cannot be linked with any of the groups so far mentioned. The bindings on a pair of presentation copies of Laurence Humphrey's *Ioannis Iuelli . . . vita et mors* (London, John Day, 1573), for example, do not seem to fit into any of the groups discussed here. One presented to Robert Dudley is now in the Pierpont Morgan Library.[69] The badge of the bear and ragged staff is from a block that seems to have been used by several different binders.[70] The other copy, now at Balliol College, Oxford, was bound for presentation to William Cecil, Lord Burghley (Fig. 33).[71]

Cambridge seems to be the only place in England besides London where gold-tooled bindings were produced in the sixteenth century. When John Denys, bookbinder and stationer, died there about 1578, a very detailed inventory of the contents of his shop was prepared by 'John Sheres & Bradshaw, booke bynders'. It is quite clear that he had a properly equipped bindery, as well as a considerable stock of bound and unbound books for sale. And among his equipment was a 'gilding coushin with the kniffe to cut gold' and 'a payer of greate corners to gilte'.[72] But none of his bindings have been identified.

Elizabeth I clearly preferred velvet to leather bindings, and many who donated books to her realized this. When in 1598 a visitor to England, Paul Hentzner (a native of Brandenburg) visited the Royal

---

[68] W. W. Greg and E. Boswell, *Records of the Court of the Stationers' Company* (London, 1930), 4.

[69] *A Catalogue of a Collection of Books formed by James Toovey . . . the property of J. Pierpont Morgan* (New York, 1901), opp. p. 136.

[70] Foot, *The Henry Davis Gift*, i. 31–2.

[71] *Fine Bindings . . . from Oxford Libraries*, no. 125.

[72] G. J. Gray and W. M. Palmer, *Abstracts from the Wills and Testamentary Documents of Printers, Binders and Stationers of Cambridge, from 1504 to 1699* (London, 1915), 36, 57–8.

Library at Whitehall, he wrote in his *Itinerarium* that it was well stored with books in various languages 'all . . . bound in velvet of different colours, though chiefly red, with clasps of gold and silver; some have pearls, and precious stones, set in their bindings'.[73] The British Library owns a red velvet binding, now very worn and faded, with a gold and enamelled centre-piece, corners, and clasps,[74] clearly the kind of thing that caught Hentzner's eye. The finest English embroidered binding of Elizabeth I's reign is in the Bodleian Library. It covers a folio Bible of 1583 that was presented to the Queen as a New Year's gift in 1584 by Christopher Barker, the printer.[75] He received in return from the Queen 11⅛ ounces of gold plate—and he deserved every ounce of it.

[73] P. Hentzner, *Itinerarium Germaniae, Galliae; Angliae; Italiae; etc.* (Nuremberg, 1612). The part relating to England was translated by Richard Bentley, *A Journey into England in the Year 1598* and published at Strawberry Hill by Horace Walpole in 1757 (for the passage quoted here see p. 31).

[74] BL 168. i. 30. W. Y. Fletcher, *English Bookbindings in the British Museum*, pl. XIX.

[75] Bodleian Library, Oxford, Douce Bib. Eng. 1583. b. 1. *Fine Bindings . . . from Oxford Libraries*, no. 163 (frontispiece). See also G. Barber, *Textile and Embroidered Bindings* (Oxford, 1971).

THREE

The First Sixty Years of the Seventeenth Century

ALTHOUGH Queen Elizabeth's own preference was for fabric or embroidered bindings rather than for gold-tooled leather ones, this did not prevent her from receiving quite a number of leather-bound books as presents, most of them probably as New Year's gifts. A copy of Isocrates, *Orationes et epistola*, printed in Paris by Henri Estienne in 1593 is bound in brown calf and tooled in gold with large corner-pieces and the royal arms.[1] It is now part of the Broxbourne Collection in the Bodleian Library. At this period the presence of royal arms or emblems on a book does not necessarily denote royal ownership; neither, as G. D. Hobson has shown,[2] does the crowned falcon. Both arms, falcon, and other royal emblems were used on trade bindings. However, a folio of this size and a work of this nature is not likely to have been put in a trade binding, and this seems to be a New Year's gift to the queen, quite possibly presented some years after the book was printed. This was not an uncommon occurrence: we can point to a copy of Andrew Willet's *Synopsis Papismi* in the British Library (C. 46. k. 4), which bears the date 1600 on the title-page but has a cancel dedication to James I as King of England. It cannot therefore have been presented to him before 1603.

Another binding, also on a book from the Broxbourne Collection,[3] covers a manuscript closely related to William Camden's first guide book to Westminster Abbey, although it does not contain the full text of the *Reges, Reginae, Nobiles & alij in Ecclesia . . . B. Petri Westmonasterij sepulti*, first published in 1600. From internal evidence

---

[1] H. M. Nixon, *Broxbourne Library: Styles and Designs of Bookbindings from the Twelfth to the Twentieth Century* (London, 1956), no. 48.
[2] G. D. Hobson, *Bindings in Cambridge Libraries* (Cambridge, 1929), 106.
[3] Nixon, *Broxbourne Library*, no. 54.

this manuscript seems likely to have been completed towards the end of 1601, and it was perhaps a New Year's gift for 1602. The brown calf binding is decorated with large corner blocks and the royal arms on a semis of small leaves. The same corner blocks were still in use as late as 1625. They are found on a copy of Smith's *Virginia* of that date, which was lot 606 in the Duke of Leeds sale at Sotheby's on 2 June 1930. Both the corners and the arms block occur on a copy of the first edition of the Bible in Welsh, probably bound for Queen Elizabeth when it was published in 1588, now in the library of Christ Church, Oxford (Fig. 34).[4]

The royal bindings of James I's reign seem mostly to be presentation copies to the king, but a binding from Dr Routh's collection in Durham University Library covers a presentation copy to Petrus Junius of the 1619 Latin edition of the king's own works.[5] Its most unusual feature is that it is bound in red turkey, which was rarely used in England before the 1650s. It shows the beginning of the reintroduction of the small tool to form a decorative border, although the main panel of the binding still has the standard centre- and corner-piece design with the background filled with a semis of a repeated single tool (Fig. 35). The only royal binding of James I's reign that shows a new and different design is a well-known example in the Old Royal Library in the British Library: although it covers a 1584 book, André Thevet's *Pourtraits et vies des hommes illustres*, it bears the arms and initials of the king and probably dates from c.1615 or later.[6] It is clearly an English imitation of the French bindings *à la fanfare*, although it lacks one of the distinguishing features of the French style. On the English binding, the interlacing ribbon that forms compartments of various shapes is bounded by a single line on each side. Another English binder, who was responsible for a group of prayer books in the chapel at Knole in Kent, also adopted the less satisfactory habit of tooling a ribbon with a single line on either side. He made up for it with a splendid collection of animal tools, including squirrels, birds, worms, moths, snails, and even a pair of military men facing two relatively enormous pigeons with true British phlegm.[7]

[4] *Fine Bindings 1500–1700 from Oxford Libraries* (Oxford, 1968), no. 122.
[5] A. I. Doyle, 'Martin Joseph Routh and his Books in Durham University Library', *Durham University Journal* (June 1956), 100–7.
[6] BL C. 22. f. 4. W. Y. Fletcher, *English Bookbindings in the British Museum* (London, 1895), pl. xxxiv. M. M. Foot, 'A London Binding, c.1638', *Book Collector*, 31 (1982), 482.
[7] G. D. Hobson, *Les Reliures à la fanfare* (London, 1935), pl. xxiv.

This shop also bound a copy of John Speed's *Theatre of the Empire of Great Britaine* (London, 1611), for James I's wife, Anne of Denmark, probably not long before her death in 1619.[8]

The most important English royal library in the early seventeenth century was not that of the king and queen but that of their eldest son, Henry, Prince of Wales (1594–1612). This library had been built up by John, Lord Lumley, on the basis of that of his father-in-law, the Earl of Arundel, which itself included much of the library of Archbishop Cranmer.[9] The rather plain bindings provided for Prince Henry nearly all seem to date from *c*.1610. As there were three blocks of the prince's arms and six separate large corner blocks, and as almost all the corner blocks are found at different times with different arms blocks, it would appear that John Norton or Robert Barker (both of whom were paid for supplying bindings at this time) farmed out the work in comparatively small batches to different binders, and lent them the blocks.[10] The Prince also owned a few more elaborate bindings which had presumably been presented to him, such as his copy of J. Ferrettus, *De re et disciplina militari*, Venice, 1575 (Fig. 36). After his death his library passed to his father and most of it reached the British Museum at its foundation with the rest of the Old Royal Library.[11] A number of Prince Henry's books, however, were sold at the disastrous sales of duplicates held between 1769 and 1832.

Charles I was much more interested in collecting pictures than in amassing a library—some of the books that reached the royal library in his reign unbound had to wait until the Restoration before they were dispatched to Samuel Mearne for binding. Like all sovereigns he acquired finely bound books as gifts. None of them show much originality in design. An example from the Cosin Library in Durham (Fig. 37) probably dates from *c*.1630, and is mainly interesting for being bound in the still-unusual red turkey leather. Another example,

---

[8] Hobson, *Bindings in Cambridge Libraries*, pl. xxxix. On this Squirrel Binder see M. M. Foot, *The Henry Davis Gift*, i (London, 1978) 52–4 [correction: the binding referred to in note 44 is decorated with the arms of Charles as Prince of Wales].

[9] S. R. Jayne and F. R. Johnson (eds.), *The Lumley Library: The Catalogue of 1609* (London, 1956). See also D. G. Selwyn, 'The Lumley Library: A Supplementary Checklist', *British Library Journal*, 7 (1981), 136–48.

[10] H. M. Nixon, *Twelve Books in Fine Bindings from the Library of J. W. Hely-Hutchinson* (London, 1953), 11, 12. The blocks may have been cast in more than one copy.

[11] For the Old Royal Library in general and Prince Henry's books in particular, see T. A. Birrell, *English Monarchs and their Books: From Henry VII to Charles II*, Panizzi Lectures 1986 (London, 1987).

on a copy of J. Schiller, *Coelum stellatum Christianum* (Augsburg, 1627), was already in Archbishop Laud's hands by 1634, when he gave it to St John's College, Oxford,[12] but at all times quite a high percentage of gifts to royalty became royal gifts in a year or two. One of the more attractive bindings the king received as a present was a copy of G. Williams, *The Right Way to the Best Religion* (London, 1636), probably presented in that year. It still shows the same style with a panel with royal arms, large corner-pieces and an outer border, but at least now the corner-pieces are composed of separate tools and the constituents of the border are more variegated and lively.[13]

Turning to the nobility who either collected books or had books thrust upon them, we meet the beginnings of one of the great English family libraries, that of the Egerton family, earls of Bridgewater. The library was founded by Sir Thomas Egerton, Viscount Brackley (? 1540–1617), who was Lord Chancellor from 1603 until shortly before his death. A splendid binding on Saxton's *Atlas* probably dates from the last years of his life (Fig. 38). His son, the first Earl of Bridgewater, greatly extended the library, which remained in the direct family line until the death of the childless third Duke of Bridgewater in 1803. It then passed to a nephew, the Marquess of Stafford, who became the first Duke of Sutherland, and then to his son, who became the first Earl of Ellesmere in 1846. Eventually the whole collection was sold to Henry E. Huntington and now forms part of his wonderful library at San Marino, California, though some duplicates were sold. Others had left the library earlier, as was the case with a copy of H. Mason, *The New Art of Lying* (London, 1624). It was presented by the author to the first Earl of Bridgewater and is now in the Bodleian Library.[14] Francis Bacon, Lord Verulam and Viscount St Albans, does not appear to have had a large library, and most of the surviving bindings with his crest (a boar passant ermine with a crescent for difference) appear to be on presentation copies of his *Instauratio magna* of 1620. But a copy now in the Bodleian Library, with a crest tooled on limp vellum, is presumably from his private library, since it covers a work by G. Lasso de la Vega, printed in Lisbon in 1619.[15]

[12] *Fine Bindings . . . from Oxford Libraries*, no. 139.
[13] BL C. 21. e. 14. M. M. Foot, 'Some Bindings for Charles I' in G. A. M. Janssens and F. G. A. M. Aarts (eds.), *Studies in Seventeenth-Century English Literature, History and Bibliography* (Amsterdam, 1984), 95–106, esp. 103 and fig. 2.
[14] *Fine Bindings . . . from Oxford Libraries*, no. 146.
[15] Ibid. no. 135.

George Villiers, Marquess and later Duke of Buckingham, was also the type of magnate who received handsome bindings as presents rather than commissioning them himself. A rather crude binding dating from c.1620 covers a copy of Holinshed's *Chronicles* (London, 1587), now at St Hugh's College, Oxford, and a more elegant white vellum binding also made for him is on James I's *Workes* (London, 1616), at Jesus College, Oxford.[16] An almost identical binding on the king's Latin Works of 1619–20 belongs to the library of York Minster. Captain John Smith's *Generall History of Virginia* (London, 1624) is a book that does not have to apologize for itself in any way, but the copy at Queen's College, Oxford, is the most desirable of all; it is the dedication copy for Frances, Duchess of Richmond and Lennox. On the title-page the author has written that it is 'for his approved kynd frend' the duchess, and the simple but well-proportioned calf binding with large corner-pieces has a well-cut block of her arms in the centre.[17]

A most attractive example of the centre- and corner-piece style occurs on an English Bible of 1602, bound in three volumes (probably c.1630) for Sir Robert Berkeley (1584–1656), Judge of the Queen's Bench.[18] In each volume is written 'Durdens Chappel', Durdans being a large house built near Epsom by the first Earl of Berkeley (1628–98). It was pulled down in the eighteenth century, but Lord Rosebery owned a house built on the same site, and it was at his sale in 1947 that the book was bought by Major J. R. Abbey. It is now in the Pierpont Morgan Library in New York.

One of the truly great collectors of this period was Sir Robert Bruce Cotton, Bt. (1571–1631). This is not the place to expatiate on his greatness as a collector of manuscripts, or on the disastrous fire at Ashburnham House, now part of Westminster School, in which a considerable number of his manuscripts were destroyed and many others were seriously damaged. Happily the greater part survived and a few are still in the red turkey bindings which Cotton had made for them. Others, mostly rebound, have retained on a flyleaf Cotton's fervent instructions to his binder. On the original paste-downs of a manuscript on vellum *Evangelia* [and] *Nomina benefactorum Dunelmensis ecclesiae* (c.840), bound in gold-tooled red turkey (Fig. 39), is

---

[16] Ibid. nos. 136, 137.
[17] Ibid. no. 140.
[18] J. R. Abbey sale, Sotheby's, 21 June 1965, lot 131.

written: 'Bind this book as strong as you can and very fair in the read leather let it be shewed [sewed] withe 3 double threads waxed and when it is backed and shewed send it me and I will mark wher you shall cutt it gett it as euen at the head as you can'. He continued at the end, presumably after he had seen it: '[Cut it] as I have marked and [round?] it not to muche in the back for fear you put som leaves so forward that the[y] may be in danger of Cutting sett flowers of gold one the back and corners and mak it very fayre and lett me have it ready this night when [I] send about 5c in the afternoone'.[19]

One of the more whimsical productions of the reign of James I was the travelling library, of which four examples are known.[20] Each consists of an olive-green or brown folio turkey leather book-box, containing three rows of 12mo, 16mo, 24mo, and 32mo books. On the inside of the cover of the box is an elaborately painted list of the books. One example, now in the Huntington Library, was evidently made for presentation to Sir Thomas Egerton, Baron Ellesmere and Viscount Brackley, and may be as early as 1615. It had always been in the Egerton family until it passed with the rest of the family library to the Henry E. Huntington Library in San Marino in 1917. At the back of the bottom shelf of the box is the name 'W: HAKEWIL. A? D. 1615'. The second in date is now in the Brotherton Library at Leeds. It appeared in Maggs's Catalogue 397 of 1920, where it was rather confusingly referred to as the 'Sir Julius Caesar' travelling library, presented by Sir Julius Caesar to John Madden, Esq. (attorney to King James I). This has the date 'Jan. 1617', a name of which it is possible to read 'G . . . l . . . l . . . H . . . il', and a coat of arms which (though it is not quite accurate) leads us once more to William Hakewill. Maggs's reason for thinking that this library had been given by Sir Julius Caesar to John Madden was based on their knowledge of the British Library example to be mentioned next, and the fact that on the Madden example the name of Julius Caesar in the list of books is in capitals. But while it is not quite certain whether a Madden was the original owner, it was clearly a present not from Sir Julius Caesar, but from William Hakewill.[21] The third and best-known example is

[19] BL MS Cotton Domitian A. VII, fos. 1, 84ᵛ.

[20] H. M. Nixon and W. A. Jackson, 'English Seventeenth-Century Travelling Libraries', *Transactions of the Cambridge Bibliographical Society*, 7 (1979), 294–304.

[21] Maggs Bros., Catalogue 397 (1920), no. 56. H. M. Nixon and W. A. Jackson, 'English Seventeenth-Century Travelling Libraries'.

in the British Library.[22] This was unquestionably made for Sir Julius Caesar (1558–1636), Master of the Rolls, and, judging from the books, not before 1619. It has Caesar's arms in the centre with those of his second and third wives. There is no sign of Hakewill's name or arms and it does not look as if they had ever been there, but it is perhaps significant that Caesar's third wife, Anne, daughter of Sir Henry Wodehouse, was the sister of William Hakewill's wife. Although—as on the Brotherton copy—Julius Caesar heads the middle column of authors on the inside of the upper cover of the box, oddly enough this name does not occur in capitals on Sir Julius Caesar's own travelling library. The fourth of these travelling libraries was made for a member of the Bacon family. It probably dates from c.1620 and is now in the Museum of Art in Toledo, Ohio.[23] It has suffered considerably from damp, and most of the books on the two top shelves were evidently so damaged that they had to be replaced. The place where Hakewill's name and arms might have been was also affected by damp, so that had they been there they would have been effaced. Sir Julius Caesar's third wife, Anne Wodehouse, already mentioned above, was also a niece of the great Francis Bacon, so that again we are dealing with members of the circle in which William Hakewill moved.

Each of these libraries has three rows of similar vellum-bound small volumes with coloured silk ties, and broadly speaking the books are the same: one shelf of theology and philosophy, one of history, and one of poetry. Not only are the texts usually the same, but frequently they are the same edition. The bindings have a single gold-tooled ornament on the sides. In the Egerton–Huntington library there are twenty-one volumes with the royal arms and eighteen with a figure who appears to be a wise virgin. There is no attempt to restrict the decoration to a particular shelf, although the four volumes decorated with a third tool—perhaps a wheatear—are all on the top shelf. One volume has a star. On the Madden–Brotherton set all the volumes have an angel carrying a scroll with the words GLORIA DEO. The Julius Caesar–British Library set has this angel on the theology and philosophy volumes on the top shelf, a rampant lion on the

[22] BL C. 20. f. 15–58. W. Y. Fletcher, *English Bookbindings in the British Museum*, pls. XLIII–XLV.

[23] D. Miner, *The History of Bookbinding 525–1950 A.D.* (Baltimore, 1957), no. 408, pl. LXXII. Nixon and Jackson, 'English Seventeenth-Century Travelling Libraries'.

historical books on the second shelf, and an olive branch oval on the poetry (Fig. 41). The Bacon–Toledo set was evidently originally decorated with the same GLORIA DEO angel; two other versions of this tool are found on the replacements. Each set originally had different coloured silk ties to the volumes on each of the three shelves.

W. A. Jackson was convinced that Charles I, when Prince of Wales, had possessed a similar travelling library. The books from this had formerly been at Britwell Court and the story went that Queen Mary possessed the box in which the books had originally been kept and that Major Christie–Miller was always terrified that she would descend upon him and demand the books. But if there was a box, and it has not been traced, it seems unlikely that it could have been in the form of a book. When the Christie–Miller set was sold at Sotheby's as lot 88 on 29 March 1971, there were sixty volumes, bound in red turkey with flat spines decorated with leafy sprays. Most of them were slightly larger than the volumes in the four travelling libraries just described, and they occupied forty-nine inches of shelf space as opposed to the twenty-seven inches of the four book-boxes. It may be that they were simply intended to fill a miniature book case. When they were described in Traylen's Catalogue 77 (1972) they were in two full crimson levant morocco boxes by Sangorski & Sutcliffe. Now they belong to Mr John Emmerson of Melbourne, Australia.[24]

Charles's elder brother Henry, Prince of Wales, had a similar small library, of which nineteen volumes survive in the Old Royal Library, one was purchased by the British Museum in 1877, and two more, which had been in the Sir Thomas Brooke sale of 25 May 1921, were bought from Maggs Bros. in 1972. Prince Henry's books were bound in dark-green turkey leather, with similar spines and with a coronetted HP monogram on the panelled sides. There is no trace of a case for this set (BL C. 66. a. 8–24; C. 64. aa. 4).

What is certainly another travelling library, but is rather later in date, belongs to the Pierpont Morgan Library. It has a much smaller box, again in book form, which is decorated in the same mosaic style as the six small devotional books that it contains. The four books that have dates in their imprints were published between 1636 and 1640, but the bindings of the books and their box with coloured onlays do

---

[24] J. McL. Emmerson, 'The Travelling Library of Charles I', *Bulletin of the Bibliographical Society of Australia and New Zealand*, 7: 3 (1983), 95–108.

not look as if they date from much before 1650. Presumably this set was originally prepared for a member of the Fountaine family, and it first appeared in the salerooms in the sale of the library of Sir Andrew Fountaine on 12 June 1902 (lot 273). Afterwards it belonged in turn to W. H. Corfield, Cortlandt F. Bishop, and Lord Rothschild.[25]

Returning to the more normal London bindings of the 1620s, we find that the smaller gold-tooled bindings are still decorated to a centre and corner design, but that both centre and corner ornaments on these books are now frequently composed at least partly of small tools. A copy of Valerius Maximus, *Dictorum factorumque memorabilium libri novem* (Hanau, 1614), bound not earlier than c.1620, is now in the Broxbourne Collection in the Bodleian Library. It has a centre and corner design, of which the central wreath and the oval line were produced by a block, as were the corner segments within the double lines of the quarter circles. But the rest of the centre and corner decoration was effected with small tools.[26] A binding in Keble College, Oxford, on a French translation of the *Book of Common Prayer*, published in London by John Bill in 1616, has been tentatively described as the work of a French refugee. However, the book was probably presented to Laud in 1628, twelve years after it had been published, and it appears to be in a typical London binding of that date (Fig. 40).[27]

The centre- and corner-piece style remained not uncommon up to c.1650; one example, again from the Broxbourne Collection, contains songs of Henry Lawes and others, and is probably not earlier than that date.[28] However, the fan centre and corners are very different from the typical ornaments of Elizabethan and Jacobean times. These particular blocks were also used on a volume containing a 1609 Bible and a 1636 Prayer Book (formerly in Major Abbey's library) that was probably bound c.1636,[29] but three of the tools on this binding,

---

[25] Pierpont Morgan Library, Rothschild 874. Corfield Sale, Sotheby's, 21 Nov. 1904, lot 40. Cortlandt Bishop sale, American Art Association Anderson Galleries, NY, 15 Nov. 1938, lot 2266. N. M. V. Rothschild, Baron Rothschild, *The Rothschild Library: A Catalogue ... formed by Lord Rothschild*, 2 vols. (Cambridge, 1954), i, no. 874, pl. XIII. See also Nixon and Jackson, 'English Seventeenth-Century Travelling Libraries'.

[26] Nixon, *Broxbourne Library*, no. 59.

[27] *Fine Bindings ... from Oxford Libraries*, no. 133. It must have been given to Laud between 1628 and 1633, as he is described as Bishop of London.

[28] Nixon, *Broxbourne Library*, no. 70.

[29] G. D. Hobson, *English Bindings 1490–1940 in the Library of J. R. Abbey* (London, 1940), no. 23.

particularly that which accompanies the rosette on the field of the panel, are typical of the Restoration period, although all were introduced into England in the late 1640s.

London was not the only town where gold-tooled bookbindings were made in the first half of the seventeenth century. Thanks to Sir Robert Birley's researches,[30] we know of bookbindings being produced at Eton, and we know the name of the binder, one Williamson. We even know that he was the first—but by no means the last— recorded English bookbinder who found at one stage of his career that alcohol improved his finishing, only to find that the improvement lasted but a short time, and soon resulted in an inability to put in any tool straight at all. Nevertheless he continued to work until c.1621, although already in 1608 Sir Dudley Carleton wrote from Eton to a friend in London:

I doe understand that the goode workemen in Fetter Lane are some of the godly brethren, and that theyr exterordinary skill they learnt at Geneva, by which they presume in Bibles that are putt to them to leave out the Apocripha. We have here a goode workeman, but he hath commonly his hands full of worke, and his head full of drinck, yet I had as leve venture my worke with this goode fellow that is sometime sober, as with them that are alwayes mad.[31]

He also bound several books for Sir Charles Somerset, when the latter left Eton in 1604, which are very nearly the first English bindings to be lettered on the spine (Fig. 42).[32] There are quite a number of Williamson's bindings in Oxford college libraries, including sets of the Eton Chrysostom at Trinity and Brasenose.[33]

Cambridge was the next town outside London where elaborate bindings were made. A considerable amount has been written on this subject since G. D. Hobson first published H. M. Davies's neat, but erroneous, views in 1929.[34] A great step forward was taken in 1953 when J. C. T. Oates wrote 'Cambridge Books of Congratulatory

[30] R. Birley, 'The History of Eton College Library', The Library, 5th ser., 11 (1956), 231–61, esp. 246–8, pls. VI, VII.

[31] Ibid. 248.

[32] The Morocco Binder preceded him with one book: Sesillius [and others] (Strasburg, 1562), Exeter Sale, Christie's, 15 July 1959, lot 110 B. See Nixon, 'Elizabethan Gold-Tooled Bindings', 237, no. 7.

[33] Fine Bindings . . . from Oxford Libraries, no. 129 (where several examples are listed).

[34] Hobson, Bindings in Cambridge Libraries, 110–17, frontispiece, pls. XLI–XLIV.

Verses, 1603–40, and their Binders',[35] in which he published a number of bills and came to the conclusion that most of these bindings were the work of Henry Moody. Later research[36] has shown that some of these bindings can be attributed to Daniel Boyse, such as two copies of the *Book of Common Prayer* [etc.] (Cambridge, 1629). One, in gold-tooled blue velvet, is now part of the Henry Davis Gift to the British Library; the other, in gold-tooled brown leather, is now in the Broxbourne Collection in the Bodleian Library.[37] While Boyse seems to have made most of the grander Cambridge bindings of this period (Pl. 4), a number of other binders must have been at work there, as at least seven main groups of bindings can be distinguished.[38] Henry Moody bound several of the Congratulatory Poems produced by the budding laureates of the university, as did John Houlden, whose work will be discussed below. It is surprising how Cambridge should have developed such a distinctive style—with equally distinctive tools—that seems to have been employed by several binders in the town, yet does not seem to have affected the binders of London in any way during the 1630s and 1640s.

One place, however, was firmly influenced by Cambridge binding: the family community at Little Gidding founded in 1626 by Nicholas Ferrar and peopled mainly by his nephews and nieces. They were dealt with most thoroughly and with perhaps undue harshness by G. D. Hobson, who described the occupation of their leisure hours—the compilation with scissors and paste of vast harmonies of the Gospels—as 'an admirable diversion for a rather backward child of eight'.[39] Among the admirers of these books were Charles I and Prince Rupert. In 1929 Hobson described fifteen of their books; since then only the Revd C. Leslie Craig has added to their number. He discovered the first of them all to be produced, which is now at Harvard, as well as three more in the possession of Lady Langman.[40] Despite Hobson's comments, the bindings are not notably less skilled in the main than contemporary professional work

[35] Cambridge Bibliographical Society, *Transactions*, 1 (1953), 395–421, pls. XX–XXIV.
[36] H. M. Nixon, *Five Centuries of English Bookbinding* (London, 1978), no. 29. Nixon, *Broxbourne Library*, no. 63. Foot, *The Henry Davis Gift*, i. 60–75.
[37] Foot, *The Henry Davis Gift*, i. 63 (pl.): Nixon, *Broxbourne Library*, no. 63.
[38] Foot, *The Henry Davis Gift*, i. 60–75.
[39] Hobson, *Bindings in Cambridge Libraries*, 122–4, pl. XLVIII.
[40] C. L. Craig, 'The Earliest Little Gidding Concordance', *Harvard Library Bulletin*, 1 (1947), 311–31. Nixon, *Five Centuries*, no. 31.

and they show a considerable variety, being bound in velvet, turkey, calf, and vellum. A velvet example in St John's College, Oxford (Fig. 43), of which there is almost a twin belonging to Lord Salisbury,[41] covers a Concordance compiled at Little Gidding in 1640. The bindings were quite a credit to the instructress at Little Gidding, a Cambridge bookbinder's daughter 'that bound rarely', as she was somewhat ambiguously described.[42] In his article in the *Transactions* of the Cambridge Bibliographical Society, Mr Oates suggested that she might have been Katharine, Henry Moody's second daughter, who was subsequently the wife of Francis Meres, Master of Uppingham from 1641 to 1666. In the early part of this century one of the most persistent myths in booksellers' versions of bookbinding history was that all English embroidered bindings of the first half of the seventeenth century were the work of the Little Gidding community. Yet it seems reasonably certain that they produced no bindings at all in this style, and that the statement in Thomas Fuller's *Worthies of England* that 'their own Needles were emploied in learned and pious work to binde Bibles: Whereof one most exactly done was presented to King *Charles*',[43] refers only to the sewing of the books which they subsequently bound in tooled velvet, leather, or vellum.

There certainly were amateur needlewomen who produced embroidery for bookbindings in the seventeenth century, such as Anne Cornwallis (born in 1612), who embroidered a splendid binding now in the Pierpont Morgan Library, with the upper cover showing the temptation of Adam and Eve and the lower cover Christ's appearance to Mary Magdalene.[44] The great majority of the embroidered bindings of this period, however, were undoubtedly professional work. In 1638 certain milliners with shops in the Royal Exchange addressed a petition to Archbishop Laud protesting against a Star Chamber decree which limited the sale of Bibles, Testaments, and Psalm Books to stationers. The milliners said that they had been selling such books bound in 'rare and curious couers of Imbrothery and needleworke', and that both they and the embroiderers would

---

[41] *Le Livre anglais: Trésors des collections anglaises. Exposition* (held at the Bibliothèque Nationale) (Paris, 1951), no. 405.
[42] J. E. B. Mayor (ed.), *Nicholas Ferrar: Two Lives* (Cambridge, 1855), 243.
[43] T. Fuller, *The History of the Worthies of England* (London, 1662), ii. 48.
[44] E. Diehl, *Bookbinding: Its Background and Technique* (New York, 1946), i, pl. 51.

suffer severely from this new regulation.[45] G. D. Hobson suggested[46] that the petition seems to have been successful, as a bill from John Morris 'Imbroiderer to the Prince his hiness' is known for supplying two Bibles in 1640. But it would presumably be perfectly simple to get round such an order by buying a couple of unbound Bibles and making private arrangements for the binding and embroidery of the covers. Moreover, 'A generall note of the prises for binding of all sorts of bookes' (London, 1619) has a section headed 'Bookes in hard bords', which suggests that Bibles, Prayer Books, and Psalm Books were available in boards, ready for the embroiderers to cover.[47]

Some of the more elaborate embroidered bindings were clearly specially commissioned, such as a 1611–12 Prayer Book and Bible from the Henry Davis Gift to the British Library, with the arms of James Montague as Bishop of Bath and Wells (a position he held from 1608 to 1616).[48] Two presentation copies are known of the 1625 edition of Bacon's *Essays* in almost identical embroidered bindings. One is in Durham University Library and has a portrait that was presumably intended as a likeness of Charles I, as the book was only entered in the Stationers' Registers a fortnight before James I died (Pl. 5). The other copy, now in the Bodleian Library, has a rather similar portrait of the Duke of Buckingham.[49] Another example from the Henry Davis Gift was also probably specially commissioned, although it shows the figures of Peace and Plenty, which appear on many of the bindings of this type that were sold ready-bound in the milliners' shops. The book, a copy of Camden's *Britain* (London, 1610), bears a contemporary poem in French and English evidently addressed to Henrietta Maria, Charles I's queen, on her arrival in England in June 1625.[50] Many of the run-of-the-mill embroidered bindings of this period show these two allegorical figures, or Faith and Hope, the latter supplied with a massive anchor.[51] Biblical scenes

[45] H. R. Plomer, 'More Petitions to Archbishop Laud', *The Library*, 3rd ser., 10 (1919), 129–38.
[46] Hobson, *Bindings in Cambridge Libraries*, 123.
[47] M. M. Foot, 'Some Bookbinders' Price Lists of the Seventeenth and Eighteenth Centuries' in G. Colin (ed.), *De libris compactis miscellanea* (Brussels, 1984), 273–319, esp. 274, 286.
[48] Foot, *The Henry Davis Gift*, ii, no. 66.
[49] C. Davenport, *English Embroidered Bookbindings* (London, 1899), pl. 31.
[50] Foot, *The Henry Davis Gift*, ii, no. 76.
[51] For examples see M. M. Foot, *Pictorial Bookbindings* (London, 1986), nos. 51, 54.

were also popular, and in addition to Adam and Eve we find Moses and Aaron, Solomon and the Queen of Sheba, David harping, Elijah in the desert and with the widow of Zarephath, and Jacob wrestling with the angel or ascending his ladder.[52] Some of the bindings have simpler, attractive floral compositions, occasionally with the addition of birds, animals and insects. The Oxford presentation bindings of this period tend to be in plain velvet.

The practice of embroidering bindings has never quite ceased in England, but it went out of fashion at the Restoration. Occasionally embroidered bindings were produced for royal use in the first year or two of Charles II's reign. A fine example from the Royal Library at Windsor, covering a 1660 *Book of Common Prayer*, is probably one of them (Fig. 44). A Bible of the same year, similarly bound, is also at Windsor, and this set is possibly the one referred to in the warrant for the year ended at Michaelmas 1662:

Item to Edmond Harrison Embroiderer . . . ffor Embroydering the Covers of one other Bible and Service Booke vpon blew Velvett w[th] Embroydered Strings . . . for Our Clossett liiij[li]v[s].[53]

The Broxbourne Collection in the Bodleian Library also contains a fine embroidered blue satin binding on a Bible and Psalms in Metre (London, 1660–1), which has on the upper cover a portrait of Charles II and on the lower cover his queen, Catherine of Braganza. The painted fore-edge bears the date 1662.[54]

From time to time the bookbinding trade has benefited from authors who thought that the dissemination of their ideas might be speeded by the presentation of their works in handsome bindings. Lord Herbert of Cherbury clearly believed that a fine binding attracted readers. Six copies of the Latin edition of his *De veritate* of 1633 and fourteen of the French translation, *De la verité*, of 1639 are now recorded in special bindings.[55] They all come from the same shop and the bindings on the French translation have Herbert's crest of a sheaf of arrows and the word ΕΥΣΤΟΧΩΣ—'well-aimed'. There are also, in the Bodleian Library, two Herbert manuscripts in a smooth

[52] For some of these see ibid., no. 52, and Y. Hackenbroch, *English and Other Needlework Tapestries and Textiles in the Irwin Untermyer Collection* (Cambridge, Mass., 1960), iv, pls. 11, 34–8.
[53] *Le Livre anglais*, no. 409. PRO, L. C. 5. 39, p. 164.
[54] *Le Livre anglais*, no. 410. Nixon, *Broxbourne Library*, no. 73.
[55] Nixon, *Five Centuries*, no. 30. Foot, *The Henry Davis Gift*, i. 52.

blue leather that seems to be morocco (rather than the fuller-grained turkey usual in England at this time), which are decorated with a different set of tools. This time Lord Herbert patronized a different binder and used a different stamp for his crest with fewer arrows and the word ΑΠΛΑΝΩΣ—'without going astray' or 'accurately'.[56]

The London binder of both Latin and French editions of *De veritate* was unquestionably the same as the man previously christened the Squirrel Binder.[57] He seems to have started work early in the seventeenth century and to have been active until the 1640s (Fig. 45). He may have been the binder who regularly worked for John Bill. Bill himself is spoken of as a bookbinder on two occasions: in the accounts of the Duke of Northumberland he is mentioned as 'Bill, the bookbinder',[58] and Sir Walter Oakeshott has quoted a letter from Lady Ralegh about the fate of Sir Walter Ralegh's books after his execution in which she says, 'But they tell me that Byll, the bookbinder and stationer, hath the very same'.[59] However, there appears to be no other evidence that Bill, an important printer, publisher, and bookseller, was himself a binder,[60] and in a lawsuit in the Chancery court in 1616 five binders—Richard Taylor, Richard Tommes, John Wollye, Christopher Wilson, and William Wrench—were said to have bound books for the booksellers Bonham Norton, John Norton, and John Bill.[61]

John Bagford, in his abortive history of the English book trade, written shortly after 1700 and now preserved among the Harleian Manuscripts in the British Library,[62] wrote 'So haue we places that haue been famous for binding as Cambridg: Eaton: and London'.

---

[56] *The Life and Raigne of King Henry the VIII* (1638), Bodley, MS Bodl. 910 and *De expeditione in Ream insulam* (1630), dedicated to Charles I, Bodley, MS e Mus. 95.

[57] Nixon, *Five Centuries*, no. 27. Foot, *The Henry Davis Gift*, i. 51–8.

[58] Historical Manuscripts Commission, Report VI (1877), appendix, p. 229.

[59] W. Oakeshott, 'Sir Walter Ralegh's Library', *The Library*, 5th ser., 23 (1968), 285–327, quotation on 292.

[60] It is possible (though by no means certain) that William Garrett, overseer of Bill's will, was a bookbinder. He was certainly a bookseller and publisher, and it may have been his bookseller's shop that was searched for books bound in sheepskin. See Foot, *The Henry Davis Gift*, i. 54.

[61] Mentioned under each of the binders' names in R. B. McKerrow, *A Dictionary of Printers and Booksellers . . ., 1557–1640* (London, 1910).

[62] MS Harl. 5943, fo. 3ʳ. Printed in C. Davenport, 'Bagford's Notes on Bookbindings', *Transactions of the Bibliographical Society*, VII (1904), 123–59 (esp. 139–40). The printed pages from MS. Harl. 5943 are among the printed books (H & SS) in the British Library.

Bagford put Cambridge first; his contemporary, Dunton, praised the work of Samuel Mearne's apprentice, Robert Steel, 'which', he said, 'for the Fineness, and Goodness of it might vye with the *Cambridge Binding*'.[63] Cambridge was indeed the place where in the 1640s the first signs occurred of the new tools, copied from France, that were to lead to the glories of English bookbinding in the Restoration period.

The most likely binder to have introduced these new tools is John Houlden. He bound two copies of the Cambridge edition of 1643 of the Venerable Bede's *Historiae ecclesiasticae gentis anglorum libri V*, which are now in the Bodleian and Cambridge University libraries (Fig. 46).[64] Both are in identical bindings, a fact which suggests (though it does not prove) that both date from the time of the book's publication. The Bodleian copy was certainly bound by 1649. It was bequeathed by John Selden in 1659, and had been given to him by Henry Rich, first Earl of Holland, Chancellor of Cambridge University, who died in 1649. The tools used on these bindings were still used in the 1660s, and Houlden, probably first heard of as John Haldyn Junior in 1633, seems to have died c.1670.[65] Houlden almost certainly bound *The Commentaries of S: Francis Vere* (Cambridge, 1657) now in the Broxbourne Collection in the Bodleian Library, which the editor, William Dillingham, Vice-Chancellor of Cambridge University, presented to Charles II at the Restoration.[66] Houlden also bound the well-known copy of the 1662 *Workes of King Charles the Martyr*, of which one volume was used as the frontispiece of G. D. Hobson's *English Bindings in the Library of J. R. Abbey*; the other volume is in the British Library.[67] The doublures of these two volumes are decorated in the typical Cambridge style, with concentric rectangles like those found on the covers of a 1662 *Epithalamia Cantabrigiensia in nuptias Caroli II* in the Library of St John's College, Oxford.[68] Houlden's binding tools appear to have passed to his son-in-law, Titus Tillet, who used them on three presentation bindings of

[63] John Dunton, *Life and Errors* (London, 1705), 345.
[64] Bodleian, S. Seld. c. 21, *Fine Bindings ... from Oxford Libraries*, no. 156; Cambridge University Library, Rel. a. 64. a. 2 is illustrated here (Fig. 46).
[65] Foot, *The Henry Davis Gift*, i. 66.
[66] Nixon, *Broxbourne Library*, no. 72.
[67] C. 108. i. 14. The Abbey copy was sold at Sotheby's, 21 June 1965, lot 187.
[68] *Fine Bindings ... from Oxford Libraries*, no. 161.

Cambridge University's book of congratulatory verses celebrating the marriage of the future King William III and Queen Mary in 1677.[69]

Although this has taken us on into the middle of the Restoration period, we must now revert to the earliest manifestations of the new movement towards the use of the much-smaller pointillé tools (tools with dotted outlines) and the much-gayer polychrome leather onlays. Surprisingly this gaiety did not wait for the Restoration, but began to appear quite early in the 1650s, in what one thinks of as the artistically depressing days of Oliver Cromwell's Protectorate. Six signed bindings are now known from the workshops of the brothers Stephen and Thomas Lewis, at the sign of The Bookbinders in Shoe Lane in the City of London. They decorated the edges of some of their bindings and signed some of them; the earliest one (now in the New York Public Library), with an edge dated 1653, has the floral volutes and single flower tools that form the specifically English contribution to the finishing tools of the Restoration binder (Fig. 47). Most of the other tools with dotted outlines introduced in England in the 1640s closely resemble French tools. The Lewis brothers at first favoured a panel design. They then introduced onlaid mosaics, as on a small Bible and Psalms of 1651–53 from the Mortimer Schiff collection, which is signed on the edge 'Lewis fecit'.[70] At a later stage the brothers may have operated independently, for there are bindings signed separately S. Lewis and T. Lewis. An example in the Edinburgh University Library on a Bible of 1648 and Psalms of 1655 has the fore-edge signed, 'Tho: Lewis fecit. Ann. Domini 1660'.[71] It shows what is perhaps the first curving version of the cottage-roof style of binding, another exclusively English design about which more below.

Another binding with a signed fore-edge that may precede the Restoration is a delightful little mosaic binding on a 1657 Bible, with the edge signed 'Evans fecit'. Major J. R. Abbey gave it to the British

[69] These bindings are now at Harvard University, ML 116.77* and at the British Library, C. 132. i. 58 and G. 17784. See Foot, *The Henry Davis Gift*, i. 67, 75 (nos. 19–21).

[70] Sotheby's, 23 Mar. 1938, lot 24 (illus.), now in the Victoria and Albert Museum. See H. M. Nixon, *English Restoration Bookbindings* (London, 1974), no. 43 (quoted below as Nixon, *Restoration*).

[71] Nixon, *Restoration*, no. 44. See also W. Kellaway, 'The Fore-Edge Paintings of Stephen and Thomas Lewis', *The Guildhall Miscellany*, no. 8 (July 1957), 27–32. An unsigned Lewis binding for Oliver Cromwell in the Pierpont Morgan Library, New York, is illus. in Nixon, *Five Centuries*, no. 32. See also Nixon, *Restoration*, 27–8, nos. 42–6.

Museum shortly before the series of sales of his great collection began at Sotheby's in 1965. It was accurately described by G. D. Hobson as 'without exception the most exquisite late seventeenth-century English binding that has been reproduced'.[72] Henry Evans was in business from 1650 until after 1676, so that a binding date of 1657 is quite possible.

Another binder who must have been active before the Restoration was a certain Fletcher, probably John Fletcher. When Charles II landed at Dover on Friday, 25 May 1660, he travelled straight to Canterbury where he stayed for the weekend. Among the many gifts he received while he was there was a copy of *The Antiquities of Canterbury* by William Somner, with a specially printed leaf reading:

To the Royall hands of his SACRED MAJESTY ... the AUTHOR, One of the meanest, but most devoted, of his loyall Subjects, From his heart congratulating his MAIESTIES safe return ... and on the bended knees of his body ... Humbly (and with hopes of Pardon for his so great presumption) Presents These his unworthy Labours.[73]

The gold tooling in the corners of this dark-brown turkey leather binding, now in the Huntington Library, link it with the copy of Foxe's 'Booke of Martyrs of the Best Paper Ruled and after the best manner bound in Turkey leather and gilt with the Kinges Armes stamped thereon in Gold', which the Stationers' Company resolved at a Court on 4 June 1660 to present to his majesty. As an afterthought the Wardens were 'desired to get it bound (by Mr Sam: Mearne a member of this company)'. He evidently passed the job on to Fletcher, for an entry in the Treasurer's Accounts for 1661 reads: 'May 14 Payd Mr Flesher for bindeing the B. Martyrs for yᵉ King 07:10: 0'. Also, at the foot of the fore-edge of the three volumes—now in the King's Library of the British Library (Fig. 48)—beneath a portrait of Charles II is the signature: FLETCHER COMPINXIT.[74] This signature also occurs on the edge of a 1638 *Book of Common Prayer* in the Royal Library at The Hague, and the presence of the same

[72] G. D. Hobson, *English Bindings ... in the Library of J. R. Abbey*, no. 38; Nixon, *Restoration*, no. 47 (now BL C. 108. n. 7).

[73] Nixon, *Restoration*, 28.

[74] Ibid. 28–30. See also Nixon, *Five Centuries*, no. 33.

tools massed in the corners of these bindings enables us to attribute to Fletcher three more bindings in the British Library.[75] John Fletcher's name occurs in the 1669 Bookbinders' Price List; he is last heard of in 1671.[76]

[75] *The Workes of King Charles the Martyr*, pt. i (London, 1662) (BL 195. g. 2): illustrated in Nixon, *Five Centuries*, no. 34. *Book of Common Prayer*: *Holy Bible*: *Whole Book of Psalmes . . . into metre* (Cambridge, 1638) (BL C. 132. i. 64).(See Nixon, *Restoration*, nos. 51, 52). N. Upton, *De studio militari libri quattuor* (London, 1654) (BL 62. h. 2): illus. in C. Davenport, *Samuel Mearne* (Chicago, 1906), pl. xv.

[76] The 1669 price list is transcribed in Foot, 'Some Bookbinders' Price Lists', 303.

FOUR

The Restoration Period

SAMUEL MEARNE was born on 20 April 1624 at Reading. In 1637 he was apprenticed to Robert Bates, a member of the Stationers' Company. He was subsequently turned over to J. Arnold, and in July 1646 he was freed by both Arnold and Bates.[1] In 1653 Mearne took the first of his twelve apprentices. Two years later, when he bound a book for one Cor: Pigeon, his address was given as 'Pellecan Courte, in Littill Brettin', and that same year a pass was granted for Cornelius Bee, Samuel Mearne, and William Minshew to proceed to Holland. In his admirable paper, 'The Great Mearne Myth',[2] Gordon Duff suggested that on this occasion Mearne may have been of service to the future Charles II, who was in Middelburg. At all events Mearne was speedily rewarded at the Restoration by being granted the office of Bookbinder to the King at a fee—which he seldom received—of £6 per annum. In 1674 he also became Stationer in Ordinary to the King and in May 1675 a new grant of the offices of Bookbinder, Bookseller, and Stationer to the King was made to Samuel Mearne and his son Charles for their lives and the life of the survivor. He was clearly a very important member of the book trade and was also active as a publisher. Mearne was not himself

---

[1] For references and further literature concerning Samuel Mearne and his work see: H. M. Nixon, *English Restoration Bookbindings* (London, 1974), 10–22 (quoted below as: Nixon, *Restoration*), from which the account that follows has been taken. According to Nixon, Samuel Mearne was apprenticed first to Robert Bates and was then turned over to Jeremy Arnold, a bookbinder. However, D. F. McKenzie, *Stationers' Company Apprentices 1605–1640* (Charlottesville, Va., 1961) and Id. *1641–1700* (Oxford, 1974), states that Samuel Mearne was turned over to John Arnold, a bookseller. McKenzie lists twelve apprentices for S. Mearne.

[2] E. G. Duff, 'The Great Mearne Myth', *Papers of the Edinburgh Bibliographical Society*, 11 (1918), 47–65.

a printer, but he had a share in the King's Printing House as one of the assigns of John Bill and Christopher Barker. His undoubted success as a business man was partly due to keeping on good terms with the Establishment as a zealous seeker-out of illegal presses, an activity which helped the government to suppress seditious pamphlets, and helped the leading members of the book trade—such as Mearne himself—to suppress possible competitors.

Mearne continued these activities till the end of his life, and on 9 July 1683 Mr Secretary Jenkins wrote to the Lord Mayor 'The late Mr Mearne was so zealous in the King's service that I think myself obliged to remember it on every opportunity of doing a good office to his son'. Samuel Mearne died in May 1683, having lived in Little Britain all his working life. The registers of St Botolph without Aldersgate contain details of the baptism of the children born to his wife Anne, of whom two sons, Samuel and Charles, and a daughter named after her mother, survived. The younger son, Charles, continued as Royal Bookbinder, Bookseller, and Stationer until his death in 1686. Robert Scott was then appointed Stationer and Bookseller to the King, but Charles's elder brother, Samuel Mearne junior, received the appointment of Royal Bookbinder, an office he held until 1688.

From 1660 onwards, Samuel Mearne the elder was much too important a figure in the book trade to have worked at the bench himself, but we know that he had a bookbinding shop on the premises of his bookselling business. For not only did Bagford record that one Suckerman was 'perhaps one of yᵉ best work men yᵗ euer tuke tule in hands, and com[m]onley worke[d] for Mʳ Merne yᵉ Binder to King Charles yᵉ 2: and King James yᵉ 2:', but he also described Richard Balley as 'bred under yᵉ tuesion of Suckerman at Mʳ Mernes'.[3]

It is therefore proper to talk about a Mearne binding, just as one talks about a Bedford or a Rivière binding, without believing that the majority of the bindings signed in these shops were the personal work of the men named. From the surviving documentary evidence and from a study of the tools used to decorate the bindings, one can identify the output of the Mearne shop with some certainty.

A list is preserved at Longleat[4] endorsed 'Catalogue of Bookes belonging to the Kings Library at Sᵗ James's In the hands of Mʳ Merne

---

[3] Bagford fragments, BL MS Harl. 5943, fo. 3ʳ.
[4] Thynne Papers, vol. lxxxiii, fos. 23ʳ–31ᵛ.

His Ma.ʸˢ Stationer. Besides 180 Volumes of Hebrew Bookes in his possession'. It lists the titles of 524 books bound at a total cost of £241.11s. The list is not dated, but the bill had not been paid by the time of Samuel Mearne's death. When his widow submitted a further demand for payment she included items for binding the 180 Hebrew books at a cost of £126 and £60 for warehousing them from 1665 to 1685. It is possible to identify with certainty both the Hebrew books and the 'severall English and Lattin Books'. The Hebrew books were eventually sold to Solomon da Costa, who presented them to the British Museum in 1759. They can now be easily traced by their uniform bindings of golden-brown turkey leather, decorated with Charles II's cypher—two Cs back to back between palm leaves surmounted by a crown—on their spines and at the corners of the panels on the covers.

The English and Latin books are of still greater interest, since they are the copies deposited during the 1670s at St James's under the terms of the Licensing Acts. These copies were delivered by the booksellers to Stationers' Hall in sheets and then sent on to St James's, where they tended to remain unbound. It was probably about 1678 when those received over the past ten years were sent to Mearne for binding. They were duly bound, but Mearne, who had already suffered much from the non-payment of royal bills, evidently refused to return the books until they were paid for, and payment was never received. Presumably Mearne's descendants were eventually allowed to dispose of them, in the same way as in 1684 the Privy Council gave his widow permission to sell the Thomason Tracts. (Mearne had bought the tracts some years before in the expectation that Charles II would add them to his library.)[5] Certainly none of the books on the Longleat list reached the British Museum with the Old Royal Library in 1757, although a certain number of them have been acquired since.

The Warrants Particular of the Lord Chamberlain's Office[6] show that Mearne was paid for binding 830 books, supplied in five batches, for the Royal Library during the years 1663 to 1667. There are three

[5] G. Fortescue, *Catalogue of Pamphlets . . . collected by George Thomason* (London, 1908), introd. XVII–XIX. The collection was presented by George III to the British Museum in 1762.

[6] PRO, Lord Chamberlain's Bill Books, L. C. 5. 39, pp. 258–60, 301–2; L. C. 5. 40, pp. 78–9, 101–2, 122–3.

separate styles among these bindings. The first group (Fig. 49) lacks Charles II's cypher; it has instead a large royal arms block, of which two variants are found on some of the more elaborate royal bindings dating from c.1660.[7] The second group has Charles II's cypher in alternate panels of the spine, but the covers have a panel with Mearne's version of a favourite Restoration-period conventional flower at the corners (Fig. 50). It may well be that these were trial designs either paid for separately at an earlier date or included among the 375 books in the 1663 bill. The third group has a gold-tooled panel with the royal cypher at the corners as well as in the panels of the spine. This is in the normal style for quartos and folios (Fig. 51).

As the standard Royal Library bindings and those on the Longleat list are almost indistinguishable, there seems very little doubt that all must have come from Mearne's shop. So did a number of more elaborate bindings from the Royal Library, such as the presentation copy of the *Poems* (London, 1667) of Mrs Katherine Philips, 'the matchless Orinda' (Fig. 52). The elaborate bindings supplied by the Mearnes and bound in the Mearne bindery fall into a number of groups: those supplied for use in the various royal chapels, for members of the royal household, for ambassadors and plenipotentiaries, and for the ceremonies of the Order of the Garter.

The majority of the bindings with the royal arms or cypher, produced in the Mearne bindery and its successor during the last forty years of the seventeenth century, were supplied to the various royal chapels. Throughout Charles II's reign the Chapel and the Closet at Whitehall appear most frequently in the accounts. The Closet was the Chapel Closet, the royal pew which formed a gallery at the west end of the Chapel. It was clearly intended that there should be a complete refurnishing of both the Chapel and Closet every three years, although as the reign progressed the intervals tended to lengthen to five years and sometimes not all the Bibles and Prayer Books were changed. When the books were replaced they normally became the perquisites of those who had used them, but the Bible and Prayer Book used by the king were the perquisites of the Clerk of the Closet. Therefore, where we can trace a Bible and Prayer Book in an elaborate binding back to one of the Clerks of the Closet,

---

[7] e.g. Nixon, *Restoration*, nos. 9, 11, 12.

there is a reasonable chance that the book was used by the king himself, rather than by a member of his household.

The Clerks of the Closet who particularly concern us are John Dolben, Dean of Westminster and Bishop of Rochester, who held office from 1664 to 1667 and Nathaniel, Lord Crewe, Bishop of Durham, whose tenure lasted from 1669 until late in 1685, when he became Dean of the Chapel Royal. Brasenose College, Oxford, owns an Ogilby's *Bible* (Cambridge, 1660) with a presentation inscription dated 1666 from John Dolben, Clerk of the Closet. This clearly became his perquisite when new books were supplied for the Closet in 1666. It has a fore-edge painting underneath the gold of Charles II's cypher with the leopards of England and the lion of Scotland above and the lilies of France and the Irish harp below. This may be one of the two Bibles supplied with two Common Prayer Books 'double ruled and richly bound for our owne Clossett' in 1664.[8] Nathaniel Crewe's long period of office would have entitled him to the royal Bibles and Prayer Books supplied in 1666 and changed in 1669, the new ones supplied in that year and changed in March 1673/4, and those supplied then which were in use until March 1678—all these were provided by Samuel Mearne. The March 1678 issue apparently lasted out Charles II's reign.

It is possible to attribute to these successive changes of the books a number of finely bound Bibles and Prayer Books that have Crewe pedigrees. The first to be considered and the most elaborate of these are a 1659 Bible and a 1662 Prayer Book which now belong respectively to the British Library as part of the Henry Davis Gift, and to the Bodleian Library as part of the Broxbourne Library.[9] They both come from Crewe Hall Library, the collection formed by Hungerford, Lord Crewe. Nathaniel Crewe died childless in 1722; the family of Hungerford, Lord Crewe, are descended from Nathaniel's second cousin. There is no certainty that these two volumes belonged to Nathaniel, Lord Crewe, in the seventeenth century. More likely candidates for one of the two pairs supplied in 1666 are the 1659 Bible and 1662 Prayer Book in Cosin's Library at Durham.[10]

⁸ PRO, L. C. 5. 39, p. 301. Nixon, *Restoration*, no. 13.

⁹ M. M. Foot, *The Henry Davis Gift*, ii (London, 1983), no. 106 and H. M. Nixon, *Broxbourne Library: Styles and Designs of Bookbindings from the Twelfth to the Twentieth Century* (London, 1956), no. 74. See also Nixon, *Restoration*, nos. 25, 26.

¹⁰ Nixon, *Restoration*, nos. 14, 15.

The inscription in the Prayer Book suggests, without definitely stating, that the date Crewe gave it to the library was 1674, the year in which he became Bishop of Durham (Fig. 53). In style the Bible and Prayer Book resemble the two pairs of books supplied in 1669. The edges are painted in the same way as those of the Dolben Bible at Brasenose, which has been attributed to 1664.

The situation for 1669 is much clearer: on 20 October of that year Samuel Mearne's bill 'For his ma[ties] Priuate Ora[ty] & y[e] Closett in y[e] Chaple' included two Bibles at £20 each and two Prayer Books at £15 each.[11] One of these Bibles and its Prayer Book 'bound Sutable' are now at Lincoln College, Oxford.[12] The Bible has an inscription to the effect that it was given to the college by Nathaniel, Lord Crewe, in 1674. The second pair was presented by him in the same year to the private chapel (and Parish Church on six Sundays in the year) at Steane Park near Brackley, where the bishop was born, died, and was buried. Both the 1660 Bible and the 1669 Prayer Book are now on deposit in the British Library.[13] The Lincoln College books and the Steane Park/British Library pair have a fore-edge painting of the crowned cypher of Charles II with a small rose in the centre.

The Bibles and Prayer Books supplied in 1674 have not been traced with certainty, though it is possible that a 1669 *Book of Common Prayer* in the British Library, similar in design to the Steane Park/ British Library set and with a similar fore-edge painting (Fig. 54), can be attributed to that year's issue.[14] One of the Bibles supplied by Mearne in 1678 is almost certainly that now in the collection of Miss Christina Foyle at Beeleigh Abbey. It is in the familiar cottage-roof style with the royal cypher on the covers and the royal arms painted on the fore-edge.[15]

The next issue were those provided by Charles Mearne in 1685 or 1686, shortly before his death; they are now in the British Library.[16] These volumes, with James II's cypher on the covers, must have lain unused in the Closet throughout his reign and were then used, as the inscription records, by William III until 1691. They were then given

---

[11] PRO, L. C. 9. 271, fo. 180[v].
[12] Nixon, *Restoration*, nos. 16, 17.
[13] C. 170. c. 26 and C. 170. c. 28. Nixon, *Restoration*, nos. 18, 19.
[14] 7. f. 13. Nixon, *Restoration*, no. 20.
[15] Nixon, *Restoration*, no. 21.
[16] 7. h. 1; 11. g. 5. Nixon, *Restoration*, nos. 22, 23. PRO, L. C. 9. 278, fo. 48 (the bill is dated 1686 and refers to 'Charles Mearne Late Stationer'.)

by Archbishop Tillotson to his predecessor in the office of Clerk of
the Closet, Gilbert Burnet. In that same year Samuel Carr provided
the Closet for the last time in the seventeenth century with its
customary supply of books, including 'two bibles Imperiall paper
painted Turkey Extraordinary inlaid'.[17] These can both be identified:
they are two Oxford folio Bibles of 1680, bound in gold-tooled red
turkey with a cottage-roof design in black and with the combined
cypher of William III and Mary II. They have very similar painted
fore-edges, with the royal arms between a cherub and a crowned
sunburst. One of these was in the library of Major Abbey and the
other is now in the Huntington Library (Fig. 55). They were probably
bound by Robert Steel.[18]

Turning to books other than those supplied for the personal use of
the king, 'One Bible of royall paper richly bound with all the
sculp[tur]es [i.e. engravings] in two volumes for the Altar in our
Chapell royall',[19] which Samuel Mearne supplied in 1665 for £50,
must be that now in the Pierpont Morgan Library (19499–500). For
if one conflates two apparently duplicated warrants for the Chapel
Royal, one of which specifying 'one Bible and a Common prayer
Book for the Altar Embossed [i.e. with bosses] as those which [are]
there now' and the other (entered later, but dated the previous day),
'One Greate Bible in two Vollums richly bound ... with all the
Sculptures to it for the Altar',[20] one arrives at an accurate description
of these books. The 'Embossed' Common Prayer mentioned in one
of the warrants does not appear to have been supplied, but a 1662
Prayer Book in the British Library[21]—without bosses—very closely
resembles the Morgan Library bindings in design. In 1675 Samuel
Mearne supplied 'for the lords in the chappell' twelve large paper
Common Prayers in turkey leather gilt at £4 each and six of the same
in 'mar[ble] leather gilt' [i.e. marbled calf] at £3 each.[22] The turkey

[17] PRO, L. C. 5. 43, fo. 30ᵛ.
[18] G. D. Hobson, *English Bindings 1490–1940 in the Library of J. R. Abbey* (London,
1940), no. 62 and Huntington Library, San Marino, California, 149044 (illus. here, Fig. 55),
Nixon, *Restoration*, p. 18.
[19] PRO, L. C. 5. 40, p. 79.
[20] PRO, L. C. 5. 138, pp. 57, 58. PML 19499–500 are 2 volumes: *Bible* (Cambridge,
n.d.), (pt. ii: 1660); *New Testament* (1659), in olive goatskin, with coloured onlays,
elaborately tooled in gold, and with metal corner and centre pieces engraved with the royal
arms.
[21] C. 14. e. 13. Nixon, *Restoration*, no. 24.
[22] PRO, L. C. 9. 274, fo. 351ʳ.

leather bindings probably resembled those made for the royal library; those in marbled calf were also decorated to a panel design with the cypher of Charles II at the corners of the panel (Fig. 56).

It is not certain whether all the service books in the royal chapels always had the arms or cypher on their covers, or whether other Bibles and Prayer Books from the Mearne bindery without royal markings may have come from royal chapels. For example, a fine 1659 Bible, formerly in Major Abbey's collection and now in the British Library,[23] has a Nathaniel Crewe pedigree. Both it and its companion Prayer Book in the Huntington Library (Fig. 57) have inscriptions saying that they were given by the Bishop of Durham to his godson, Devereux Knightley, in September 1681. Both are decorated in a totally different style from that of the other Mearne bindings that have been considered, although they exhibit the Mearne bindery's characteristic tools. Their design is based on French fanfare bindings of one hundred years earlier, and they have the Crucifixion painted on the fore-edge under the gold. More typical is a red turkey cottage-style binding on a Prayer Book at Keble College, Oxford,[24] which shows a flame burning on an altar in the centre of the covers. This binding, reminiscent of the king's own bindings of 1666, also has a painted Crucifixion on the fore-edge.

One of Mearne's steadiest lines must have been supplying Bibles and Prayer Books to ambassadors. Unfortunately, none of these have yet been identified with certainty. An important set of bindings for which Samuel Mearne was responsible covers the five copies of the Prayer Book of 1662 ordered by the Act of Uniformity to be deposited among the Records at the Tower and in each of the four Courts of Justice (Fig. 58). These all now survive in their original bindings in the Public Record Office. Richard Royston supplied the five Prayer Books for £7.10s., and Mearne charged £4 each for binding them in turkey leather.[25] The bindings are particularly interesting in that they have in the centre of the covers the coat of arms found on the earliest royal library bindings, while at the corners of the panel and on the spine appears (probably for the first time) Charles II's cypher in two sizes. Another authenticated group of bindings sup-

---

[23] C. 108. tt. 6. Nixon, *Restoration*, no. 27

[24] Nixon, *Restoration*, no.28.

[25] PRO, L. C. 5. 39, pp. 304, 259. The five copies are at C. 95. 1; C. 95. 2; K. B. 118. 1 (Nixon, *Restoration*, no. 12: illus.); C. P. 14.1; E. 163/32.

plied by Mearne is well documented. These are the books supplied to the Dean of Windsor as Register of the Order of the Garter during Charles II's reign. The Wardrobe Warrant to Michaelmas 1661 ordered payment of £35 to Samuel Mearne, bookbinder, for 'One and twenty Statute bookes bound in turky Leather and foure Registers bound in velvet . . . for the Order of the Garter'. Earlier in the same warrant is a payment to the embroiderer Edward Trussell for 'crimson velvet watchet velvet and black velvet to cover three bookes for the Register of the Garter' and 'purple velvet to cover our owne Register Booke at Windsor'.[26] These registers all survive in velvet of the correct colours (watchet is light blue) at Windsor, but were apparently rebound in the nineteenth century. The book that was originally bound in purple velvet is now in a typical Samuel Mearne binding of red turkey leather, probably made about 1677 (Fig. 59).[27] It was evidently nearly full in 1684, when Charles Mearne was ordered to supply a new one; this presumably bore the cypher of Charles II. There was very little activity in the Order, however, between 1684 and the coronation of William and Mary, so that this 'Yellow Book', or 'Liber aureus' as it was more grandly called, was supplied by Samuel Carr in a similar binding with the cypher of William and Mary.[28]

The Mearne bindery also supplied the manuscript copies of the Statutes presented to the newly installed knights. They were all thin quarto-shaped books bound in very dark-blue turkey and originally had two pairs of blue ties. The earliest type has the royal arms block found on some of Mearne's earliest royal bindings. A copy now in the British Library[29] is probably one of the twenty-one copies supplied in 1661 when the original registers were rebound. The Duke of Lauderdale's copy may be one of 'five vollum of Statutes of the order of the garter att fifty shillings abooke' for which Samuel Mearne submitted a bill on 28 June 1673.[30] One of the five, however, does not seem to have been used for another ten years, for the third Duke of Hamilton's copy, now in the Pierpont Morgan Library, is almost identical and he did not become a Knight of the Garter until 25

[26] PRO, L. C. 5. 39, pp. 77–8, 44, 45.

[27] Nixon, *Restoration*, 21.

[28] Ibid. 21–2. The 'Liber Carolinus' remained in use up to 1689.

[29] Add. MS 6294. Nixon, *Restoration*, no. 30. Another, very similar binding, on a copy of the Statutes and Ordinances of the Garter, MS c.1673–5, for Charles Fitzroy, Earl of Southampton, is now Add. MS 68922.

[30] BL Add. MS 6291, Nixon, *Restoration*, no. 31, PRO, L. C. 9. 273, fo. 136ʳ.

September 1682 (Fig. 60). The Statutes received by Thomas Osborne, Duke of Leeds, at his installation in April 1677[31] were bound in a slightly simpler style. At least one other design was used in Charles II's reign. It has a later version of the royal arms as well as the king's cypher.[32]

Two bindings in the fanfare style from the Mearne bindery have already been mentioned. The Pierpont Morgan Library has another one on a French translation of the Book of Common Prayer, published in London in 1678 (Fig. 61). It has a decorated fore-edge with a cartouche containing the name of Charles Bland and the date 1678, while beneath it can just be made out 'CM fecit'. In this instance CM evidently stands for Charles Mearne, by 1678 in partnership with his father, while Charles Bland was probably the Page of his Majesty's Robes who was responsible for the supply of garter ribbon registers or markers for the royal service books with their gold 'fringes'.[33] The tools used on this binding are found on several copies of Sir Thomas Browne's *Certain miscellany tracts*, 'Printed for *Charles Mearn*, Bookseller to his most Sacred Majesty' in 1683, one of which is in the Pierpont Morgan Library, while another one belongs to the Henry Davis Gift to the British Library.[34] They were evidently the presentation copies that would presumably be bound in Mearne's shop. These are the latest books on which the tools link clearly with those found on the bindings attributed to the Mearne bindery. On the Bibles supplied by Charles Mearne in 1685/6 for the Closet most of the tools are new, although they are close copies of the earlier ones. It is these new tools which appear on the royal bindings for the remainder of the century, but one or two older ones, such as two pairs of French corners, continue to be used with them. It seems slightly more likely that Charles Mearne had many of his tools recut, or ordered new ones in 1684 or 1685, than that he closed down his own bindery and sent his work out to Steel.

Robert Steel was apprenticed to Samuel Mearne from 1668 to 1675. By 1677 he was established as a master binder and between then and 1710, when he is last heard of, he had eleven apprentices, and in the latter year he was living in Little Britain—where Samuel and Charles

[31] BL Eg. MS 3375. Nixon, *Restoration*, no. 32.
[32] e.g. Nixon, *Restoration*, no. 33.
[33] PRO, L. C. 5. 42, p. 112; L. C. 9. 279, fo. 62.
[34] Nixon, *Restoration*, 23, no. 34. Foot, *The Henry Davis Gift*, ii, no. 111.

Mearne had lived.[35] Two books that belonged to one Richard
Graham, a minor author of the day, bear a Latin inscription in the
form 'Robertus Steel Bibliopegus dono dedit R. Graham'. One, a
copy of Dryden's version of Du Fresnoy with Graham's own
supplement, was published in 1695 and is decorated with tools that
form a distinct group linking with Charles Mearne's bindery. It was
illustrated in Maggs Bros. Catalogue 665 (September 1938, no. 36).
The binding has two pairs of tools which occur on the Bible and
Prayer Book supplied for the king's own use by Charles Mearne in
1686. It links with a group of bindings[36] which include a service
book supplied to William and Mary and the dedication copy to the
Earl of Pembroke of Thomas Greenhill's *Art of Imbalming* (London,
1705), now in the British Library (Fig. 63). Some of the large leaf
tools that occur on these bindings are found on Pepys's copy of
Narborough's *Voyages* (London, 1694),[37] also a member of the
group. Oddly enough, the other book that Steel gave to Graham has
a completely different set of tools and does not seem to come from
his own bindery.[38]

   In addition to the Mearne bindery and its successor, numerous
other binders were active during the last forty years of the seventeenth
century. Our primary sources are Dunton's *Life and Errors*, published in 1705, in which he devotes several pages to the binders who
had worked for him, and the notes of John Bagford (c.1650–1716),[39]
a shoemaker turned superior bookseller's runner, who finished by
searching for books both in England and abroad for such collectors
as Harley, Sloane, and Bishop Moore. Among Bagford's notes is a
very short—but quite invaluable—section on the binders of his day.
We have also the records of the Stationers' Company, as recorded in
Ellic Howe's *List of London Bookbinders 1648–1815* (London, 1950),
and the list of bookbinders who signed an agreement on prices with
the booksellers in 1669, to which Howe first called attention. Other
evidence comes from the tools used on the bindings themselves. It is

[35] Nixon, *Restoration*, 23–4. See also D. F. McKenzie, *Stationers' Company Apprentices,
1641–1700* and Id. *1701–1800* (Oxford, 1978).
   [36] Nixon, *Restoration*, nos. 22, 23, 35–9, p. 24.
   [37] H. M. Nixon, *Catalogue of the Pepys Library at Magdalene College, Cambridge: Vol.
VI Bindings* (Cambridge, 1984), frontispiece, pl. 52 (P.L. 1365).
   [38] G. D. Hobson, *Thirty Bindings . . . Selected from the First Edition Club's Seventh
Exhibition* (London, 1926), pl. XXVII.
   [39] BL MS Harl. 5943, fo. 3ʳ. See also Nixon, *Restoration*, 26.

possible to group the bindings into the products of different binderies by a study of these tools, which were engraved in brass and not cast. As patterns were frequently repeated for different binders, great care must be taken in making absolutely sure that a tool is identical with another before citing it as evidence. One must constantly bear in mind the dictum of a learned judge, quoted by Duff: 'When you say things are practically the same, you really mean they are different'.[40] Once the groups are established, a clue may give us the name of the binder who owned these tools.

A group of a dozen bindings has been attributed to the Royal Heads Binder, so named after the portrait heads of Charles II and his queen which lurk among the masses of tooling in the angles of the panel on two manuscript volumes of anthems used in the Chapel Royal (Fig. 64).[41] The shop also bound a number of copies of the 1662 *Book of Common Prayer*, two of them with the royal arms.[42] No book printed later than 1664 belongs to this group, and it seems likely that the tools used by this bindery may have been lost in the Great Fire of 1666.

In the 1670s new binders and tool types begin to appear. The Naval Binder, employed (probably by Pepys) to bind some of the naval documents to be placed before senior officials of the Admiralty, remained faithful to panel design with corners and a central ornament of massed tooling. He was one of the finest London craftsmen of the day, and worked from about 1670 till at least 1695 (Fig. 62).[43] One of the new tools was the so-called drawer handle, actually the capital of an Ionic column, which lent itself both to all-over patterns and to combination with a panel, as on the dedication copy of Loggan's *Oxonia illustrata* (London, 1675) to Charles II (Fig. 65). In *Bindings in Cambridge Libraries* (pl. LVIII), G. D. Hobson listed twenty-eight bindings which he attributed to a Queens' Binder, with 'Queens'' in the plural, because he bound books for both Catherine of Braganza and Mary of Modena. A closer examination of this group, however, has shown that four different binderies are represented in this list. Seventeen of the books come from the shop which bound at least

[40] E. G. Duff, 'The Great Mearne Myth', 63.
[41] See Nixon, *Restoration*, no. 53. The other one is at the Boston Athenaeum, Boston, Mass.
[42] Nixon, *Restoration*, 30–2.
[43] Ibid. 37, nos. 79–83.

three books for Catherine of Braganza, as well as the Loggan illustrated here. This shop, now known as that of Queens' Binder A, bound in a number of different styles, sometimes with drawer handle tools and sometimes without. A huge two-volume *English Atlas*, printed in Oxford for Moses Pitt (1680–1), now in the British Library, shows this binder's addiction to the fanfare style, but here it is applied in a personal variation in which the design does not occupy the whole of the covers.[44] He also used a curved version of the cottage-roof style (Fig. 66). He was the most prolific binder of the 1670s and 1680s and clearly employed a number of finishers, for the quality of the tooling is variable.[45]

In the catalogue of the bindings in the Pepys Library an attempt was made to establish the identity of this binder. The majority of Pepys's elaborate bindings are either on books that Pepys particularly valued, or on books dedicated to him or given to him by a friend, or on books that reached him in the course of official business as a *douceur* from a seeker after preferment. Another category is those which Pepys obviously bought 'for the love of the binding'. One specially bound book should, from the number of its pressmarks, have been in the library during the *Diary* period; it cannot be accounted for under the first three headings. This is *A Conference about the Next Succession to the Crowne of Ingland*, by Robert Parsons, published in 1594. The finishing is not particularly expert, but the binding is decorated with tools belonging to the Queens' Binder A and this may have been the book referred to in the *Diary* on 12 March 1668/9, where he wrote: 'I took him [W. Howe] in my coach with W. Hewer and myself toward Westminster, and there he carried me to Nott's, the famous bookbinder that bound for my Lord Chancellor's library. And here I did take occasion for curiosity to bespeak a book to be bound, only that I might have one of his binding'. It is possible, but by no means proven, that Nott was the Queens' Binder A.[46]

Pepys also possessed three bindings from the workshop of the Queens' Binder B,[47] who was responsible for four bindings on

[44] 1 Tab. 16–17. Nixon, *Restoration*, nos. 58, 59.
[45] Nixon, *Restoration*, 32–4.
[46] R. Latham and W. Matthews (eds.), *The Diary of Samuel Pepys*, ix (London, 1976), 480. H. M. Nixon, *Catalogue of the Pepys Library*, vi, pl. 40 (P.L. 518).
[47] H. M. Nixon, *Catalogue of the Pepys Library*, vi, pls. 44, 45 (P.L. 1603, 15, 16).

Hobson's list.[48] This shop's speciality was painting edges over the gold with large naturalistic flowers which, unlike those of his contemporaries such as the Mearnes, show when the book is closed. Pepys's three volumes, which are all manuscripts, have these edges and they are among the most beautiful bindings in his library (Fig. 67). They could have been bound to Pepys's order, for they seem to have entered his library in the second half of the 1670s, the decade when this bindery seems to have been at work. An even finer binding from this shop—they are all of excellent quality and were probably all tooled by the same finisher—covers a copy of Jeremy Taylor, *Antiquitates Christianae* (London, 1675) in the New York Public Library.[49] The Queens' Binder C operated on more conventional lines. The only bindings by him in Hobson's list are numbers iii and iv, the first Viscount Stair's *Institutes of the Law of Scotland* (Edinburgh, 1681) in two volumes. He also bound (probably ten years after publication) a 1666–8 Cambridge *Book of Common Prayer* and *Bible*, now in the British Library (Fig. 68), and two presentation copies of Thomas Binning's *A Light to the Art of Gunnery* (London, 1676). All these bindings have his characteristic version of the conventional four-petalled flower tool.[50]

Three more books on Hobson's list[51] come from yet another bindery employing very similar tools, that of Queens' Binder D. The first of these is a book bound for Mary of Modena. This is a copy of the third edition of Edmund Waller's *Poems* published in 1668 (Fig. 69), with a manuscript dedication and extra poems in the author's hand. Since it bears Mary's arms as Duchess of York, the poet cannot have presented it to her before her marriage to the future James II in 1673.[52]

Much easier to distinguish from his contemporaries than these four Queens' Binders is the work of the man G. D. Hobson named the Devotional Binder.[53] He used slightly fatter drawer handle tools than

[48] G. D. Hobson, *Bindings in Cambridge Libraries* (Cambridge, 1929), pl. LVIII, nos. IX, X, XIII, XVIII. See also Nixon, *Restoration*, 35.

[49] D. Miner, *The History of Bookbinding 525–1950 A.D.: An Exhibition Held in the Baltimore Museum of Art* (Baltimore, Md., 1957), no. 416, pl. LXXXIII.

[50] Nixon, *Restoration*, nos. 70–2.

[51] Hobson, *Bindings in Cambridge Libraries*, pl. LVIII, nos. VI, XXII, XXV.

[52] Nixon, *Restoration*, no. 73. See also Id., *Restoration*, 35–7, nos. 74–7.

[53] Hobson, *Bindings in Cambridge Libraries*, pl. LXII. See also Nixon, *Restoration*, 38, nos. 84–7.

most of the binders of this period, but his most distinctive tools are his version of the conventional four-petalled flower, in which the petals are united instead of being distinct, and a half-open flower with pointed petals and a rounded heart, seen sideways on (Fig. 70). Most of the bindings from this shop, which was active between 1675 and 1685, are well tooled.

For about fifty years from 1670 onwards the practice of binding Service Books and works of piety in blind-tooled black turkey, often with black edges, was exceedingly common; it must have been carried out by almost all the binders of the time. In *Bindings in Cambridge Libraries*, G. D. Hobson postulated a 'Sombre Binder', but later he realized that several binders worked in this style.[54] The sombre binding on a copy of the *Eikon Basilike* of 1648 in the Pepys Library, illustrated by Hobson, shows characteristic profile head, hand, and moth tools and is decorated with closely-set hatched lines. Very few bindings from this particular Sombre Binder's shop are known (Fig. 71).

The cottage-roof style of binding was still current in the 1670s, although the next shop—named after the very small carnation tool used four times in the centre of the binding of G. J. Grelot, *Relation nouvelle d'un voyage de Constantinople* (Paris, 1680)[55]—usually employed it in a simple and rudimentary form (Fig. 72). On other bindings this Small Carnation Binder made use of a panel design with a repeating pattern within the panel. This bindery was working between 1676 and 1685. A different tool group is attributed to the Centre–Rectangle Binder, who was active during the same period but who was still at work as late as 1696. He was addicted to using a rectangular onlay in contrasting colour in the centre of the covers, and he also possessed two curious naked seated figures—not very cherubic—engaged in fishing with an outsize strawberry as bait and catching a swag (Fig. 73).[56]

A binder who also worked during the 1680s gets his name from a Common Prayer, Bible, and Psalms in metre (Cambridge, 1683), now in the Pierpont Morgan Library (Fig. 74). It has on the original

[54] Hobson, *Bindings in Cambridge Libraries*, pl. LVIIB. Nixon, *Restoration*, 42, 45, no. 113. See also Hobson, *English Bindings . . . in the Library of J. R. Abbey*, no. 64 (not by the Sombre Binder).
[55] Nixon, *Restoration*, no. 88; see also p. 38, nos. 89–91.
[56] Nixon, *Restoration*, 38, 40, nos. 92–4.

leather of the second panel of the spine the words: 'ELIZABETH DICKINSON HER BOOK 1688' tooled in gold. This bindery had a fondness for tulip tools, grapes, and thistles, but despite the latter it appears to have been located in London.[57] Another binder bound three presentation copies of Barlow's *Aesop* in 1687. The copy now in the Cracherode library of the British Library is in blue turkey (Pl. 7). Pepys's copy is in red with a black interlace, and so is the dedication copy to the Earl of Devonshire, formerly at Chatsworth.[58] The Spaniel Binder gets his name from a tool that seems to represent a King Charles spaniel, although he does not seem to have been at work before the Glorious Revolution of 1688. He was still in business in the first decade of the eighteenth century and produced what were probably presentation copies for both William III and Queen Anne (Fig. 75). He had other somewhat eccentric tools besides the spaniel, such as a butterfly with three large spots on its wings, a couple of winged cherubs, and a pair of perky little birds.[59]

We come finally to four London binders who can be identified by name. The first, John Harding, worked in the 1660s and 1670s;[60] three others started work in the 1680s. If, as Bagford stated, Richard Balley (the second binder) was 'bred under ye tuesion of Suckerman at Mr Mernes', he was probably in business on his own in the 1680s. Bagford also reported that he had 'contriued to bind a Booke that at sight you could not know ye forege from ye backe bouth being cut & gulded alike'.[61] Five examples are known of such books, all decorated with the same tools (Pl. 6).[62] His tools can be found on a number of other bindings from this period, such as a remarkable architectural binding in Cambridge University Library, depicting the Holy Table with the Ten Commandments above it.[63] Balley was probably active until at least 1711.

The third binder of this period whom we can identify with certainty by name is Alexander Cleeve, who was apprenticed to John Harding

[57] Ibid. 40, nos. 95–7.

[58] Pepys Library, 2637 (H. M. Nixon, *Catalogue of the Pepys Library*, vi, pl. 51); the Chatsworth copy is now in the BL C. 132. i. 63 (Nixon, *Restoration*, no. 99, see also no. 98).

[59] Nixon, *Restoration*, 41, nos. 101–3.

[60] H. M. Nixon, *British Bookbindings Presented by Kenneth H. Oldaker to ... Westminster Abbey* (London, 1982), no. 3.

[61] BL MS Harl. 5943, fo. 3^r.

[62] Nixon, *Restoration*, 42.

[63] Ibid. no. 111. M. M. Foot, *Pictorial Bookbindings* (London, 1986), fig. 3.

in 1678. A 1680 Prayer Book, now in the Victoria and Albert Museum, has the word CLEEVE at the foot of the upper cover and FECIT on the lower.[64] A binding in black turkey, in the Henry Davis Gift to the British Library, is signed on a leather strip above the turn-in of the lower cover CLEEVE FECIT.[65] That Alexander Cleeve is our man, and not Isaac the bookseller, is suggested by a binding given by J. W. Hely-Hutchinson to Eton College (Fig. 76). This has tools found on both the signed bindings, including the characteristic leopard-headed vase, and on an inserted end-leaf, one side of which has been painted purple, is a manuscript inscription in gold: 'Mrs Dorcas Gale is desired to accept of this Book from her Obliged Friend and Valentine A. C. 1691'.[66] The fourth named London binder is John Berresford or Beresford. He was made free of the Stationers' Company in 1682, took his first apprentice in 1696, and is last mentioned in the Stationers' Company Records in 1716. He worked for Samuel Pepys and bound several of the most important books in Pepys's library (Fig. 78).[67]

During the whole of the Restoration period London was the centre of fine binding. Outside London, only Oxford and Cambridge produced elaborately tooled bindings of the type that have been described above. As we have seen, the first signs of the new tools, copied from France, that were to become so prominent during this period occurred in Cambridge in the 1640s. The work of the man who might have introduced them, John Houlden, and of that of his son-in-law and successor, Titus Tillet, has been discussed in the previous chapter.

During the first half of the seventeenth century most of the Oxford presentation books had been bound in velvet, or ordered from London; it was not until Roger Bartlett, a London bookbinder, arrived in Oxford shortly after the Great Fire, that any first-rate gold-tooled leather bindings seem to have been produced there. Bartlett's career has been well documented by I. G. Philip[68] and, as

---

[64] Nixon, *Restoration*, no. 104.
[65] Ibid. no. 105. Foot, *The Henry Davis Gift*, ii, no. 142.
[66] Nixon, *Restoration*, 41, nos. 106.
[67] H. M. Nixon, *Catalogue of the Pepys Library*, vi, pp. XXIII–XXIV, pls. 22, 53. D. F. McKenzie, *Stationers' Company Apprentices 1641–1700*.
[68] I. G. Philip, 'Roger Bartlett, Bookbinder', *The Library*, 5th ser., 10 (Dec. 1955), 233–43. See also Nixon, *Restoration*, 45–7 (with literature) and H. M. Nixon, *Five Centuries of English Bookbinding* (London, 1978), no. 38.

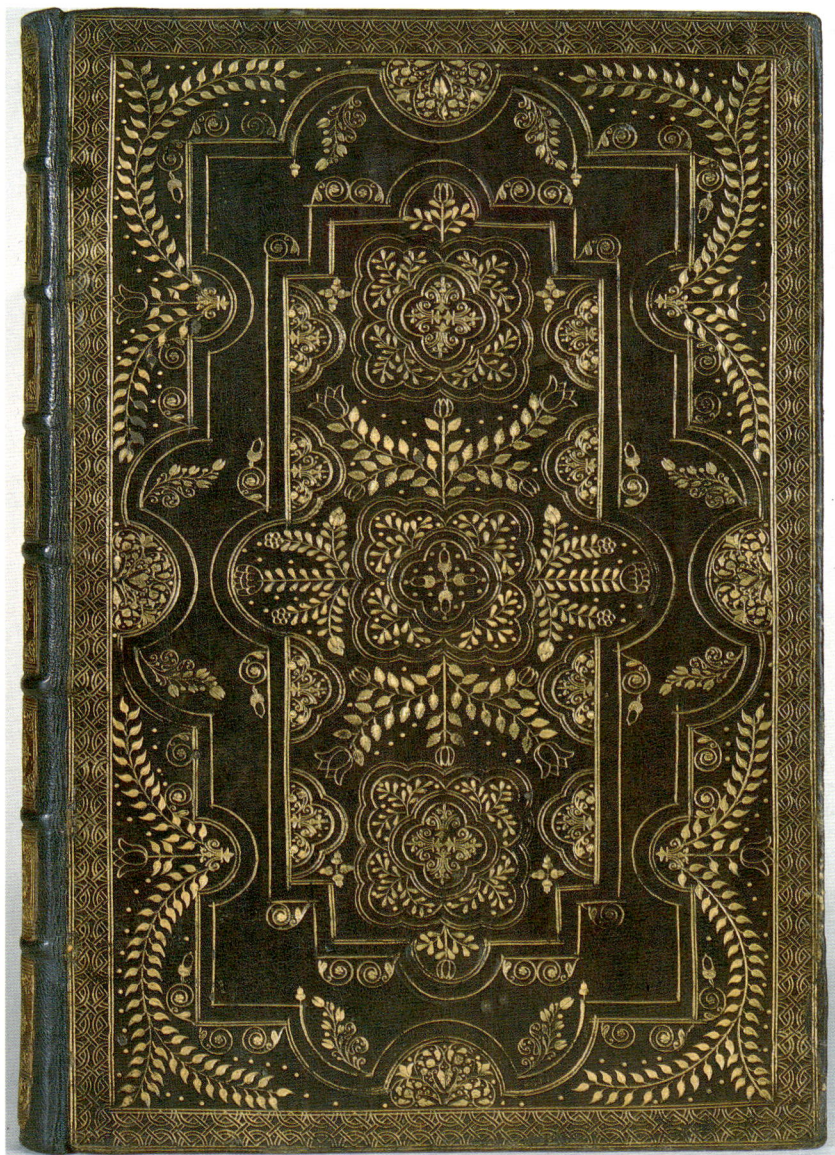

Pl. 7 Aesop, *Fables*, London, 1687. Blue goatskin, gold tooled.
BL 671.l.6. 370 × 250 × 40 mm.

PL. 9 *Book of Common Prayer*, Cambridge, 1760. Transparent vellum, gold tooled, painted decoration on the undersurface of the vellum. Queen Charlotte's arms are on the upper cover.

PL. 8 John Theobald, *Albion*, Oxford, 1720. Red goatskin, onlaid in black and citron, painted in black and gold tooled, with the arms and motto of Gerald, Lord Kinsale.

his bindings form a very homogeneous group, it has been possible now to identify over thirty of them (Fig. 77).[69] The attribution of these bindings to Bartlett, first made by G. D. Hobson, is probably more certain than any other of the period, since it is based on Oxford University and college accounts of sums paid to a man who was clearly a working bookbinder, with one (illegal) apprentice, and not a stationer or bookseller with a large business, who might farm out some or all of his bookbinding work. He is known to have been paid 'for the rich binding of the Oxford Antiquitys for the duke of Florence',[70] a copy of Anthony à Wood's *Historia et antiquitates Universitatis Oxoniensis* (Oxford, 1674), sent to Cosimo de Medici in that year, which fortunately survived the 1967 flooding of the Biblioteca Nazionale in Florence. In 1680 he bound the Benefactors' Book of Magdalen College, Oxford; he was also responsible for binding the Book of Benefactors of St Edmund Hall.[71] All these books are decorated with a distinctive set of tools and distinctive designs in which a simple cottage roof, decorated with floral volutes along the tiles, occurs time after time. This design persisted in Oxford for the remainder of the century.

The Accounts of the Delegates of the Oxford University Press furnish us with two more names of Oxford binders. In 1681 a William Ingram was paid for some 'extraordinary work' upon books presented to Charles II. As these have not been identified we do not know which of the Oxford bindings of the early 1680s came from this shop. But in 1699 a payment of £4.13s. was made 'To Mr Sedgley the Binder for binding of the 3d Vol: of Dr. Wallis's works to present ye King'.[72] The work in question is John Wallis's *Opera mathematica*, published in three volumes between 1693 and 1699. A large paper copy of volume 3, bound in blue turkey and tooled in gold to a panel design, is now in the King's Library in the British Library (Fig. 79). The tools used on this binding occur on a group of bindings on Oxford books, starting in the late 1670s or early 1680s, and these may well be the work of Richard Sedgley. Thomas Hearne recorded on 22 October 1719, 'Yesterday died Mr Sedgley, a Bookbinder of Oxford, in the 72d Year of his Age. He was an extraordinary good Binder'.[73]

[69] Hobson, *English Bindings . . . in the Library of J. R. Abbey*, nos. 40–2.
[70] Anthony à Wood, *Life and Times* (Oxford, 1895), iv. 71.
[71] Nixon, *Restoration*, nos. 117, 118; see also nos. 119–21.
[72] Ibid. 47, no. 122. Nixon, *Five Centuries*, no. 54.
[73] T. Hearne, *Remarks and Collections*, vii (Oxford, 1906), 58.

FIVE

The Eighteenth Century

O NE of the best-documented printed books in English literary history is Clarendon's *History of the Rebellion*, first
printed at the Oxford University Press in 1702–4 in three
volumes. In the IPEX exhibition, *Printing and the Mind of Man* at
Earl's Court in 1963, almost every step in the production of this book
was shown. There were the manuscript copy used by the printers, the
warehouseman's accounts, the punches and matrices for the types
used in the book, the artist's drawings for the ornaments, the copper
plates for those ornaments and for the frontispiece, and the completed
book. But although two copies of the book are known in identical
bindings—two volumes in George III's library in the British Library
(Fig. 80) and a complete three-volume set in the Royal Library at
Windsor—the one piece of information that has failed to survive is
the bill for the presentation copies. Nor, so far, has the binder been
identified.

Another anonymous craftsman who was active in the first two
decades of the eighteenth century has been named the Geometrical
Compartment Binder, from his determination to introduce—not
always very successfully—some new designs to replace the all-
pervading cottage-roof style or all-over patterns of his contemporaries
(Fig. 81). A number of his bindings recall the French fanfare bindings
of the late sixteenth century.[1] For the first quarter of the eighteenth
century there is, however, very little new in the way of design. Only
one set of bindings stands out from the rest, those associated with the

---

[1] H. M. Nixon, *Five Centuries of English Bookbinding* (London, 1978), no. 56 (cited
below as Nixon, *Five Centuries*). H. M. Nixon, *British Bookbindings Presented by Kenneth
H. Oldaker to . . . Westminster Abbey* (London, 1982), no. 10. M. M. Foot, 'A Binding by
the Geometrical Compartment Binder', *Book Collector*, 35 (1986), 76–7.

name of Elkanah Settle, the self-styled 'City Poet'. Unfortunately, it is for their oddity rather than their beauty that they are remembered. Settle (1648–1724) was considered a rising playwright in the 1670s, but by the beginning of the eighteenth century he had degenerated into a hack poet scraping a precarious living by retailing copies of topical political verse, *Eusebia Triumphans* or *Carmen Irenicum*, and equally topical but non-political verses celebrating the births, marriages, or deaths in the families of the nobly born or newly wealthy. Put in turkey leather, embellished with crude gold tooling and the arms of a suitable recipient, these copies were offered by the humble author in the hope of a commensurate reward (Fig. 82). In some cases the title-page and the flyleaf were decorated in gold with impressions of the same tools that are found on the bindings. If spurned, Settle cancelled the leaf that contained specific references to the particular event and substituted one referring to some new event. A new coat of arms on a new piece of leather was pasted on the covers, and Settle called hopefully at a second grand house. On at least one occasion he was successful only at the third attempt.[2]

By the 1720s we begin to find that the majority of the groups of bindings that have been isolated are attributable to named binders, although this does not mean that there is not a great deal of work to be done in isolating and attributing other groups. The first library for which we have clear information on the binders who worked for it is the famous Harleian library, founded by Robert Harley, first Earl of Oxford, and greatly enlarged by his son Edward, Lord Harley. After the father's fall from office in 1715, the son took over the management of the library. It became the main interest in his life, and he greatly expanded it until it contained over 7,000 manuscripts (now one of the foundation collections of manuscripts in the British Library) and some 50,000 printed books which had to be sold in the 1740s. Most of the bills for binding books for the Harleian library have survived in the Duke of Portland's collection and are now on deposit in the British Library.[3] In his early days Harley patronized Richard Sedgley

---

[2] W. E. Moss, 'Elkanah Settle: The Armorial Binding Expert', *The Book Collectors Quarterly*, 13 (1934), 7–22; 14 (1934), 91–6. G. D. Hobson, *English Bindings 1490–1940 in the Library of J. R. Abbey* (London, 1940), 92–6. Nixon, *Five Centuries*, no. 57.

[3] H. M. Nixon, 'Harleian Bindings' in *Studies in the Book Trade in Honour of Graham Pollard* (Oxford, 1975), 153–94 (where references can be found for the passages quoted below).

of Oxford, John Graves (probably of London), and Thomas Dawson of Cambridge, but by 1715 he was sending his books to one of the best binding shops in London, that of Jane Steel, daughter of the Robert Steel who had been apprenticed to Samuel Mearne, the royal bookbinder, from 1668–75. Three of her bills survive from the years 1715–17, and a number of her bindings can be identified. One covers a Lucan printed in Rome in 1469; it cost 18 shillings to bind in red turkey (Fig. 83).

By 1719, however, Thomas Elliott appears as one of Harley's two main binders, and as he in turn had been apprenticed to Robert Steel, it may be—as so often happened—that he married his late master's daughter and took over the business. Certainly his wife was in the trade, for when in 1721 he bound one of the treasures of the library, the Codex Aureus,[4] she is mentioned as working with her husband at Harley's house in Dover Street on 10 July, and was probably doing the headbanding as 'Gold and Silver twist for headbanding' was bought the same day. Elliott seems to have been a fairly cheerful soul, who was frequently reproved for careless lettering by Harley's admirable (but at times somewhat officious) librarian, Humphrey Wanley. After one of these complaints Elliott appears to have got his own back by returning two books without 'middle pieces', but with the letters of his name hidden in circles in the centre of the spine decoration, an exceedingly unusual practice at this time (Fig. 84). Dr C. E. Wright, who together with his wife produced an excellent and extremely useful edition of Wanley's diary,[5] first spotted this joke of Elliott's. Wanley's diary also shows that the other main binder employed by Harley in the 1720s was Christopher Chapman. While most of Elliott's bills have survived, we have none of Chapman's, although fortunately there is just enough information in Wanley's diary to identify his work, and it is evident that he played an equally important part as his rival, Elliott, in the binding of the library. He started binding for the library in January 1719/20, and at first his work seems to have satisfied Wanley (Fig. 85). But gradually— perhaps because Harley settled his bills less and less frequently during his life—Chapman took longer and longer to return the books.

[4] BL MS Harl. 2788. H. M. Nixon, art. cit. 168. Reproduced in Nixon, *Five Centuries*, no. 60.

[5] C. E. and R. C. Wright (eds.), *The Diary of Humfrey Wanley, 1715–1726* (London, 1966) (the passages from Wanley's diary, quoted below, are taken from this edition).

Finally when on 23 December 1725 Chapman called, Wanley 'gave him no Work; chiding him for being so slow in my Lords former business, which he had frequently postponed, that he might serve the Booksellers the sooner'. For the remaining six months of Wanley's life only Elliott was binding for the Harleian library.

Superficially the bindings produced by Elliott and Chapman are very similar. They used the same batch of skins for their red morocco bindings, with rather thick boards and projecting squares, and with the same type and colour of headbands. Many of the covers are decorated with roll-tooled borders and diamond-shaped 'middle pieces', but most of the tools employed to effect the designs are distinctly different and can be used to distinguish the work of these two binders.

The Harleian library was one of the first to use Moroccan goatskins rather than those from Turkey, which had been normally used in England up to this time. John Beaver, the husband of Wanley's stepdaughter, acquired 288 skins of this leather during a visit to Gibraltar in 1720–1. He obtained them from 'a Merchant in Barbary, who has sent me the cream of the Countrey'.[6] Although many of these skins have lasted well, they are clearly not of the quality of the best skins from Turkey.

Elliott and Chapman were both practising heads of not very large binding firms doing first-rate work. John Brindley was a successful business man of the Samuel Mearne type, who added bookselling and publishing to his bookbinding business and probably did not work at the bench himself in later life. He held the appointment of Bookbinder to George II's queen, Caroline of Ansbach. A binding on a copy of Cavendish's *General System of Horsemanship* (London, 1743), which he published, is now in the King's Library at the British Library (64. i. 4).[7] Earlier he had specialized in painted armorial decoration on the fore-edge of the leaves of the book, thus almost filling the apparent gap between the painted edges of the Restoration period and the pictorial edges of Edwards of Halifax. Brindley's first connection with the Harleian library appears to have been on 3 February 1719/20, when Wanley recorded that 'Mr Brindley came to

---

[6] Letter from Beaver, dated 22 January 1720/1 in BL MS Harl. 3777, fo. 179. See also Nixon, art. cit. 164–5.

[7] Nixon, *Five Centuries*, no. 64. Nixon, art. cit. 184–6.

know if my Lord had any work for him; & say's that his Lordship lately gave him a Book to Bind'. Wanley 'referred him to his Lordship' and the binder certainly obtained no work until after Wanley's death. But four bills among the Portland papers on deposit in the British Library, which cover the years 1733 to 1738, show Brindley not only selling books to the library but also binding for it.[8] The most interesting books in these bills are copies of Oricellarius, *De bello Italico* (London, 1724), bound for George I, and Richard Holland, *Observations on the Small Pox* (London, 1728), bound for Queen Caroline; both apparently were sold to Harley for one guinea each on 11 October 1736. Copies of these books are now respectively at Windsor and in the King's Library at the British Library (Fig. 86). Both have the arms of the recipient on the foreedge. The problem remains as to whether—as often has happened with royal gifts—both books were given away by their recipients and had found their way back to Brindley, their publisher, by 1736, or whether he had duplicate bindings made, and retained them until 1736. Both books can be traced in Osborne's Harleian sale catalogues, but neither of the copies now known bears Osborne's easily erased pencil price.

Bindings of distinction were produced both in Oxford and in Cambridge during the first half of the eighteenth century. The leading binder at Oxford, Thomas Sedgley, has been identified by John P. Chalmers,[9] and his elaborate onlaid bindings are quite distinctive (Pl. 8). He was probably the son of Richard Sedgley, although this cannot be proved with certainty, and he was binding for the Bodleian Library before the end of 1721. Many of his bindings are to be found in the Bodleian and among George Clarke's books at Worcester College, Oxford. He shared with Alexander Thompson the binding of the Oxford University verses on the death of Queen Caroline in 1737. He died late in 1761 or early in 1762.

The leading Cambridge binder of the eighteenth century, Edwin Moor or Moore, was at work in the period 1740 to 1769. Stylistically he was conservative, working in the Harleian style with a central lozenge built up of small tools and several borders (Fig. 87). But his bindings nearly always look better than those of the Harleian books,

[8] BL, Loan 29/111, Misc. 1(C). Nixon, art. cit. 185.
[9] J. P. Chalmers, 'Thomas Sedgley Oxford Binder', *Book Collector*, 26 (1977), 353–70.

since he continued to bind in turkey leather, rather than morocco, and his finishing was considerably better than Elliott's or Chapman's.[10] The work of William Bonnor, active in Cambridge between 1727 and 1739 has also been identified, but it is not very distinguished.[11]

An unidentified binder made a number of elaborate, if not very beautiful, bindings in the 1740s, some of them with coloured onlays. An example in the British Library bears the arms of George, third Earl of Cholmondeley, and covers, as do two of the others, Faerno's *Fabulae Centum*, published in London by Guillaume Darres and Claude Du Bosc in 1743 (Fig. 88). A 1741 Plutarch in blue morocco with red morocco doublures, by the same binder, is one of three books from this shop bound for John Carteret, second Earl Granville.[12]

W. O. Hassall first drew attention to the work of Jean Robiquet,[13] a French binder living in London, who bound many of the books in the Long Library at Holkham. Jane Steel was paid £31.10s. for binding up to Lady Day 1719, and then Brindley both sold books to and bound books for Lord Leicester until 1738. He was obviously kept very busy and from Lady Day 1719 until 1729 his bills for binding alone seldom dropped below £50. The majority of his bindings were in red morocco or brown russia. Then Robiquet took over the binding work for Holkham and did almost all of it until the death of the first Earl of Leicester (second creation) in 1759; the majority of his bindings are in plain calf with gilt spines. He had two long spells working at Holkham: in 1742 he spent 19 weeks with his wife and a man, and then in 1748 he spent '44 weeks and 5 days Binding Books' at a cost of £67.10s.; he also had three men with him for three weeks. This probably got the Long Library at Holkham fairly straight, and for the next eleven years the binding bill was

[10] Nixon, *Five Centuries*, no. 65. M. M. Foot, *The Henry Davis Gift*, i (London, 1978), 80–3; ii (London, 1983), no. 171.

[11] Nixon, *Five Centuries*, no. 62.

[12] Ibid. no. 63.

[13] W. O. Hassall, 'Portrait of a Bibliophile II, Thomas Coke, Earl of Leicester, 1697–1759', *Book Collector*, 8 (1959), 255–6. The information below is based on notes by H. M. Nixon, made at Holkham Hall, concerning Holkham Journal Book, Codex 7375, and Holkham Accounts (library expenses). I am grateful to Bryan and Kate Ward Perkins, Lord Leicester's librarians, for their help during my visit to Holkham Hall. See also H. M. Nixon, 'Some Huguenot Bookbinders', *Proceedings of the Huguenot Society of London*, 23 no. 5 (1981), 326–7.

usually in the nature of £2 or £3 a quarter, with the exception of bills
for binding and lettering 60 portfolios in 1755 for £12, and £11.19s.
'for book binding' in 1757. Little else seems to be known of
Robiquet's work beyond a binding in the British Library (Fig. 89) in
red morocco with the arms of Horace Walpole and a contemporary
note on the flyleaf saying 'bound by Robiquet'. It is encouraging to
note that one tool used on this binding is found on ten books at
Holkham, three of which were mentioned in the two surviving
Robiquet bills there in which the books are individually named.[14]
Most of the payments to him are for a quarter's binding, but
occasionally the name of a single book is given in the accounts, such
as Chishull's *Travels in Turkey* (London, 1747) [LL. E. 6] and
Anson's *Voyage* (London, 1748) [LL. E. 4], both bound in 1748, and
five volumes of Bolingbroke's *Works* (London, 1754) [LL. E. 4],
bound in the year of publication.

Another binder whose work at this period has been identified is
Christopher Norris, who bound for the antiquary Maurice Johnson.
Four of Norris's bindings, evidently bound c.1751 for Johnson, were
sold at Sotheby's on 23 March 1970 in a collection that had descended
through W. A. Marsden, Keeper of Printed Books in the British
Museum from 1930 to 1943.[15] One of these, covering an early
seventeenth-century heraldic manuscript illustrating the arms of English and Norman families, came to the British Library with the Henry
Davis Gift. Chistopher Norris was one of a family of bookbinders.
He was freed by patrimony in 1703. Several apprentices were registered to him and he lived in the Old Change (1709), Hatton Garden
(1724), St Paul's Alley (1725), and Chapter House Alley (1726), the
address given by Maurice Johnson for his bookbinder. By 1751
Norris was probably too old to stand at the bench himself but he
could well still have been at the head of a bindery. He died in 1763,
and in his will left his working tools to his son, Christopher.
Christopher junior had been apprenticed to his father from 1736 to
1745, when he took up his freedom. In 1750 he is mentioned as living
in St Paul's Churchyard, where he stayed at least until 1753; by 1767

[14] LL. D. 3. C. Buonamici, *Commentariorum de bello Italico libri*, 2 vols. (Leiden, 1750),
51; LL. E. 12. H. Saint John, Viscount Bolingbroke, *Letters on the Study and Use of
History*, 2 vols. (London, 1752); SR. back left 1/4. John Hill, *Review of the Works of the
Royal Society* (London, 1751).
[15] Lots 10, 157, 174, 179. For Norris see Foot, *The Henry Davis Gift*, i. 87–94.

he was living in Old Fish Street. Four apprentices were registered to him between 1762 and 1767 and he died in 1792.

A German, Andreas Linde, also made his mark as a binder in the 1750s. He held the appointment of Stationer and Bookbinder to Prince George before the death of the prince's father, Frederick, Prince of Wales. His work will be discussed below, together with that of the considerable number of German binders who came to work in London in the last quarter of the eighteenth century.

Richard Montagu was one of the leading London binders of the 1750s and 1760s, and seems to have specialized in producing bindings with doublures or inner linings of leather, hitherto a rare occurrence in English binding. An example of his work covers a volume by Akenside and Glover, now in the British Library (Fig. 90). One of his best patrons was that staunchly patriotic republican, Thomas Hollis, who used him for the more elaborate bindings which he presented to Harvard and Berne, as well as for a set of Milton's works which he presented to the 'academy of La Crusca' and which are now in the Biblioteca Nazionale in Florence.[16] Montagu also bound for Hollis to present to Sir John Dick a remarkable set of six volumes, each bound in a different leather, and the set of forty copies of the Book of Common Prayer that were provided for the Installation of the Knights of the Bath in Henry VII's Chapel, Westminster Abbey, on 26 May 1761. Hollis's simpler presentation bindings, again more common at Harvard or Berne than in England, were the work of one Matthewman between c.1761 and 1769. These are of comparatively plain red leather with different tools of republican significance in gold in the centre of the covers, and often tooled in black on the end-leaves (Fig. 91). Matthewman's shop and all his tools were destroyed by fire in June 1764; it was 1767 before the complete set had been replaced with similar but distinguishable new ones by Pingo, the seal engraver.[17]

A character somewhat resembling Thomas Hollis was Jonas Hanway (1712–86), never mentioned without reference to a record (apparently quite untrue) that he was the first person to have used an umbrella in London. He was another eccentric philanthropist who

[16] Nixon, *Five Centuries*, nos. 67–8; E. Howe, *A List of London Bookbinders 1648–1815* (London, 1950), 69.

[17] Nixon, *Five Centuries*, no. 74. See also W. H. Bond, *Thomas Hollis, of Lincoln's Inn* (Cambridge, 1990).

sought to further the good causes he favoured by presenting elaborately bound books on such subjects to possible subscribers. His
favourite causes varied from paving, cleaning, and lighting the streets
of Westminster, through the reform of prostitutes and the protection
of young chimney sweepers, to his particular favourite, the Marine
Society, which he founded and which still exists. G. D. Hobson
pointed out that he seems to have used two binders, but neither of
them has yet been identified by name.[18] The first, whom he patronized
until 1765, worked in an old-fashioned style comparable to the
Harleian bindings of the 1720s (Fig. 92). Hanway's later bindings
include emblematic tools, similar to but different from those found
on Hollis bindings, as well as some rococo elements.

Styles of binding decoration tend to lag behind the latest designs in
other arts, often by as much as twenty years. A marked exception to
this occurred in the first half of the 1760s, when the two leaders in
the neo-classical style of architecture, James Stuart and Robert Adam,
designed neo-classical bindings at a time when there had been hardly
any rococo ones. The bindings covered two splendid folios: James
Stuart and Nicholas Revett's *The Antiquities of Athens*[19]—the first
volume of which appeared in 1762, the second in 1787, and the third
in 1794—and Robert Adam's *Ruins of the Palace of the Emperor
Diocletian, at Spalatro*, published in 1764.[20] Several copies are known
of Stuart and Revett's book in red morocco with the same design,
although volume 1 has tools that differ slightly from those used on
volumes 2 (Fig. 93) and 3. A set in brown calf was exhibited at the
28th Antiquarian Book Fair (1987). Numerous examples of Adam's
Spalatro are found with slightly differing designs; copies for members
of the royal family were bound in red (Fig. 94), for members of the
Order of the Garter in blue, and for members of the Order of the
Thistle in green. There is also an extremely satisfactory neo-classical
binding of 1764 among George III's books in the British Library on
the 1764 Strawberry Hill edition of *The Life of Edward, Lord Herbert*

---

[18] Hobson, *English Bindings . . . in the Library of J. R. Abbey*, 120–4. Nixon, *Five
Centuries*, no. 78. See also Nixon, *British Bookbindings Presented by Kenneth H. Oldaker
to . . . Westminster Abbey*, nos. 18–19.
[19] Nixon, *Five Centuries*, no. 69. Mr A. G. Thomas also possesses vol. iii (1794) in a
presentation binding.
[20] Ibid. no. 70.

of Cherbury.[21] Rather surprisingly, Horace Walpole took little interest in bookbinding. This volume seems to have been a present to George III from Lord Powis, who owned the manuscript and was, in return, given part of the edition by Walpole. These three bindings have no tool in common, nor did they set any new fashion.

The work of Richard Dymott has been studied by Giles Barber.[22] Dymott is a typical example of the way a London binder doing first-rate work can be traced back for a century or more in a series of apprenticeships all in first-class shops. In Dymott's case he was apprenticed to Benjamin Stichall, who had been bound to Thomas Elliott, the apprentice of Robert Steel, who in turn was the apprentice of Samuel Mearne. Of these Stichall is the least known, but he bound two volumes of Catesby's *History of Carolina* for Holkham in 1744. Dymott was one of the earlier eighteenth-century binders to sign his name, as on a binding on Apuleius's *Golden Asse* (London, 1566) from the Britwell collection, now in the Huntington Library (Fig. 95). Another binding by him, on a *Book of Common Prayer* (Amsterdam, 1711), formerly in the Sullivan, Schiff, and Abbey collections, is signed 'Dymott fecit' at the head and tail of the spine.[23] From the tools used on these two bindings it has been possible to identify a number of other examples of his work, including a copy of volume i of Appian's *Roman History* in Latin (Venice, 1477; IB. 20487a) in the British Library. A third signed binding, in the Broxbourne Collection at the Bodleian Library, covers a Baskerville Virgil (Birmingham, 1757) but seems to have no tools in common with the others. Dymott was active between 1757 and 1778 or 1779. After his death his widow carried on the firm for a number of years.

In the second half of the eighteenth century there was evidently quite a good trade in elaborate Masonic bindings. It is possible that the first binder who specialized in these was Robert Black of Tower Hill, who was also a stationer dealing in 'all sorts of Books of Navigation, Sea Charts, Mathematical Instruments [etc.]'.[24] Two bindings by him are known (though without Masonic tools), one of

[21] Ibid. no. 71.

[22] G. Barber, 'Richard Dymott, Bookbinder', *The Library*, 5th ser., 19 (1964), 250–4 (with references to bindings mentioned below), pl. xxii. E. Howe, *A List of London Bookbinders*, 31–2.

[23] Hobson, *English Bindings . . . in the Library of J. R. Abbey*, no. 77.

[24] Sotheby's, 2 Mar. 1937, lot 19. Howe, *A List of London Bookbinders*, 13–14. Nixon, *Five Centuries*, no. 75 (last para: Loveday is a misprint for Lovejoy).

which is signed. Four generations of his family carried on the business until 1850. John Lovejoy, said by Ellic Howe to have worked mainly for the booksellers in calf or calf gilt, also made Masonic bindings[25] (Fig. 96). He became free of the Stationers' Company in 1771 and did not die until 1818 or 1819.

The next bindings to be discussed are those of Edwards of Halifax.[26] The firm was established by William Edwards in Halifax, at least as early as 1755, the year before his most famous son, James, was born. It was probably before William's sons James and John had started their London bookshop in Pall Mall in 1784 that the three specialities of the firm had been developed—scenes painted on the fore-edge, Etruscan bindings in stained calf with a border of classical ornaments, and vellum bindings with scenes and portraits painted on the under-surface of the vellum, rendered transparent by a patented process and backed with white paper. All three activities appear mainly to have been practised in Halifax, although the transparent vellum technique was not patented until James Edwards had come to London.

As has already been mentioned, the painting of designs under the gold on the fore-edge of books dates back in England to the 1650s. It was quite common during the Restoration period, and was continued in the first half of the eighteenth century by John Brindley. The Edwards family not only carried on the art, but enlarged it from the mainly floral and heraldic early efforts, with occasional religious scenes and royal portraits, to embrace views of well-known country houses set in landscapes. From time to time they also produced religious scenes, such as that on the Bible that has been in the possession of the Farrer family since it was bound, which has a wash drawing on the edge of St Paul preaching to the Athenians, signed 'Edwards fc'',[27] or the Prayer Book of Queen Charlotte in the British

[25] Howe, *A List of London Bookbinders*, 61. Hobson, *English Bindings . . . in the Library of J. R. Abbey*, 146–8. Foot, *The Henry Davis Gift*, ii, no. 207.
[26] T. W. Hanson, 'Edwards of Halifax', *The Bookbinding Trades Journal*, ii, no. 7 (1911), 100–3; id., '"Edwards of Halifax": A Family of Book-Sellers, Collectors and Book-Binders', *Transactions of the Halifax Antiquarian Society* (1912), 141–200; id., 'Edwards of Halifax bookbinders', *Book Handbook*, 6 (1948), 329–38. Hobson, *English Bindings . . . in the Library of J. R. Abbey*, nos. 99, 100. H. M. Nixon, *Broxbourne Library: Styles and Designs of Bookbindings* (London, 1956), no. 93. Foot, *The Henry Davis Gift*, ii, nos. 186–7.
[27] Nixon, *Five Centuries*, no. 77. The fore-edge of Queen Charlotte's Prayer Book is illustrated in M. M. Foot, *Pictorial Bookbindings* (London, 1986), fig. 30. An early 19th-century binder who continued this tradition was Bartholomew Frye; see: M. M. Foot, 'A

Library (Pl. 9) with a picture of the Resurrection painted under the gold.

The Etruscan style was produced by the Halifax firm and was continued, after William Edwards' retirement, by his fourth son, Thomas. These books were bound in calf, with a centre panel of acid-stained tree calf outlined by a small gilt Greek-key roll. Outside this a frame of light calf was decorated with classical ornaments in two shades of terracotta; the outer border had a gilt roll of alternating vertical dashes and roundels. T. W. Hanson, in his article in *Book Handbook*, noted that he knew of thirteen copies of John Watson's *History . . . of Halifax* (London, 1775) bound in this style; and it may well have been developed not long after this date.

The best known of the Edwards specialities is that of painting cover designs under the vellum. From time to time during previous centuries, bindings had been produced with arms or decoration painted on the outer surface of white vellum covers, but these have often been damaged by wear. The Edwards patent of 1785 described the method of rendering vellum transparent by soaking it in water in which a small quantity of pearl ash had been dissolved and by pressing it hard until it became transparent. It can then be drawn upon and painted; the completed decoration must be lined with paper attached with flour paste.[28] The blue paint frequently found in the gold-tooled rolls in the borders of the covers and on the spine was usually applied to the outer surface of the vellum. Painted designs included portraits, coats of arms, Biblical scenes, landscapes, and, most commonly, allegorical figures. The Farrer Bible mentioned above has on the lower cover a painting of Belshazzar's feast; the bindings on a five-volume set of Walpole's *Anecdotes of Painting in England* (Strawberry Hill, 1762), formerly in Major Abbey's collection, show various portraits.[29]

The most famous English binder of the latter half of the eighteenth

Binding by Bartholomew Frye, c.1820', *Book Collector*, 37 (1988), 92–3. The great majority of fore-edge paintings now in existence are 20th-century paintings on the edges of otherwise difficult-to-sell books in contemporary leather bindings of the period 1800–30. See H. M. Nixon's review of C. J. Weber's *Fore-Edge Painting* (New York, 1966) in the *TLS*, 29 June 1967, 588.

[28] The patent is quoted in T. W. Hanson, *Papers, Reports, etc. Read before the Halifax Antiquarian Society* (1912), 193–4.

[29] Hobson, *English Bindings . . . in the Library of J. R. Abbey*, no. 100.

century is Roger Payne.[30] His reputation has been enhanced by his partiality for strong drink and his elaborate, not always wholly truthful, bills. His typical and best-known bindings were usually in brown russia; red, blue, or green straight-grain morocco; or smooth olive morocco, with purple end-leaves and tall green headbands. They seem to date from the last eight or nine years of his life, when he was mainly working for his namesake, the bookseller Thomas Payne. One of his earliest-known bindings, made when he was working at Eton, belonged to Sir Geoffrey Keynes and was bound in 1764.[31] It is particularly interesting in that it shows his preference for small tools and the use of a dotted background, though it is a far cry from this to his later fully developed style. Sir Robert Birley wrote about some of the simpler signed bindings by him and his brother Thomas found in A. M. Storer's library at Eton. Another signed Payne binding of the period 1775–85 is in the Pierpont Morgan Library and now seems equally uncharacteristic.[32]

The typical Payne bindings of the 1790s have very elaborate small-tooled spines, frequently with two or three panels lettered and the date of printing nearly always in roman numerals. This pattern can be seen on the brown russia bindings of a set of Sir William Dugdale's *Works* (London, 1658–1730) bound for Sir Richard Colt Hoare, which is now widely scattered. One of these belongs to the Henry Davis Gift to the British Library and another, the three-volume *Monasticon Anglicanum* (1658–73) at Harvard, contains two letters from Roger Payne dated 1796. A binding of smooth olive morocco covers a Lascaris (Venice, 1494/5) in the Cracherode collection in the British Library (Fig. 97).

The invasion of German binders played an important part in the West End binding trade in the last quarter of the eighteenth century. The first of them to arrive was Andreas Linde, who by 1751 was in London as stationer and bookbinder by appointment to the future George III. A signed binding on a German Psalter in octavo (Fig. 98) and another on its companion New Testament, both in the British

---

[30] C. Davenport, *Roger Payne* (Chicago, 1929); R. Birley, 'Roger and Thomas Payne: With some Account of their Earlier Bindings', *The Library*, 5th ser., 15 (1960), 33–41; Foot, *The Henry Davis Gift*, i. 95–114.

[31] Nixon, *Five Centuries*, no. 72: this binding is now in Cambridge University Library, Keynes T. 6. 23. See also M. M. Foot, 'An Eton Binding by Roger Payne', *Book Collector*, 32 (1983), 202–3.

[32] D. Miner, *The History of Bookbinding 525–1950* (Baltimore, Md., 1957), no. 505.

Library (218. d. 3 and 217. f. 24), are anything but beautiful with their winged and tail-coated waiters supporting the Prince's initials. But there are two handsome folios by Linde at Windsor, illustrated by Holmes; an attractive quarto from the Pierpont Morgan Library, covering Lord Orrery's translation of Pliny's *Letters* (London, 1751) (PML, 936–7), is also a success.[33] It is not known when Linde died, but the next important German to come to London was John Baumgarten, who seems to have been well established by 1771. When Baumgarten died in 1782, he received a brief notice in the *Gentleman's Magazine* (unusual for a binder at this time), which described him as 'a native of Germany, and a man of uncommon excellence in his profession'.

An eighteenth-century German bookbinder tended to be much better educated than his English counterpart, and was in the habit of taking a book through all the binding processes himself. There is a fascinating account in J. G. Hüttner's *Englische Miscellen* (*Bd.* 6, Tübingen, 1802) of the state of the binding trade in England at this period, which explains in detail the difference in method and outlook between English and German binders, and accounts for the success of the immigrants. Prospects in England were much better than in Germany. A German prince would probably have his whole library bound in calf, but a simple British gentleman like Cracherode or H. G. Quin, whose small but very distinguished library is now at Trinity College, Dublin,[34] would have much of his library bound in the more expensive morocco.

Baumgarten's initials, J. B., are to be found on several of his bindings, including two copies of James Beattie's *Essay on Truth* (London, 1774), one of which is in the Pierpont Morgan Library, the other in the British Library (Fig. 99). Some confusion has been caused by the same initials appearing on Masonic bindings of the period, but here the significance is apparently purely Masonic.[35] Baumgarten was

---

[33] R. R. Holmes, *Specimens of Royal Fine and Historical Bookbinding, Selected from the Royal Library, Windsor Castle* (London, 1893), pls. 57, 58, 65, 66; Nixon, *Five Centuries*, no. 66. For a general discussion of German binders in London see also H. M. Nixon, *Twelve Books in Fine Bindings from the Library of J. W. Hely-Hutchinson* (London, 1953), 69–73; J. G. Marks, 'Bookbinding in London about 1880', *Book Collector*, 33 (1984), 449–56.

[34] V. Morrow, 'Bibliotheca Quiniana' in P. Fox (ed.), *Treasures of the Library Trinity College Dublin* (Dublin, 1986), 184–96.

[35] H. M. Nixon, 'Baumgarten's Will' in *Festschrift Ernst Kyriss* (Stuttgart, 1961), 397–404. See also E. Howe, *A List of London Bookbinders*, 8–10.

probably responsible for introducing the rococo style into English bookbinding, although there had been some rococo features in Linde's work. Several other binders in London were producing rococo bindings in the 1770s. One made the bindings on a set of Prayer Books, probably bound c.1776 for Philip Stanhope, fifth Earl of Chesterfield. The dedication copy of Marmaduke Stalkartt's *Naval Architecture* (London, 1781), which is in George III's collection in the British Library (62. g. 8), and another copy of the same book at Harvard (Houghton Library, Typ. 705. 81. 807 PF.), are in very similar morocco bindings decorated with yet another set of tools.[36] Baumgarten died after a seizure in 1782, and the depositions which were required to ensure the acceptance of his unsigned will throw a little light on the circumstances of his death.[37] His one-time apprentice, partner, and successor was another German immigrant, Christian Samuel Kalthoeber, whom Hüttner, writing in 1802, considered to be the outstanding figure in the English binding trade (Fig. 100). It is clear that his reputation had reached Russia by the 1780s, for Catherine the Great evidently made considerable efforts to lure him to St Petersburg. One of his bindings, priced at thirty guineas, aroused so much interest that George III had it brought to Buckingham House (later the Palace) for his inspection; at the same time it was no doubt seen in the king's private bindery, which produced a number of bindings in the same sort of style on the most important books in the royal library—now at the British Library. Soon after Hüttner wrote Kalthoeber's fortunes seem to have declined, and his business was taken over by another binder with a German name, Frederick Deschlein.[38] It is most likely that the Kalthabert who was employed by the French *immigré*, August Marie, Comte de Caumont, as his 'premier ouvrier' from 1808 till 1814 was C. S. Kalthoeber himself. The Comte de Caumont ran a bindery in London from 1796 until his return to France in 1814.[39]

[36] For Chesterfield bindings see M. M. Foot, *The Henry Davis Gift*, ii, no. 185. Nixon, *Five Centuries*, no. 76. See also M. M. Foot, 'A London Rococo Binding', *Book Collector*, 28 (1979), 110–11.

[37] Nixon, 'Baumgarten's Will', 397–403.

[38] Nixon, *Twelve Books*, 69–73. E. Howe, *A List of London Bookbinders*, pp. xxxv, 53, and 30. See also H. M. Nixon, *British Bookbindings Presented . . . to Westminster Abbey*, nos. 21–2.

[39] C. Boisset-Astier, 'A French Bookbinder in London', *Book Collector*, 30 (1981), 182–215. See also H. M. Nixon, *British Bookbindings Presented . . . to Westminster Abbey*, no. 30 (with further literature).

Henry Walther was another of the Germans to come to England. A note in the Jaffray manuscript, quoted by Ellic Howe,[40] says that he worked for a time with Baumgarten. His two most elaborate bindings cover copies of the 1790 James Edwards reprint of *Novelle Otto*. One of these, with a repeating pattern of blue onlays in the style of Padeloup, was bound for Colonel Thomas Stanley and is part of the Henry Davis Gift to the British Library.[41] It is signed and dated in the joint: 'Bound by H. Walther 1791'. The other, with an outer border of gilt pinnacles and the Spencer crest on the blue onlays, is in the John Rylands University Library in Manchester.[42] It seems likely that Henry Walther survived to a great age, although there may be some confusion with his son, Charles D. Walther, who was also a binder.

Another of the German firms that was established before the end of the eighteenth century was that of Staggemeier and Welcher. Like most of these German immigrants, Staggemeier came from Hanover, in his case from near Osnabrück. Ellic Howe[43] has shown that Staggemeier first worked on his own, and a book with the ticket 'Bound by L. Staggemeier', which was lot 165 in the Wheeler sale in Paris in 1932, was probably bound in 1793 or very soon thereafter. By 1799, however, he was in partnership with Samuel Welcher, and this probably continued for at least ten years (Fig. 101), although Wheeler also owned a book of 1810 with the ticket: 'Bound by Welcher, 12, Villiers Str', Strand' (lot 166 in his sale). In his *Bibliographical Decameron* of 1817,[44] Dibdin describes as the '*ne plus ultra*' of Staggemeier's 'bibliopegistic skill' a severely neo-classical binding, which Thomas Hope presented on 27 March 1805 to the Royal Institution in London. Dibdin further noted that 'Mr. Hope gave the binder his plan . . . of book-embellishment'. Not unusually, Dibdin was not quite accurate, for, as might be expected from the date of the binding, it has a yellow ticket reading: 'Bound by *L. Staggemeier & Welcher. No. 11. Villiers S*. *York Build*. LONDON'. It is now in the British Library (C. 180. cc. 4).[45]

[40] Howe, *A List of London Bookbinders*, 97.
[41] Nixon, *Twelve Books*, pl. 14; Foot, *The Henry Davis Gift*, ii, no. 195 (with literature).
[42] Nixon, *Five Centuries*, no. 80.
[43] Howe, *A List of London Bookbinders*, 88.
[44] ii. 520.
[45] Nixon, *Five Centuries*, no. 81.

An important shop which has not yet been mentioned was that of Charles Hering. He started his business in 1794 and died in 1815, but the firm was carried on by other members of his family until 1845.[46] Many of Charles Hering's early bindings are in the style of Roger Payne, and after the latter's death Hering worked for the leading bibliophiles of the period. In 1841 the firm produced a nineteenth-century rarity, now in the Royal Library at Windsor, a velvet binding with a delightful miniature. It portrays Mrs Henrietta Digby Sprye, accompanied by her seven children, presenting a 'Memorial', in which she petitioned for an appointment at court, to Queen Victoria, enthroned and supported by her husband in full regimentals (Pl. 10).

Another German binder who arrived in the eighteenth century was John Bohn. He was born in Weinheim in 1757, came to England in 1790, and started up on his own in London in 1795. He bound until 1815 and then took to bookselling. He bound two famous illuminated manuscripts, both in Westminster Abbey Library, the *Liber Regalis* and the Litlyngton Missal (Fig. 102). He died in 1843. His son was the famous mid-nineteenth-century publisher H. G. Bohn.[47]

A binding shop that had been totally forgotten until the 1940s was the private bindery at Buckingham House, which operated from the 1780s until a few years after George III's death in 1820. When in 1828 the new King's Library at the British Museum was completed and the books were transferred to it, the few remaining members of the bindery staff accompanied them and became library assistants. The finishing tools they left behind eventually reached Windsor Castle, where they remained unrecognised until the end of the Second World War, when Sir Owen Morshead realized what they must be. The discovery was most opportune, as a number of books had been damaged by a bomb in Bloomsbury before the evacuation of the King's Library to Oxford had been carried out. After the war, the original tools were borrowed from Windsor by the HMSO bindery at the British Museum and used to finish the repaired spines of books on which they had been originally used nearly one hundred and fifty years before. During the war Ellic Howe had also discovered something about the history of this bindery among the recollections of

[46] J. G. Marks, 'Bookbinding Practices of the Hering Family, 1794–1844', *The British Library Journal*, 6 (1980), 44–60.
[47] Howe, *A List of London Bookbinders*, pp. xxviii, 14. Nixon, *Five Centuries*, no. 82. See also 'Bookbinding', *The Art Journal* (1881), 196.

elderly binders preserved by John Jaffray in the 1840s, and included this in his *The London Bookbinders, 1780–1806* (London, 1950). Before, or possibly still during, the 1780s James Campbell and Walther Shropshire had held the office of Bookbinder to the King; later in the decade the king decided to have the work done in the Palace and apparently obtained men for the purpose from Campbell.[48] Among them was John Polwarth, who was head finisher at the Palace for six years before opening his own bindery in what is now Buckingham Palace Road, opposite the entrance to the Royal mews.[49] The majority of elaborate bindings executed in George III's bindery were in the Roger Payne style, with small tools and what Payne called 'fine studded work', such as occurs on the bindings of the two volumes of George III's forty-two-line Bible.[50] But during the last ten years of George III's reign there was a complete change of style, resulting in bindings in the 'Gothick' taste, with false bands, double boards and recessed panels, and decoration in blind as well as in gold, based on Gothic architectural features (Fig. 103).[51] These bindings are probably among the earliest in the Gothic revival which hit English binding so severely in the middle of the nineteenth century.

[48] M. M. Foot, 'A Binding by James Campbell', *Book Collector*, 34 (1985), 214–15 (with literature).

[49] Howe, *A List of London Bookbinders*, pp. xxxiv–v, 19–20, 77.

[50] H. M. Nixon, *Royal English Bookbindings in the British Museum* (London, 1957), pl. 16A.

[51] Ibid. pl. 16B. Nixon, *Five Centuries*, no. 84.

SIX

====

From 1800 until the Beginning of the Modern Movement

B Y 1810 the influx of German binders had largely ceased and
English or Scottish names—with one or two notable excep-
tions—had become normal once more. Although John Mackinlay was born c.1737 and was already active as a bookbinder in
London by 1778, the more elaborate of his bindings which have been
identified all seem to date from the nineteenth century. His Bow
Street shop burned down with Covent Garden Theatre in 1808, but
he continued in business at Southampton Street, Strand, until his
death in 1821.[1] A binding by him on a copy of Aristotle, *De Poetica*
(Oxford, 1794), in the Grenville collection in the British Library (G.
8032), is not signed but has four tools in common with the set of
Dugdale's works also in the Grenville Library (G. 11795–G. 11811,
G. 11958–G. 11965, G. 11969–G. 11977) (Fig. 104). This set was
certainly bound by Mackinlay, 'the very mention whereof causeth the
tingling of the blood', according to Dibdin.[2]

A binding in the Broxbourne Collection in the Bodleian Library
possibly appears here under false pretences. It is signed 'Macnair',
and this may be the binder Alexander Macnair, who was working in
London from c.1795 until at least 1813, though a Robert Macnair was
at this time binding in Glasgow. It covers James Christie's *Disquisi-
tion upon Etruscan Vases* (London, 1806) and has a note in the
original owner's hand, saying that 'This learned work was written by
James Christie the auctioneer a man of high classical attainments &
what is much better of great moral worth . . . It was bound by a

---

[1] E. Howe, *A List of London Bookbinders 1648–1815* (London, 1950), 64. H. M. Nixon,
Five Centuries of English Bookbinding (London, 1978), no. 83 (cited below as Nixon, *Five
Centuries*).
[2] T. F. Dibdin, *The Bibliographical Decameron* (London, 1817), ii. 519.

Scotchman of the name of Macnair.'³ The next binder to be mentioned is one of the great names of English nineteenth-century binding, Charles Lewis. He was indeed born in London in 1786, though the son of an Hanoverian immigrant, Johann Ludwig; he was apprenticed in London, to another German immigrant, Henry Walther and spent all his life there. After obtaining his freedom in 1807 and working in several West End shops, he set up in Scotland Yard, moved to Denmark Court, the Strand, and thence to Duke Street, St James's, where he became unquestionably London's best-known binder, patronized by all the great collectors of the day. His early bindings are more interesting than his later ones, but the fashion for bindings imitating (not very accurately) earlier styles took hold of most English collectors in the 1820s and, for the next fifty years, binders had few opportunities for displaying originality in design, except for a very occasional fling at an international exhibition. A binding from the Grenville collection originally bound for Sir Mark Masterman Sykes, with his arms on the covers and those of Grenville added to the doublures, shows Lewis at his best (Fig. 105). An over-large copy of a Duodo binding (a type of binding then thought to have been made for Marguerite de Valois) shows the kind of pastiche to which he was reduced by his clients. It covers the presentation copy to Dibdin of volume 1 of the second edition of Brunet's *Manuel du libraire* (Paris, 1814), but it was evidently bound to the recipient's instructions at a considerably later date (Fig. 106). Charles Lewis died in 1836, and the firm was carried on under the ownership of his widow until 1854. From 1836 to 1841 it was managed by Francis Bedford.⁴

Dawson & Lewis is a binding firm about which not much is known, although it was clearly of importance during the 1820s (Fig. 107). The business first appears in the directories in 1817 and continues there until 1832. Henry Dawson carried on for another two

³ H. M. Nixon, *Broxbourne Library: Styles and Designs of Bookbindings from the Twelfth to the Twentieth Century* (London, 1956), no. 99 (cited below as Nixon, *Broxbourne Library*).

⁴ E. Howe, *A List of London Bookbinders*, 58–9. C. Ramsden, *London Bookbinders 1780–1840* (London, 1956), 36, 96. Nixon, *Five Centuries*, no. 85. In 'Our Portrait Gallery, No. 11—W. T. Morrell', *The British Bookmaker*, 4:47 (1891), 11, it is stated that 'Mrs Lewis's business [fell] into the hands of H. Stamper, who controlled it until 1861'. But the London Directories show that Lewis's Duke Street business ceased in 1854 (last mentioned), while H. Stamper does not appear till 1860 and then at 17 Frith Street, where he is last mentioned in 1866.

or three years, but by 1836 the shop had disappeared. A copy of Gell and Gandy's *Pompeiana* (London, 1817–19), in the Broxbourne collection in the Bodleian Library, is probably quite an early effort; most of the gold tooling on this binding is copied from ornaments illustrated in the book.[5]

A firm that started up at much the same time as Dawson & Lewis is that of John Mackenzie, although the presence in London of both a Joseph and a John Mackenzie as binders makes it difficult to be quite certain about dates. John Mackenzie held the office of Bookbinder to both George IV and William IV. He was probably proposed for the Benefit Society in 1811 at the age of 23 by Thomas Armstrong the younger, and was then perhaps working at Staggemeier's. About 1843 he moved to 4 and 5 Crown Street, Westminster, and he had retired or was dead by 1850. The firm was carried on by Charles Mackenzie, presumably his son, but did not exhibit in the 1851 Great Exhibition. Despite the fact that Mackenzie held the royal appointments, he was nothing like so successful a binder as his contemporary Charles Lewis. He had an unpleasant passion for hard-grain morocco, which seldom takes gold tooling well. It is very noticeable in the Grenville collection at the British Library that Mackenzie, who did much uninspired work for Grenville, seems to have played second fiddle to Lewis, to whom Grenville sent his more important books. A binding in the Broxbourne Collection is one of Mackenzie's earlier examples in the cathedral style.[6] Although it covers J. T. Smith, *Antiquities of Westminster*, publication of which was completed in 1809, the binding is not likely to be much earlier than 1820. The Gothic revival style first became popular in England c.1812. An unsigned example from the Broxbourne Collection covers a copy of the second edition of James Bentham's *History and Antiquities of the . . . Cathedral Church of Ely*, published in Norwich in that year.[7] At least one provincial binder was probably decorating bindings in the Gothic style by 1820, if not earlier, namely William Lubbock of Newcastle (Fig. 108). Ramsden records him as being at work between

[5] Nixon, *Broxbourne Library*, no. 100. Ramsden, *London Bookbinders*, 59. M. M. Foot, *The Henry Davis Gift*, ii (London, 1983), no. 212.
[6] Howe, *A List of London Bookbinders*, 63. Nixon, *Broxbourne Library*, no. 101. Ramsden, *London Bookbinders*, 101–2.
[7] *Le Livre anglais: Trésors des collections anglaises. Exposition* (held at the Bibliothèque Nationale) (Paris, 1951), no. 440.

1811 and 1821. Another example of his work, in the Broxbourne Collection, covers volume i of an Edinburgh Bible of 1811, but it also may have been bound a few years later.[8]

Thomas Gosden, bookbinder and bookseller specializing in sporting subjects (particularly angling), is first found in the directories as a bookbinder in 1805. In his article in the Spring 1975 issue of the *Book Collector*,[9] A. N. L. Munby recorded that his stock as a print seller was sold by auction in 1826, but that he continued to bind until his death in 1840. G. D. Hobson[10] says that he died bankrupt, but Munby noted a 'tantalizing reference' by W. Loring Andrews to an auction of Gosden's library which fetched £800 and therefore cannot be the 1826 sale of his stock which made £1169.17s.6d. Gosden as a binder favoured bevelled wooden boards with unbevelled corners decorated with various types of emblems (Fig. 109), a style of binding which Andrews rather harshly called 'a libel upon bibliopegy'.[11]

About 1823, with the introduction of bookbinders' cloth, a big change was finally effected by which almost every book in a bookseller's shop was available in a publisher's binding or casing. The latter process was introduced sometime between 1825 and 1830. A decisive factor in this development was the gradual mechanization of binding processes that took place from the 1820s onwards. When the publisher took over the responsibility for the final appearance of the book, certain types of book also emerged, such as the annuals of the early 1830s, that were available in different styles; some of these qualify as fine bindings. A copy of *The Remembrance. MDCCCXXXI* (London [1831])[12] in maroon morocco embossed by Remnant and Edmonds probably dates from 1831, a few years after the process of embossing bindings with a fly-embossing press had been introduced.

[8] C. Ramsden, *Bookbinders of the United Kingdom (outside London) 1780–1840* (London, 1954), 111. Nixon, *Five Centuries*, no. 87. For bindings in this style see: E. Jamieson, *English Embossed Bindings 1825–1850* (Cambridge, 1972).

[9] A. N. L. Munby, 'Notes on Thomas Gosden', *Book Collector*, 24 (1975), 13–16.

[10] G. D. Hobson, *English Bindings 1490–1940 in the Library of J. R. Abbey* (London, 1940), no. 107. See also ibid. no. 108; Howe, *A List of London Bookbinders*, 41; Ramsden, *London Bookbinders*, 73; Nixon, *Five Centuries*, no. 88; Foot, *The Henry Davis Gift*, ii, nos. 204–5.

[11] W. Loring Andrews, *An English XIX Century Sportsman, Bibliophile and Binder of Angling Books* (New York, 1906), 42.

[12] Nixon, *Broxbourne Library*, no. 105. See also Howe, *A List of London Bookbinders*, 80–1. Ramsden, *London Bookbinders*, 121.

That some caution is required in dating this type of binding is made clear by an advertisement for *'FRIENDSHIP'S OFFERING*: a literary album ... for 1832. *Price* 12s. *in full gilt binding, elegantly embossed'*, that appeared in the 1832 *Comic Offering* in the British Library (PP6615). The advertisement then continues by stating that as there had been demand 'for complete sets of FRIENDSHIP'S OFFERING, from its commencement in 1824, the publishers have the satisfaction to state, that, after great trouble, they have succeeded in completing *a few sets*, which may now be had in 9 vols., price 5*l*.10s. uniformly done up in the improved binding.' The firm that bound *The Remembrance* [1831] in the Broxbourne Collection traces back to Thomas Remnant, who by 1785 was established in Lovell's Court, Paternoster Row, and lasted as Remnant and Edmonds (Fig. 110) until 1873, when it was taken over by Simpson and Renshaw. Other examples in this style were produced by De la Rue & Co., Westley & Clarke, and A. Bain.

Another type of publisher's fine binding that was popular in the 1840s was made of illuminated vellum and was normally blocked in gold and colours. The style seems to have been introduced by J. S. Evans by 1835, and quite a number of bindings of this type from different shops were exhibited in the Great Exhibition of 1851. An example in the British Library (Fig. 111), however, is not blocked but hand tooled and covers the copy of the libretto of M. W. Balfe's *The Bohemian Girl* (London, 1843). This was presented to Prince Albert when, on 1 February 1844, after the ardours of a State opening of Parliament, the Queen and 'her illustrious Consort honoured Drury Lane Theatre with their presence'.[13]

A third type of elaborate publisher's binding was that made in black moulded *papier mâché* on a metal frame, with an elaborate Gothic design in imitation of carved ebony. They were produced in the 1840s, 1850s, and 1860s. The earliest imprint of a book in such a binding is 1843; several were made on the instigation of Longman within a few years around 1850, such as *The Good Shunammite* (London, 1847) (Fig. 112).[14] These books were obviously designed to lie about the Victorian parlour with the other bric-à-brac and not to

[13] Nixon, *Five Centuries*, no. 89.
[14] Another example belonged to H. M. Nixon and was sold at Bloomsbury Book Auctions, 6 Oct. 1983, lot 244. See R. McLean, *Victorian Publishers' Book-Bindings in Paper* (London, 1983), 12–13, 50–9.

be shelved in a bookcase, where they could inflict considerable damage on neighbouring polished calf. From about 1830 most fine binding was carried out for wealthy collectors of valuable books, who liked to have their best books bound in what they—or their binders—considered suitable 'antique' styles. They were very seldom at all accurate copies of old bindings and few books in a nobleman's library received a pastiche of even the right century. An exception was Joseph Walker King Eyton, a collector who is not mentioned in any of the standard books on English book-collecting and who encouraged his binder, James Hayday, to produce bindings in a modern style. A very interesting design on the Maitland Club's 1830 edition of Pitcairne's *Babell*, in the Huntington Library, shows Hayday's complete originality and his prefiguration of the modern preference for producing a design by the use of onlays rather than by gold tooling (Fig. 113). After Eyton's library had been dispersed in 1848, Hayday seems to have been reduced to providing for the popular taste. The example he showed at the Great Exhibition of 1851 'in morocco in a style suitable for ecclesiastical books' does not sound very thrilling, and by 1861 he was bankrupt.[15] He subsequently carried on binding in partnership with William Mansell.

A great many binders were at work in London and in the provinces during the nineteenth century. Only some of these shops are discussed here and may serve to indicate the kind of fine work that was predominant during this period.

Francis Bedford is one of the few English bookbinders to have been included in the *Dictionary of National Biography*. He was Charles Lewis's foreman and after 1836 continued to run the shop for five years for Lewis's widow. He then went into partnership with John Clarke as Clarke and Bedford, and finally set up on his own in 1851. For the next thirty-two years, until his death in 1883, he was the unquestioned leader of his profession in England. Many of his bindings—the great majority in fact—were rather dull imitations of earlier designs, for this was what his customers required. A Roger Payne pastiche, for example, merely lacks all the life of the original article.[16] A Grolieresque binding in the British Library (Fig. 114) on

[15] Ramsden, *London Bookbinders*, 78–9. Nixon, *Five Centuries*, no. 90. Foot, *The Henry Davis Gift*, ii, no. 222.
[16] Hobson, *English Bindings . . . in the Library of J. R. Abbey*, no. 115.

the other hand is not so strict a copy—although all the tools used are close imitations of those used in Paris in the 1540s and 1550s. An obituary of Bedford in the *Athenaeum* (16 June 1883) stated that he had no capacity for design whatever. If so, he must have had someone on his staff in 1866 who could design, for a binding of that date on Higden's *Polychronicon* (Westminster, W. Caxton, 1482), despite the statement on the bill that it was tooled 'after an old Design', owes nothing to any known previous binding.[17] After Bedford's death the firm was acquired by John Shepherd, who certainly had ideas of his own on binding design. A very untypical binding with its modern-looking diagonal stripes, now in the New York Public Library, clearly indicates Shepherd's tastes, but the firm did not long survive its publication in the *British Bookmaker* for October 1892.[18]

The next great London firm in the second half of the nineteenth century is that of Zaehnsdorf, a firm which still survives. Its founder, Joseph Zaehnsdorf, was born in the Austrian Empire in 1814, and worked in Stuttgart, Vienna, Freiburg, Baden-Baden, and Paris before coming to London, where his brother was already established as a jeweller. He worked for a time with Westley, then moved to Mackenzie, and in 1842 decided to set up on his own. Progress was slow for a time, but when, some years before his death in 1886, he handed the business over to his son, Joseph William Zaehnsdorf, it was booming. In 1890 the firm moved into very grand new premises on the corner of Shaftesbury Avenue and Cambridge Circus, occupying all four floors with a staff of over one hundred. J. W. Zaehnsdorf was Bookbinder by appointment to Edward VII as both Prince of Wales and king, and controlled the firm until 1920, when he in turn handed it over to his son, Ernest. The latter then managed it until after the Second World War, when it passed out of the family's possession. For a time it survived only as a few men working by hand in a machine bindery, but although the latter moved away and disappeared, Zaehnsdorf's still survives south of the river.[19] The

[17] Nixon, *Five Centuries*, no. 91.

[18] *The Bookbinder*, 1 (1888), 55–6; *The British Bookmaker*, 6:64 (1892), 77–8, pl. facing p. 116; D. Miner, *The History of Bookbinding 525–1950 AD : An Exhibition Held at the Baltimore Museum of Art* (Baltimore, Md., 1957), no. 567. See also Ramsden, *London Bookbinders*, 36.

[19] *The British Bookmaker*, 4:37 (1890), 8–9; no. 41 (1890), 12–16. Nixon, *Broxbourne Library*, no. 116. Ramsden, *London Bookbinders*, 155. Foot, *The Henry Davis Gift*, ii, nos.

binding illustrated (Fig. 115) is one of the comparatively few non-retrospective bindings the firm managed to produce among a welter of retrospective bindings in the nineteenth century.

From the middle of the nineteenth century until shortly before the outbreak of the Second World War, Zaehnsdorf's main rival was the firm of Rivière & Son. Robert Rivière, though of Huguenot descent, came of a family that had been resident in England for over a century when he was born in 1808; his nephew was Briton Rivière, a well-known RA. Robert's first experience in the trade was as a bookseller in Bath, and c.1840 he established himself in London as a bookbinder in Great Queen Street, being apparently entirely self-taught.[20] He had made his name by 1851 and his firm was chosen as the binders of the special presentation edition of the Great Exhibition catalogue after its close in 1851. Robert Rivière had no sons, but two of his daughter's sons, Percival and Arthur E. Calkin, carried on the firm after his death in 1882. The firm remained in the Calkin family until it ceased business in 1939, when its tools passed to Bayntun's of Bath. Like Bedford's and Zaehnsdorf's, much of their work consisted of pastiches of earlier styles (Fig. 116). A remarkable series, unfortunately often on quite unsuitable books, was bound for Lord Howard de Walden; the books are now in the Brotherton Library at Leeds. Two catalogues that Rivière's issued in 1919 and 1920, the second of bindings which they had exhibited in Leipzig just before the First World War and which had only just been recovered, were in the modern idiom but seemed to owe much to the influence of Alfred de Sauty and Sangorski & Sutcliffe.[21]

While the majority of the best English bindings of the second half of the nineteenth century are signed, a practice (which dates back at least to 1874) grew of fashionable booksellers in the West End of London signing bindings actually bound for, and not by, them.

218-21. H. M. Nixon, *British Bookbindings Presented by Kenneth H. Oldaker to ...
Westminster Abbey* (London, 1982), nos. 50-2. F. Broomhead, *The Zaehnsdorfs
(1842-1947) Craft Bookbinders* (London, 1986).

[20] *The Bookbinder*, 1 (1888), 150-1; *The British Bookmaker*, 4:44 (1891), 5-7 (according to this article Rivière went back to London in 1830). See also C. Ramsden, *Bookbinders of the United Kingdom (outside London) 1780-1840* (London, 1954), 140; Ramsden, *London Bookbinders*, 123; H. M. Nixon, 'Some Huguenot Bookbinders', *Proceedings of the Huguenot Society*, 23:5 (1981), 328-9.

[21] Nixon, *Five Centuries*, no. 98. The 1919 catalogue contains six bindings which had spent the war in Leipzig and were not returned to the binders until June 1920.

Usually they put their name in a manner that suggested that they had bound the book, but did not expressly say so. Such an example covers a pious work, *Daily Light on the Daily Path: The Morning Hour* (London, [? 1862]), presented together with a Bible to the Duchess of Edinburgh shortly after the birth of her eldest son, as a belated wedding present, on 16 November 1874 by the Maidens of the United Kingdom. The name of Houghton and Gunn, 162 New Bond Street, is tooled in gold on the turn-in of the upper cover. They were a firm of stationers, subsequently taken over by Asprey's, and there is no evidence that they ever bound a book.[22]

Although most of the more elaborate bindings of the Victorian age were executed in London, there were several outstanding shops in the provinces. One of these was that of Fazakerley of Liverpool. Thomas Fazakerley, after being apprenticed to John Sutton of the city in 1813, eventually became his foreman, until, in about 1833 he took over the business of Messrs. Robinson. After a year or two in partnership with F. Davis, he started a new business on his own in 1835, which he continued until 1877. He was succeeded by his son, John Fazakerley, who carried on a successful business dealing with every type of binding, but taking particular interest in 'extra' work. Under him the firm continued until the beginning of the First World War.[23] The binding illustrated covers Uzanne's *La Reliure moderne*, published in Paris in 1887 and probably bound soon after that date (Fig. 117).

Another provincial firm with an even longer history, is that of Birdsall of Northampton. It can be traced back to 1757 as a bookselling business under John Lacy—probably also including bookbinding as one of its activities at that time—and was acquired by William Birdsall in 1792. From then until it closed in the 1960s it was run by five generations of the family and fine binding was one of the firm's activities (Fig. 118). Its collection of finishing tools passed in 1968 to the University of Toronto Library and the last owner of the firm, Anthony Birdsall, died in 1972.[24]

On 24 June 1883, when Mrs William Morris said to the largely unemployed barrister T. J. Cobden-Sanderson, 'Then why don't you

[22] Nixon, *Five Centuries*, no. 93.
[23] *The British Bookmaker* 5:51 (1891), 57–8. Ramsden, *Bookbinders of the United Kingdom*, 71.
[24] *The British Bookmaker*, 4:42 (1890), 5–7. E. Evans and R. Grover, *The Birdsall Collection of Bookbinders' Finishing Tools*, (Toronto, 1972).

learn bookbinding?',[25] she inaugurated the 'amateur' movement which has played such an important part in the subsequent history of the craft in England. On 4 July Cobden-Sanderson had his first lesson from Roger de Coverly, who had been apprenticed to Zaehnsdorf, worked ten or eleven years at J. & J. Leighton's, and established a workshop in October 1863.[26] For a fortnight Cobden-Sanderson concentrated on sewing and then on 17 July noted in his *Journal* (i. 96–7) 'In a few minutes I shall go to my bookbinder master to have a lesson. Oh, for the quiet of a handicraft trade, and for the thinking of high thought the while!'. After spending from the beginning of August until the middle of November abroad, he applied himself assiduously to his new craft and by 25 June 1884, having bound fifty-two books (most of them in half morocco), he set up on his own. In July he produced his first gold-tooled binding; when he had completed his second in October, his friends were enthusiastic at the result. After an initial panic that his hands and his arms were not going to stand up to the labour, he settled down, and until 1893 he bound all his books personally, except for the sewing (some of which was done by his wife)[27] and the edge-gilding which, like that of most other London binders of the day, was done by Gwynn.

Cobden-Sanderson had bound and tooled over two hundred volumes when, on 20 March 1893, his thoughts having turned to printing and the establishment of the Doves Press, he opened the Doves Bindery, with Bessie Hooley as sewer, Charles Wilkinson as forwarder, and Charles McLeish as finisher; Cobden-Sanderson himself acted from then onward only as designer and supervisor. The three members of his staff all came—fully trained—from Rivière's, but there was also an apprentice, Douglas Cockerell, who was to play an important part in the furtherance of Cobden-Sanderson's ideas.[28] The professionalism of the Rivière-trained members of the staff predominated and it is noticeable that the Doves Bindery output, while always interesting, aims consistently for the highest professional accuracy and lacks the spontaneity and life of Cobden-Sanderson's own highly

[25] T. J. Cobden-Sanderson, *The Journals of Thomas James Cobden-Sanderson, 1879–1922*, 2 vols. (London, 1926), i. 94.

[26] *The British Bookmaker*, 5:56 (1892), 179–80. According to this article William Morris was a customer of De Coverly.

[27] The earliest mention in the *Journals* (i. 237) of Annie sewing a book is on 17 Jan. 1886.

[28] Hobson, *English Bindings . . . in the Library of J. R. Abbey*, 164–8. M. Tidcombe, *The Bookbindings of T. J. Cobden-Sanderson* (London, 1984).

skilled work. He had one habit which enraged the professional binders of his day. Instead of a heavily rounded spine and strongly concave fore-edge which was *de rigueur* with the trade binders, he favoured a flat spine and had no objection to the fore-edge being slighlty convex. None of his successors, perhaps, has followed his practice quite so closely here. He also seems deliberately to have avoided the brilliantly accurate, directly vertical tooling of the skilled Victorian professional finisher, which produced a rather dull mechanical effect. Cobden-Sanderson's own bindings have a liveliness and personality about them which is lacking in most of McLeish's impeccably finished Doves Press bindings.

The binding illustrated on Pl. 11 is Shelley's *Revolt of Islam* (London, 1818), bound in April 1888, which Cobden-Sanderson gave to his wife, Annie, the daughter of Richard Cobden. Another binding for Annie, bound in November of the same year, also covers a work by Shelley, his *Adonais* (London, 1886). Rather surprisingly Cobden-Sanderson himself, and not his wife, presented it to the British Museum in 1920 (C. 68. i. 1). In an accompanying note he recorded that as he bound it, 'I thought at once of Shelley's ashes' grave and of the grave of Adonais, and whilst overhead I seemed to see the stars, on the earth I seemed to see tall flowers pendulent over them.'[29]

One of the best of Cobden-Sanderson's designs for the Doves Bindery is a binding made in 1903, finished by Charles McLeish, on perhaps the finest of all the Doves Press books, Milton's *Paradise Lost* (1902). Like a number of the very best of Cobden-Sanderson's own bindings, this copy belonged to his wife. It is now in the Broxbourne Collection in the Bodleian library.[30] One of the books bound at the Doves Bindery, but with a binding designed by William Morris, very appropriately covers the Kelmscott Chaucer of 1896. Douglas Cockerell forwarded and finished the first of these bindings, which he took for Morris to see only a few weeks before his death.[31] A number of others were bound by Wilkinson and finished by Cockerell, and Cobden-Sanderson produced a second design, also in pigskin and tooled in gold, of which there is an example in the British Library (Fig. 120).

Cockerell was the apprentice at the Doves Bindery from its opening

[29] Nixon, *Five Centuries*, no. 94.
[30] Nixon, *Broxbourne Library*, no. 108.
[31] Hobson, *English Bindings ... in the Library of J. R. Abbey*, no. 119.

in 1893 until 1897, when he was appointed teacher at the L.C.C. Central School of Arts and Crafts. He set up on his own in 1898 and soon afterwards had George Sutcliffe and Francis Sangorski working for him for two or three years before they established their own firm. The majority of the best of Cockerell's bindings were designed in the period 1898 to 1905, when he became manager of W. H. Smith's bookbinding department, a position he held until the outbreak of the war in 1914. A binding on Milton's *Poems* (Cambridge, 1899) in the Broxbourne Collection at the Bodleian dates from 1904.[32] Another example of Cockerell's work of the same date is now in the British Library (Fig. 119). During the war he was at the Ministry of Munitions and afterwards, until 1924, he was printing adviser to the Imperial War Graves Commission. He then started up the firm of Douglas Cockerell and Son at Letchworth. He died in November 1945, and his son, Sydney Morris Cockerell, continued the firm until his own death in November 1987.

The rise of the amateur school of English bookbinding was accompanied by another phenomenon, the appearance of ladies in the craft. The first and probably the best of these was Sarah T. Prideaux, who began to bind in 1884, only a year after Cobden-Sanderson. She studied with Zaehnsdorf in London and Gruel in Paris, and then during the 1890s did her binding in Rivière's shop, but apparently did everything herself. The result was a very satisfactory professional standard of binding combined with contemporary standards of design. A binding on the *Rubáiyát* of Omar Khayyám (London, 1889) dates from 1901 and is now in the Broxbourne Collection at the Bodleian.[33] A year later she bound J. A. Symonds's *Walt Whitman* (London, 1893) in gold-tooled green morocco (Fig. 121). She seems to have given up binding soon after 1904, although she lived until 1933. She was also a noted writer on the history of bookbinding: her 'Bibliography of Bookbinding', published in *The Library* for 1892, and *An Historical Sketch of Bookbinding* (London, 1893), are both scholarly and intelligent.

One of the more successful of Sarah Prideaux's pupils, of whom

[32] Nixon, *Broxbourne Library*, no. 109. See also Hobson, *English Bindings . . . in the Library of J. R. Abbey*, no. 120. Nixon, *British Bookbindings Presented . . . to Westminster Abbey*, no. 53. *Cockerell Bindings 1894–1980: An Exhibition . . . Fitzwilliam Museum* (Cambridge, 1981).

[33] Nixon, *Five Centuries*, no. 95.

she took several in the 1890s, was Katharine Adams (Mrs Edmund Webb), who studied under her for three months and then spent a month with Douglas Cockerell, before setting up on her own. Her father had been at school and at Oxford with William Morris and her first commission came from Mrs Morris. She was soon binding for famous collectors such as Yates Thompson, Fairfax-Murray, Dyson Perrins, and Sir Sydney Cockerell. Her designs were markedly feminine in character, especially those used on smaller books (Fig. 122). Unlike Miss Prideaux she continued binding until about five years before her death at the age of 90 in 1952.[34] Possibly her last completed bindings, made in 1947, cover two huge volumes of Cervantes, *Don Quixote* (London, 1927–8), in the Henry Davis Gift to the British Library.[35] Another lady binder who started in the 1890s was Elizabeth M. McColl, who also took lessons from Miss Prideaux. She developed an entirely distinctive style working freehand with a small wheel, but relied on her brother, D. S. McColl, successively director of the Tate Gallery and of the Wallace Collection, for her designs. The physical demands of the procedure were evidently great and she never produced very many bindings, finally giving up in 1924. In 1892 she bound a copy of the catalogue of the first exhibition of the Arts and Crafts Exhibition Society (London, 1888) for C. R. Ashbee, who in a note on the flyleaf described the scene on the binding as 'The poor Peacock of the Arts & Crafts with his proud tail exploding in fireworks'.[36]

One of the more interesting binders in London at the turn of the century was Alfred de Sauty, the son of a successful engineer who was himself trained as one. He gave it up in favour of bookbinding and for a time in the 1890s worked as a finisher with Rivière's. Then he worked as designer to the Hampstead Bindery established by Frank Karslake. About 1908 he first visited the United States, and from 1923 was the first manager of the hand-bindery of R. R. Donnelley in Chicago.[37] Most of his best work dates from the first decade of the twentieth century.

Besides the Hampstead Bindery, founded in 1898 with a staff of seven, Frank Karslake was responsible for a more loosely knit organ-

[34] Nixon, *Broxbourne Library*, no. 111. Nixon, *Five Centuries*, no. 99.
[35] Foot, *The Henry Davis Gift*, ii, no. 236.
[36] Nixon, *Broxbourne Library*, no. 107.
[37] Ibid. no. 110. Nixon, *Five Centuries*, no. 97. Nixon, *British Bookbindings Presented . . . to Westminster Abbey*, no. 56.

PL. 10 Mrs Henrietta Digby Sprye, *Memorial*, MS 1841. Purple velvet, embroidered in gold thread and coloured silks, with a painted medallion on the upper cover showing Mrs Sprye delivering her petition to Queen Victoria. The lower cover is embroidered with the royal arms.
Royal Library, Windsor Castle. 390 × 260 × 13 mm.

PL. 12 J. Bunyan, *The Pilgrim's Progress*, London, 1859. Brown goatskin, onlaid in citron, green, red, and fawn, gold tooled. BI.C. 108.b. 17, 200 × 142 × 41 mm.

PL. 11 P. B. Shelley, *The Revolt of Islam*, London, 1818. Red goatskin, gold tooled.

ization called the Guild of Women-Binders, which operated for much the same period, from 1898 to 1904. It included women binders' guilds of distinctly varied levels of craftsmanship, the best represen- tatives being Constance Karslake, Edith and Florence de Rheims, and Miss Edwards, who bound Bunyan's *Pilgrim's Progress* (London, 1859) in brown morocco, onlaid and tooled to a typically art nouveau design (Pl. 12).[38]

The designer of nearly all the bindings discussed so far had been at some time in his or her life a practising bookbinder. At the turn of the century, we find non-binders beginning to design bookbindings. One of the most successful of these was Charles Ricketts (1866–1931), whose extremely simple but beautifully judged linear designs for the Vale Press bindings were produced between 1896 and 1903.[39]

Francis Sangorski and George Sutcliffe, as already mentioned, worked with Douglas Cockerell before setting up in partnership as Sangorski & Sutcliffe in 1901. The firm is still active in Poland Street in London, but its great days from a design point of view were the pre-First World War years. After an initial natural tendency to imitate Cockerell's floral designs, they developed their own elaborate style particularly suited to binding the *Rubáiyát* of Omar Khayyám; their masterpiece, on a copy of this work, was lost on the fatal voyage of the Titanic.[40] One of the bindings they made for T. J. Wise enshrines his faked Reading *Sonnets* of 1847 (Fig. 123). The doublure of the first cover contains a lock of Mrs Browning's hair, and this is followed inside the book by a letter authenticating the lock of hair.[41] After the unbound copy of the *Sonnets*, in a suitable sunk mount, follows another perfectly genuine letter authenticating a lock of Robert Browning's hair inlaid in the doublure of the second cover. The whole was quite clearly contrived to leave a visitor, already dazzled by the genuine treasures of Wise's library, with the idea that he had seen a copy of the Reading *Sonnets* authenticated by either Elizabeth

[38] Nixon, *Five Centuries*, no. 96. See also G. E. Anstruther, *The Bindings of To-morrow* (London, 1902). Nixon, *British Bookbindings Presented . . . to Westminster Abbey*, no. 55.

[39] Hobson, *English Bindings . . . in the Library of J. R. Abbey*, no. 122. G. Barber, 'Rosetti, Ricketts, and some English Publishers' Bindings of the Nineties', *The Library*, 5th ser., 25 (1970), 314–30 (especially 323–30). Foot, *The Henry Davis Gift*, ii, no. 228.

[40] J. H. Stonehouse, *The Story of the Great Omar, bound by F. L. Sangorski, and Its Romantic Loss* (London, 1933). The binding was in fact designed by Sangorski, forwarded by S. Byrnes, and finished by G. Lovatt.

[41] The letter has been transferred to the Department of Manuscripts.

Barrett or Robert Browning, or better still by both.[42] From 1939 onwards Kenneth Hobson was Sangorski & Sutcliffe's main designer for some twenty years.

The London bookselling firm of Sotheran's has never had a bookbinding branch, but it was responsible for a style of binding featuring painted miniatures inlaid in gold-tooled leather. They called these Cosway bindings, possibly named after G. C. Williamson's *Richard Cosway*, remaindered and advertised in 1909 as having been bound in this way. The earliest of these bindings date from 1902, and were invented by J. H. Stonehouse (1864–1937), who finished as managing director of the firm. An example in the British Library has miniatures by Miss C. B. Currie of Margaret Chalmers and Robert Burns on the upper and lower covers of the 1927 facsimile of the Kilmarnock edition of Burns's 1786 *Poems* (Fig. 124). Some of the bindings of this type were by Sangorski & Sutcliffe, but the great majority were made by Rivière's. Miss Currie's name is first mentioned in Sotheran's illustrated Coronation catalogue of 1911. She also specialized in signed fore-edge paintings, of which she executed nearly two hundred, although never, apparently, on the edges of a Cosway binding.[43]

The last arrival on the English bookbinding scene in the days before the First World War was Sybil Pye. She and her sister were friends of Rupert Brooke. She differs from all the other amateur binders of her day in that she took no lessons in bookbinding at all, teaching herself from Douglas Cockerell's *Bookbinding, and the Care of Books* (London, 1901). This is all too clear in the weakness of her forwarding. When she started to bind in 1906 she was at first influenced by the sober linear designs of Charles Ricketts. Then, shortly before the First World War, she fell under the influence of the Cubists and adopted an entirely personal style using inlaid leather, often of the brightest colours (Fig. 125). She died c.1957.[44]

[42] T. J. Wise, *The Ashley Library: A Catalogue of Printed Books, etc.*, i (London, 1922), 98. See also *Le Livre anglais*, no. 454.

[43] Mr. J. Chidley of Sotheran's kindly provided H. M. Nixon with this information, which corrects that given in Nixon, *Five Centuries*, no. 100. A number of Cosway bindings, some featuring several miniatures on each cover, were sold at the third Estelle Doheny Sale, Christie's, New York, 1–2 Feb. 1988.

[44] Hobson, *English Bindings . . . in the Library of J. R. Abbey*, no. 125. *An Exhibition of Modern English and French Bindings from the Collection of Major J. R. Abbey* (held at the Arts Council) (London, 1949), 13. Nixon, *Broxbourne Library*, no. 113.

Between the wars, there was not a great display of new English talent. Rivière, Zaehnsdorf, and Sangorski & Sutcliffe carried on, but with reduced staffs, for the new fashion for original condition among English and American collectors hit them cruelly. The most important new binder was an Englishman working in Wales, George Fisher at the Gregynog Press. Fisher (1879–1970) had been apprenticed as a finisher in the shop of Rivière's. He owned a small-holding in Hampshire and devoted most of his time to farming. In 1925 he was enticed to work for the Gregynog Press where he stayed for 20 years, returning to Hampshire in the summer to help his wife with the hay harvest. Originally the designs for the special bindings were the work of designers, including William MacCance and Blair Hughes-Stanton, who did not themselves bind. The binding on Fortescue's *The Story of a Red-Deer* (Newton, 1935) (Fig. 126) was designed by Fisher himself and is probably one of the most successful of the whole series.[45]

A binder who had much in common with Fisher was William F. Matthews. He was born in 1898 and apprenticed, before and after the First World War, to W. T. Morell, then employing a staff of nearly a hundred. In 1923 he started a long career as a teacher, and many of the leading English binders of today were among his pupils. Three years later he set up as a binder on his own and continued to work, single-handed or with a pupil, until his death in 1977. He was a first-rate craftsman, he cut his own tools—his finishing was particularly brilliant—and he was an excellent teacher. Shortly before his death he bound a copy of John Donne's, *X Sermons* (London, 1923) in gold-tooled black goatskin (Fig. 127).[46]

It is not the intention to discuss here the work of binders who are still alive, but one exception must be made for the father of the modern movement in English binding design, Edgar Mansfield. Born in London in 1907, he was taken to New Zealand at the age of 4 and did not return to England until he was almost 27. He studied bookbinding under William Matthews and Elsa Taterka. His influence began when he started to teach design to bookbinders at the London School of Printing in 1948 and lasted until he returned to New

[45] D. A. Harrop, 'George Fisher and the Gregynog Press', *Book Collector*, 19 (1970), 465–77. D. A. Harrop, *A History of the Gregynog Press* (Pinner, 1980).

[46] D. A. Harrop, 'Craft Binders at Work 1, William F. Matthews', *Book Collector*, 21 (1972), 524–31. Obituary in *The Times*, 14 April 1977.

Zealand in 1964. During that period it was very strong, although his style turned out to be intensely personal and deeply felt, and few of his pupils really mastered it. The example illustrated in Fig. 128 covers the first of a dozen copies of the 1936 Gollancz edition of *Through the Woods* by H. E. Bates, which he bound between 1951 and 1961.[47]

[47] E. Mansfield, *Modern Design in Bookbinding: The Work of Edgar Mansfield* (London, 1966). I. Robinson, 'A Bookbinding Discussed . . . a Tribute to Edgar Mansfield', *The New Bookbinder*, 7 (1987), 19–32.

INDEX

Mansfield, Edgar, binder vii, 113–14, fig. 128
Marguerite de Valois 99
Marine Society 88
Marsden, W. A. 86
Mary I, Queen 30
Mary II, Queen 59, 68, 70, 72, fig. 55
Mary of Modena, Queen Consort 73, 75, fig. 69
Mary of Teck, Queen Consort 50
Mason, Henry 46
Masonic bindings 89–90, 93, fig. 96
Matthewman, John, binder 87, fig. 91
Matthews, William F., binder 113, fig. 127
Mearne bindery 63, 69, 70, 71, 75
Mearne, Charles, binder 62, 63, 67, 70, 71–2, fig. 61
Mearne, Samuel I, binder 45, 58, 60, 62–5, 66–72, 77, 82, 89, figs. 49–54, 56–60
Mearne, Samuel II, binder 63
Medallion Binder 27–8, 32, fig. 21
Medici, Cosimo de, Duke of Florence 79
Meres, Francis 54
Mersea Priory, Essex 7
Merseyside County Museums 23, fig. 16
metal bookcovers 18–22, pl. 3
Michon, Louis-Marie 25
Middleton, Bernard C., binder v n.
miniatures on bindings 96, 112, pl. 10, fig. 124
Minshew, William 62
Mitchell, William S. vi
M., M., initials fig. 71
Montagu, Richard, binder 87, fig. 90
Montague, James, Bishop 55
Moody, Henry, binder 53, 54
Moody, Katharine 54
Moor(e), Edwin, binder 84–5, fig. 87
Moore, John, Bishop 40, 72
Morell, W. T., binder 113
Morgan, Paul 28
Morocco Binder 36, 52 n., pl. 2
Morris, John, embroiderer 55
Morris, William 4, 108, 110
Morris, Mrs. William 106–7, 110
Morshead, Sir Owen 96
Moss, W. E. 34
Munby A. N. L. 101

Naval Binder 73, fig. 62
Needham, Paul 3
Newcastle binder 100–1, fig. 108
New York Public Library 33, 59, 75, 104, fig. 47

Nicholas Bokebynder 13
Norris, Christopher I, binder 86
Norris, Christopher II, binder 86–7
Northampton binders 106, fig. 118
Northumberland, Sir Robert Dudley, Duke of 57
Northumbrian binding 3
Norton, Bonham 57
Norton, John 45, 57
Nott, William, binder 74
Nottingham, Charles Howard, Earl of 27

Oakeshott, Sir Walter 57
Oates, John C. T. 52–3, 54
Octagonal Rose Binder 14, 18
Oldham, John B.:
    Blind Panels 15, 16, 17, 18
    English Blind-Stamped Bindings 10, 12, 13, 16
    study of blind-tooled binding 8, 14
Osborne, Thomas, Duke of Leeds 71
Oxford:
    Bodleian Library: MSS in 5–6, 25, 56–7, figs. 2, 7, 19; printed books in 27, 39, 42, 46, 55, 58, 84, fig. 30; see also Broxbourne Collection
    city: binders in 13–14, 78–9, 82, 84, pl. 8, figs. 77, 79; blind-tooled bindings from 6, 7, 8, 10, 12, 13, 14, fig. 10; velvet bindings from 56
    Colleges: Balliol 41, fig. 33; Brasenose 52, 66, 67; Christ Church 44, figs. 31, 34; Corpus Christi 14–16; Jesus 47; Keble 51, 69, fig. 40; Lincoln 67; Magdalen 13, 79; Merton 30; New College 27; Oriel 13; Queen's 47; St Edmund Hall 79; St Hugh's 47; St John's 28, 46, 54, 58, fig. 43; Trinity 29, 30, 52; University 38, fig. 29; Worcester 84
    University Press 79, 80
Oxford, Earls of, see Harley

Padeloup, A. M., binder 95
panel stamps 8, 14–18, figs. 11–13
Pantzer, Katherine F. 35 n.
papier mâché bindings 102–3, fig. 112
Paris bindings 5, 36, 39, 104
Parker, Matthew, Archbishop 36, 38, 39–40, fig. 31
Parron, William 7
Payne, Roger, binder 92, 96, 97, 103, fig. 97
Payne, Thomas, binder 92
Payne, Thomas, bookseller 92

1. Hegesippus, *Historia de excidio Judaeorum*, MS *c*.1150. Brown calf, blind tooled. Winchester Cathedral Library, MS XVII. 290 × 210 × 52 mm.

2. Petrus Lombardus, *Sententiarum libri quatuor*, MS late 12th c. Brown hide, blind tooled.
Bodleian Library, MS Rawl. C. 163 (lower cover). 345 × 245 × 95 mm.

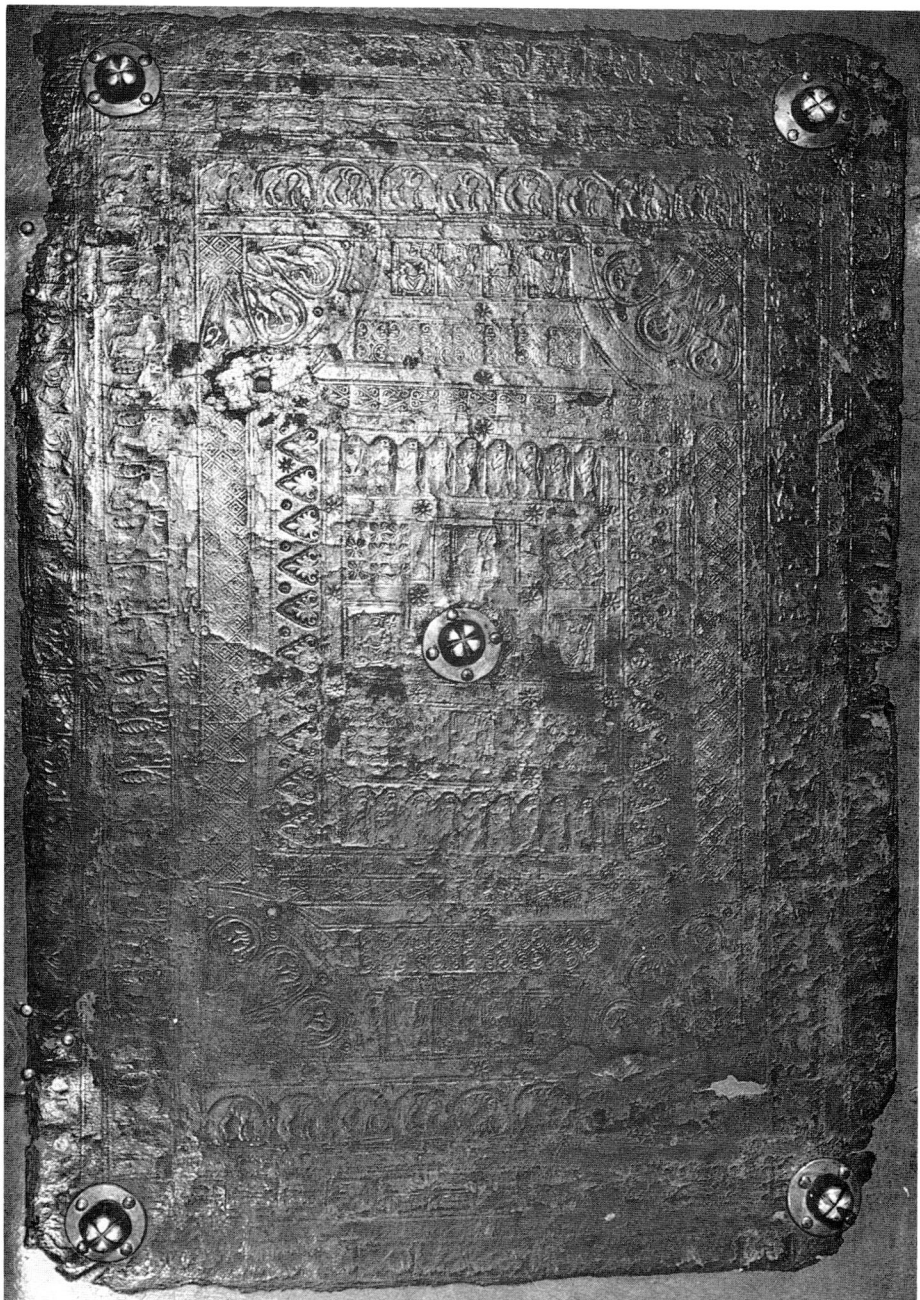

3. *Biblia*, MS *c.* 1170–80 (vol. 4). Rebound with original covers onlaid: brown hide, blind tooled.
Durham Cathedral Library, MS A. II. 1 (lower cover). 494 × 342 × 70 mm.

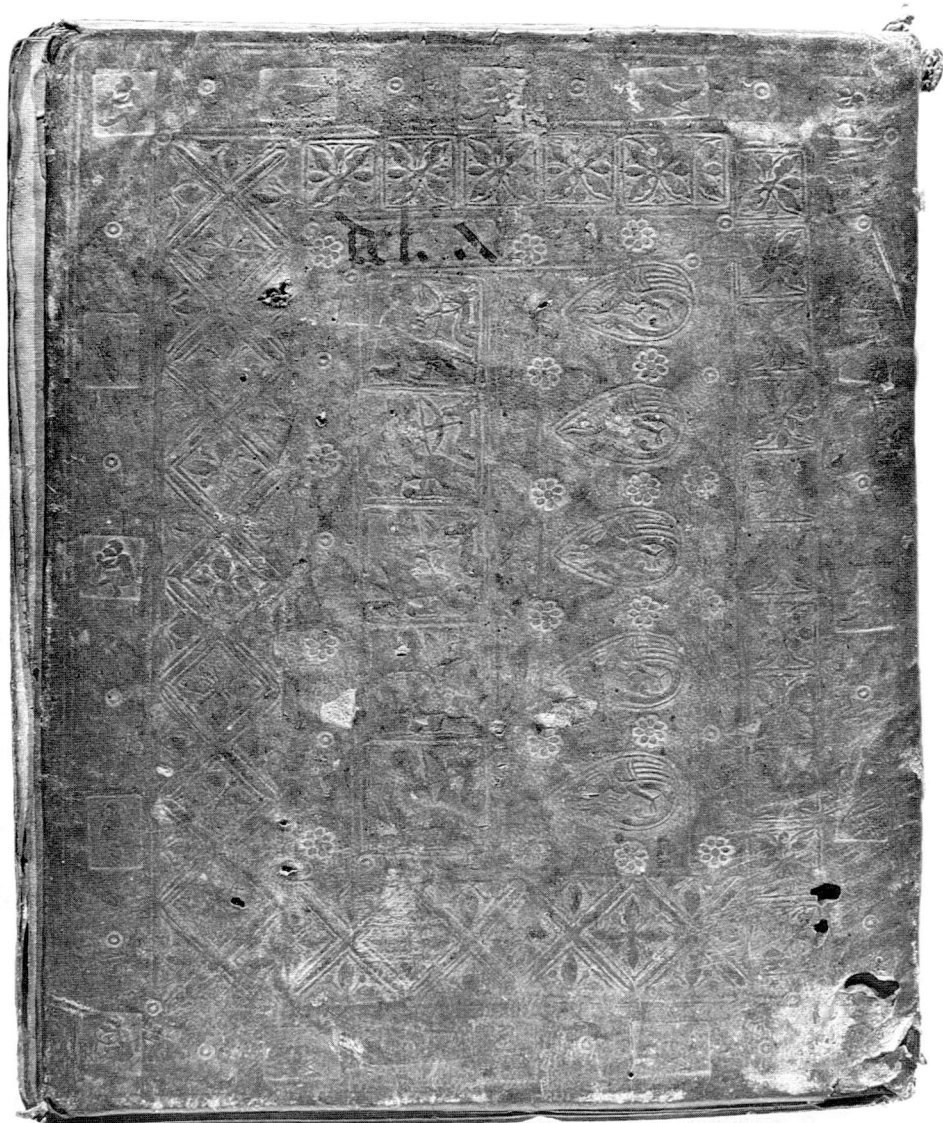

4. *Medica*, MS on vellum, 13th c. Whittawed leather, blind tooled.
St John's College, Cambridge, MS 132 (lower cover). 212 × 169 × 40 mm.

5 (left). Terence, *Vulgaria*, [London, *c*.1483]. Rebound with original covers onlaid: brown hide, blind tooled.
BL IA. 55454. 182 × 128 × 37 mm.

6 (right). The abridgement of the Book of Assizes, MS *c*.1456–65. Brown calf, blind tooled.
BL Add. MS 65194. 205 × 145 × 37 mm.

7. Gulielmus Alvernus, *Works* [Latin], MS first half 15th c. Rebound with the original blind-tooled brown calf covers onlaid.
Bodleian Library, MS Bodley 281. 417 × 290 × 80 mm.

8 (left). Anthology of Middle English verse and prose, MS 2nd half 15th c.–3rd quarter 16th c. Brown calf, blind tooled.
BL Add. MS 60577. 220 × 152 × 62 mm.

9 (right). St Augustine, *Confessiones*, Cologne, 1482. Brown calf, blind tooled.
BL IA. 3941 (lower cover). 216 × 140 × 43 mm.

10. J. Nider, *Consolatorium timoratae conscientiae*, Paris, 1478 [and two other works, n.d. and 1480]. Brown calf, blind tooled.
BL IA. 39102 (IA. 39118; IA. 39175). 220 × 140 × 43 mm.

11 (left). *Horae B.M.V. ad usum Sarum*, London, Wynkyn de Worde, [1494]. Brown calf, blind tooled.
Lambeth Palace Library, 1494.6 (lower cover). 215 × 140 × 55 mm.

12 (right). Desiderius Erasmus, *Precationes*, MS *c.*1550. Brown calf, blind tooled with two impressions of a panel showing the royal arms.
Westminster Abbey, CD 38. 222 × 154 × 15 mm.

13 (left). Robert Whittinton, *De octo partibus orationis*, [Southwark, (?) 1531] [and other grammatical tracts, (?) 1522–34]. Brown calf, blind tooled with the arms of Henry VIII and Anne Boleyn. BL C. 40. e. 2. 198 × 140 × 47 mm.

14 (right). Thomas More, *Utopia*, Basel, 1518. Brown calf, blind tooled. BL C. 67 d. 8. 220 × 159 × 40 mm.

15 (left). Sherborne Chartulary, MS *c.*1146. Wooden boards, hollowed out with remnant of Limoges enamel (detail, shown right way up).
BL Add. MS 46487. Enamel: 52 × 57 mm.

16 (right). Carved whalebone book cover.
Merseyside County Museums, Liverpool, M8016. 203 × 98 mm.

17. *Psalterium*, MS early 14th c. Embroidered canvas inlaid in 18th-century calf. BL Sloane MS 2400 (lower cover). 239 × 165 × 44 mm.

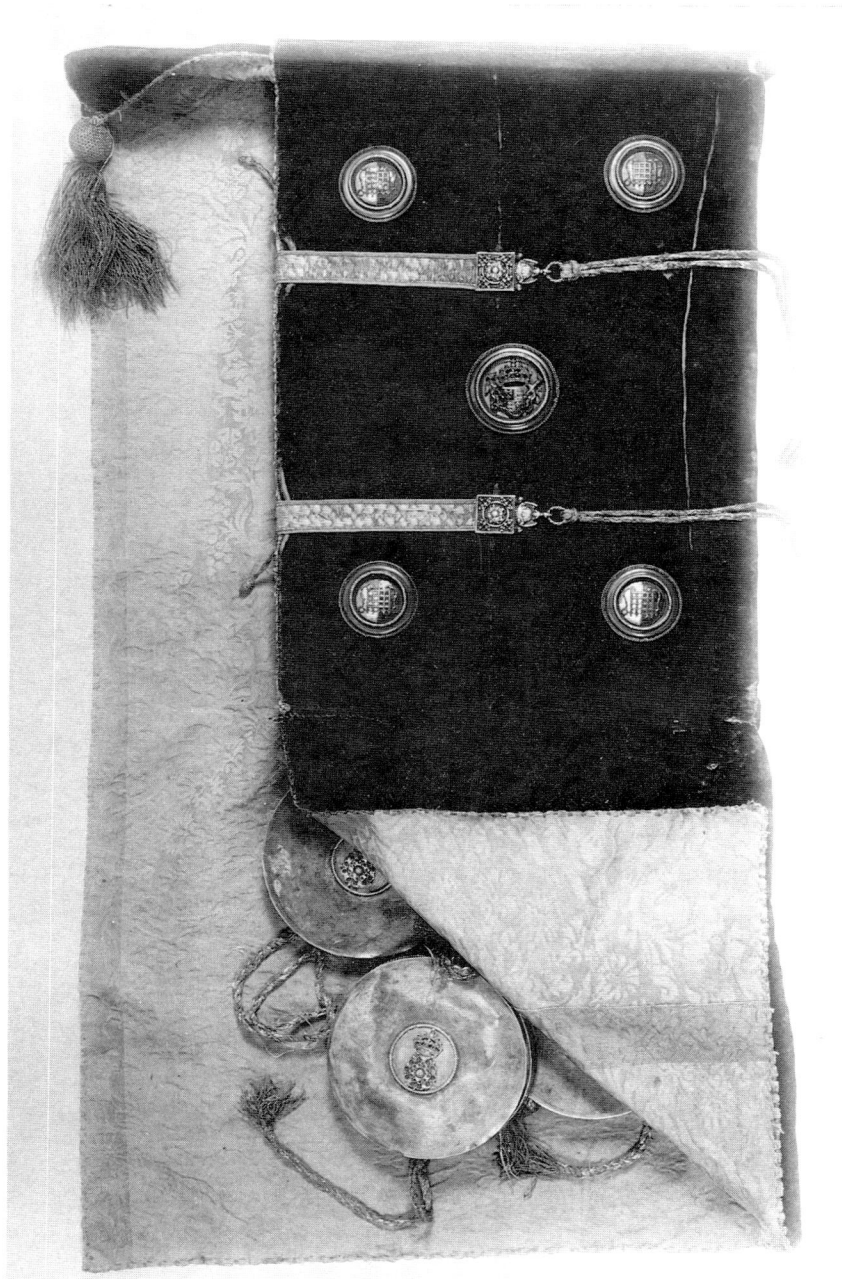

18. *Indenture made between . . . King Henry VII . . . and John Islippe Abbot of . . . Westminster*, MS 16 July, 1504. Red velvet, silver-gilt and enamelled medallions and clasps. BL MS Harl. 1498 (lower cover). 385 × 280 × 50 mm.

19. R. Whittinton, *Epigrams*, MS *c*.1519. Brown calf, gold tooled.
Bodleian Library, MS Bodley 523. 240 × 160 × 13 mm.

20. *Determinatio Negativa Collegij Doctorum Regentium alme Universitatis Aurelianensis, super binas Quaestiones* [and other tracts], MS 1529–30. Brown calf, gold tooled. BL MS Harl. 1338. 301 × 205 × 24 mm.

21. Flavius Josephus, *Opera*, Basel, 1544. Rebound with original covers onlaid: brown calf, gold tooled, with the arms and initials of Edward VI.
BL G. 7851. 345 × 230 × 62 mm.

22. [Sir Richard Morison], Plan, addressed to Henry VIII, for a codification in Latin of the common law. MS *c.*1540–6. Rebound with original covers onlaid: mottled brown goatskin, gold tooled with the arms and initials of Henry VIII [outer fleurons have been re-tooled].
BL MS Royal 18. A. L. (lower cover). 225 × 157 × 10 mm.

23. Xenophon, *La Cyropedie*, Paris, 1547. Brown calf, gold tooled and decorated with black paint; with the arms and initials of Edward VI.
BL C. 48. f.3 (lower cover). 224 × 167 × 22 mm.

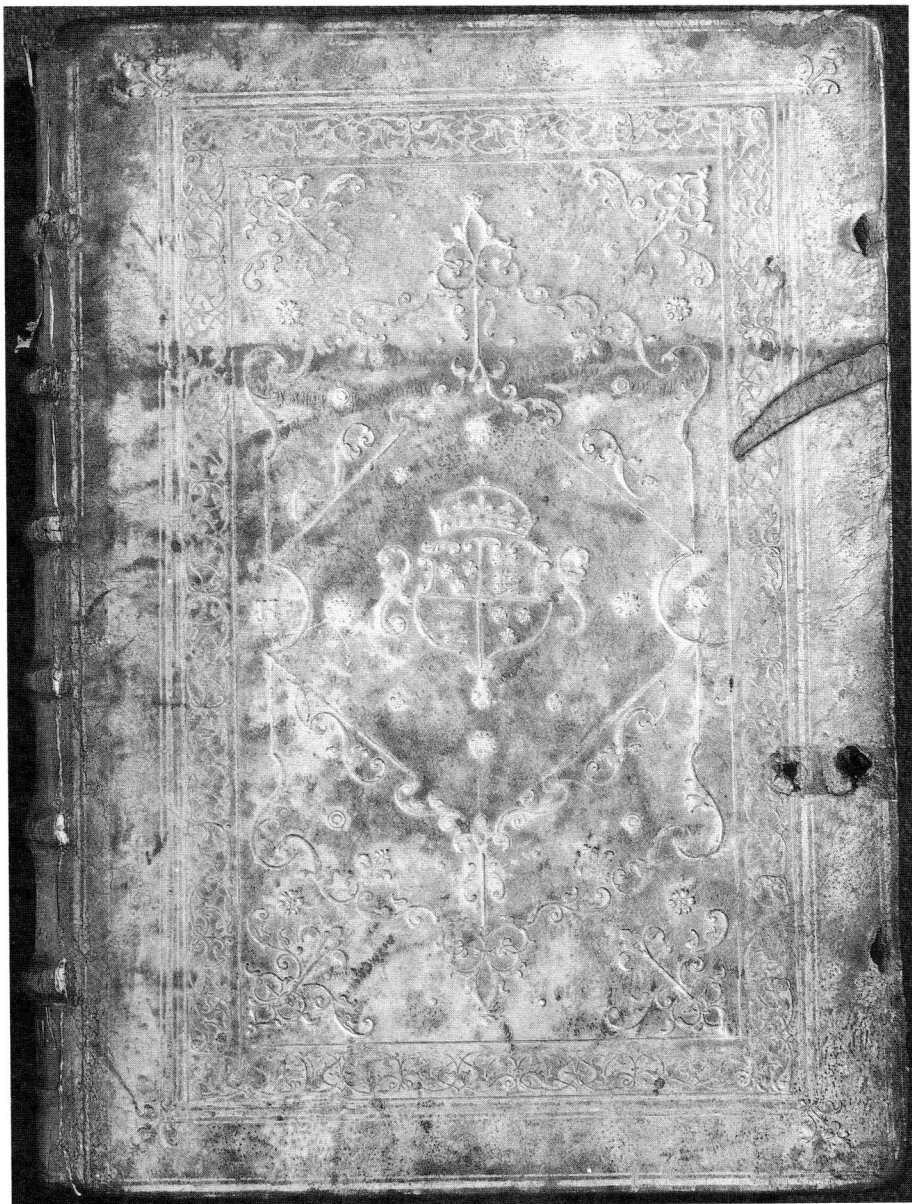

24. Prosper of Aquitaine, *Opera*, Lyons, 1539. White leather, gold tooled, with the arms and initials of Henry VIII.
Chetham's Library, Manchester, E. 3. 37. 330 × 230 × 52 mm.

25. *Novum Testamentum* (ed. W. Deleen), London, 1540. Brown calf, gold tooled, with the arms and initials of Henry VIII.
Lambeth Palace Library, E. 1945/1540 (lower cover). 252 × 185 × 50 mm.

26 (left). Trogus Pompeius, *Justini ex Trogi Pompeii historia libri 44*, Cologne, 1556. Brown calf, gold tooled, with the badge and initials of Robert Dudley, Earl of Leicester. BL C. 64. b. 2 (lower cover). 157 × 100 × 27 mm.

27 (right). Plato, *Convivium, aut de amore, colloquium morale*, Paris, 1543. Brown calf, gold tooled, traces of black paint, with the badge of Robert Dudley, Earl of Leicester. BL C. 19. c. 23 (lower cover). 228 × 151 × 13 mm.

28. Clemens Alexandrinus, *Τα Ευρισκομενα άπαντα*, Florence, 1550. Brown calf, gold tooled, remnants of dark paint, with the badge and initials of Robert Dudley, Earl of Leicester.
BL G. 11780. 342 × 225 × 50 mm.

29. W. Forrest, *History of Joseph: a poem*, MS (first part), *c*.1569. Brown calf, gold tooled.
University College, Oxford, MS 88. 330 × 235 × 50 mm.

30 (left). [Aelfric, *Grammaticus*], *A Testimonie of Antiquitie*, London, [(?) 1566]. Brown calf, tooled in gold and silver, with the badge of Robert Dudley, Earl of Leicester. Bodleian Library, Gough Sax. Lit. 127 (lower cover). 147 × 88 × 16 mm.

31 (right). [G. Acworth], *De visibili Rom'anarchia contra Nich. Sanderi monarchiam*, London, 1573. Brown calf, gold tooled, with the arms and initials of Archbishop Matthew Parker. Christ Church, Oxford, e. 4. 19 (lower cover). 221 × 153 × 20 mm.

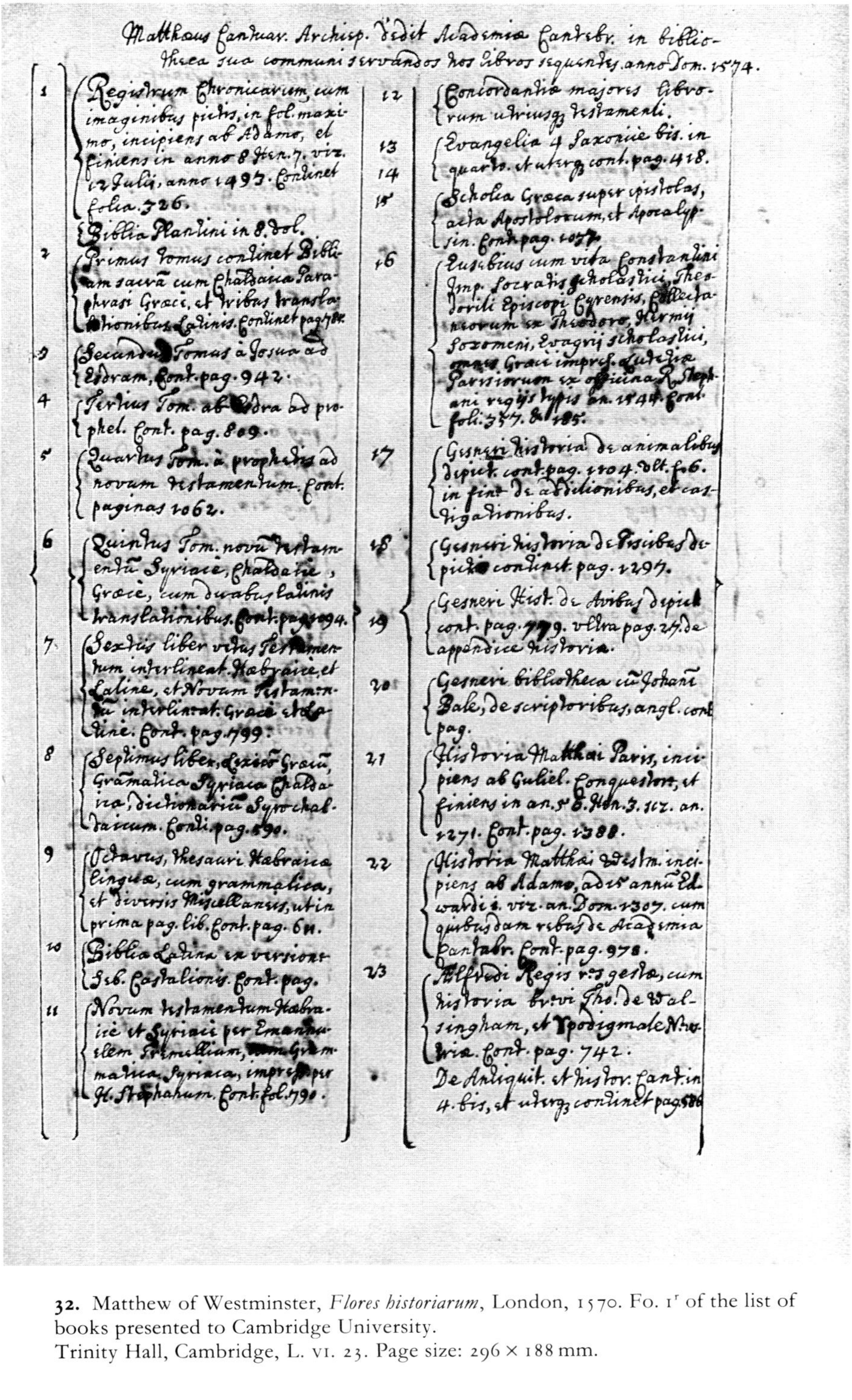

Matthæus Cantuar. Archiep. dedit Academiæ Cantebr. in bibliothecâ sua communi servandos hos libros sequentes. anno Dom. 1574.

1 Registrum Chronicarum, cum imaginibus pictis, in fol. maximo, incipiens ab Adamo, et finiens in anno 8 Hen. 7. viz. 12 Julii, anno 1493. Continet folia 326.

Biblia Plantini in 8. vol.

2 Primus tomus continet Bibliam sacrã cum Chaldaica Paraphrasi Græci. et tribus translationibus Latinis. Continet pag. 788.

3 Secundus Tomus à Josua ad Esdram, Cont. pag. 942.

4 Tertius Tom. ab Esdra ad prophet. Cont. pag. 809.

5 Quartus Tom. à prophetis ad novum testamentum. Cont. paginas 1062.

6 Quintus Tom. novũ testamentũ Syriacè, Chaldaicè, Græcè, cum duabus Latinis translationibus. Cont. pag. 994.

7 Sextus liber vetus testamentum interlineat. Hebraicè, et Latinè, et Novum testamentũ interlineat. Græcè et Latinè. Cont. pag. 799.

8 Septimus liber, Lexicon Græcũ, Gramatica Syriaca Chaldaica, dictionariũ Syrochaldaicum. Conti. pag. 590.

9 Octavus, thesauri Hebraicæ linguæ, cum grammatica, et diversis Miscellaneis, ut in prima pag. lib. Cont. pag. 611.

10 Biblia Latina ex versione Seb. Castalionis. Cont. pag.

11 Novum testamentum Hebraicè et Syriacè per Emmanuelem Tremellium, cum Grammatica Syriaca, impress. per H. Stephanum. Cont. fol. 790.

12 Concordantiæ majores librorum utriusq; testamenti.

13 Evangelia 4 Saxonice bis. in
14 quarto. et uterq; cont. pag. 418.

15 Scholia Græca super epistolas, acta Apostolorum, et Apocalypsin. Cont. pag. 1037.

16 Eusebius cum vita Constantini Imp. Socratis scholastici, Theodoriti Episcopi Cyrensis, Collectaneorum ex Theodoro, Hermij Sozomeni, Evagrij scholastici, omnia Græce impress. Lutetiæ Parisiorum ex officina Roberti Stephani regijs typis an. 1544. Cont. foli. 357. & 185.

17 Gesneri historia de animalibus depict. cont. pag. 1104. ult. fo. 6. in fine de additionibus, et castigationibus.

18 Gesneri historia de Piscibus depict. continet pag. 1297.

19 Gesneri Hist. de Avibus depict. cont. pag. 779. ultra pag. 27. de appendice historia.

20 Gesneri bibliotheca cũ Johañi Bale, de scriptoribus, angl. cont. pag.

21 Historia Matthæi Paris, incipiens ab Guliel. Conquestore, et finiens in an. 5° 8. Hen. 3. scz. an. 1271. Cont. pag. 1388.

22 Historia Matthæi Westm. incipiens ab Adamo, ad 15 annũ Edwardi 1. viz. an. Dom. 1307. cum quibusdam rebus de Academia Cantabr. Cont. pag. 978.

23 Alfredi Regis res gestæ, cum historia brevi Tho. de Walsingham, et Ypodigmate Neustriæ. Cont. pag. 742.

De Antiquit. et histor. Cant. in 4. bis, et uterq; continet pag. 586

32. Matthew of Westminster, *Flores historiarum*, London, 1570. Fo. 1r of the list of books presented to Cambridge University.
Trinity Hall, Cambridge, L. VI. 23. Page size: 296 × 188 mm.

33. L. Humphrey, *Ioannis Iuelli Angli, . . . vita et mors*, London, 1573. Brown calf, gold tooled, with the arms of William Cecil, Lord Burghley.
Balliol College, Oxford, Arch. A. 11. 2 (lower cover). 202 × 148 × 33 mm.

34. *Y Beibl.* London, 1588. Brown calf, gold tooled, with the arms and initials of Elizabeth I.
Christ Church, Oxford, MS Room 409 (lower cover). 337 × 225 × 67 mm.

35. James I, *Opera*, London, 1619. Red goatskin, gold tooled, with the arms of James I.
University Library, Durham, SR. 5. F. 2 (R. LXX. B. 5). 336 × 219 × 42 mm.

36. J. Ferrettus, *De re et disciplina militari*, Venice, 1575. Brown calf, gold tooled, with the arms of Henry, Prince of Wales.
BL C. 18. b. 13. 300 × 204 × 55 mm.

37. B. Hertfelder, *Basilica SS. Udalrici et Afrae Augustae Vindelicorum Historice descripta*,
Augsburg, 1627. Red goatskin, gold tooled, with the arms of Charles I.
University Library, Durham, + GACA. C27H (Cosin, R. III.15). 299 × 194 × 35 mm.

38. C. Saxton, *Atlas* (set of 35 maps of England, Scotland, and Wales, dated 1574–79). Black goatskin, gold tooled, with the crest of Sir Thomas Egerton. Huntington Library, 110105. 430 × 300 × 24 mm.

39 (left). *Initia IV. Evangelia* [and] *Nomina benefactorum Dunelmensis ecclesiae*, MS *c*.840. Red goatskin, gold tooled, with the arms of Sir Robert Bruce Cotton. BL MS Cotton Dom. A. VII. 213 × 147 × 40 mm.

40 (right). *La liturgie angloise*, London, 1616. Brown calf, gold tooled. Keble College, Oxford. 214 × 155 × 40 mm.

41a (left). F. Toletus, *Cardinal, Compendium*, Sammieli, 1613. White vellum, gold tooled.
BL C. 20. f. 20. 95 × 50 × 22 mm.

41b (middle). G. Bellendenus, *Ciceroni princeps, rationes et consilia*, Paris, 1608. White vellum, gold tooled.
BL C. 20. f. 58. 116 × 62 × 14 mm.

41c (right). Quintus Curtius Rufus, *De rebus gestis Alexandri magni*, Antwerp, 1613. White vellum, gold tooled.
BL C. 20. f. 34. 107 × 60 × 17 mm.

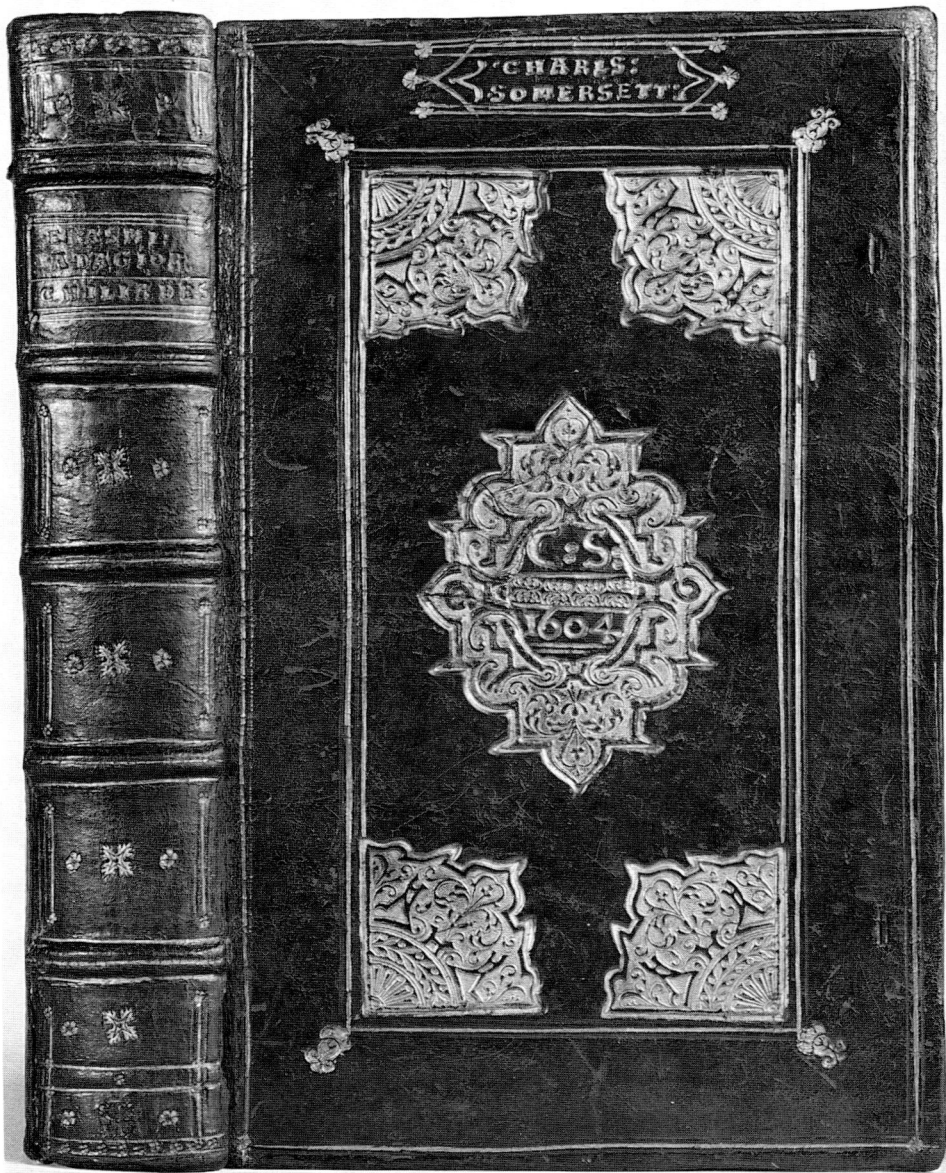

42. D. Erasmus, *Adagiorum Chiliades iuxta locos Communes digestae*, [Frankfurt], 1599. Black calf, gold tooled, with the name and initials of Sir Charles Somerset and the date 1604.

BL C. 128. k. 3. 367 × 225 × 80 mm.

43. *The Whole Law of God as it is Delivered in the Five Books of Moyses*, Little Gidding, 1640. Purple velvet, gold tooled.
St John's College, Oxford, MS 262. 500 × 370 × 42 mm.

44. *The Book of Common Prayer ... with the Psalter*, [Cambridge], 1660. Blue velvet, embroidered with gold and silver thread and coloured silks, with the arms and initials of Charles II.
Royal Library, Windsor Castle. 468 × 305 × 30 mm.

45. M. Raderus, *Bavaria Pia*, Antwerp, 1628. Olive-brown goatskin, gold tooled, with the arms of Charles I.
BL C. 24. c. 4. 348 × 230 × 28 mm.

46. Bede, *Historiae ecclesiasticae gentis anglorum libri V*, Cambridge, 1643. Brown goatskin, gold tooled.
University Library, Cambridge, Rel. a. 64. 2. 350 × 230 × 45 mm.

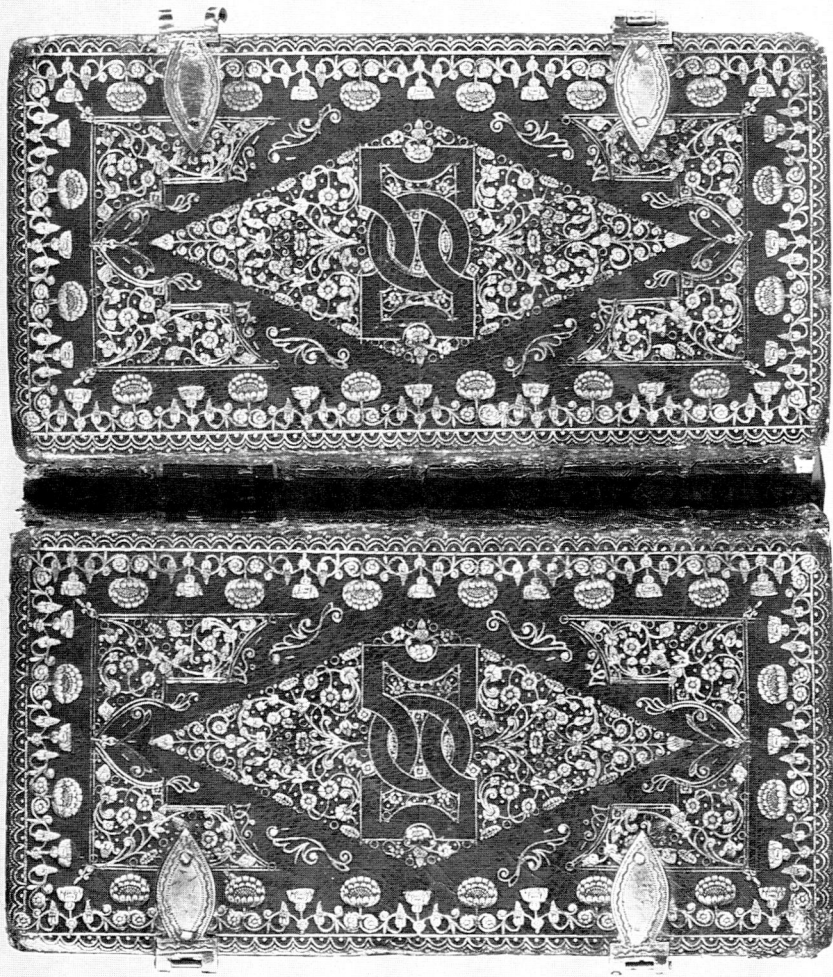

47. *Holy Bible*, London, 1651 [and] *A Brief Concordance*, London, 1652. Black goatskin, gold tooled. New York Public Library, Spencer Coll., Engl. 1651. 143 × 75 × 35 mm.

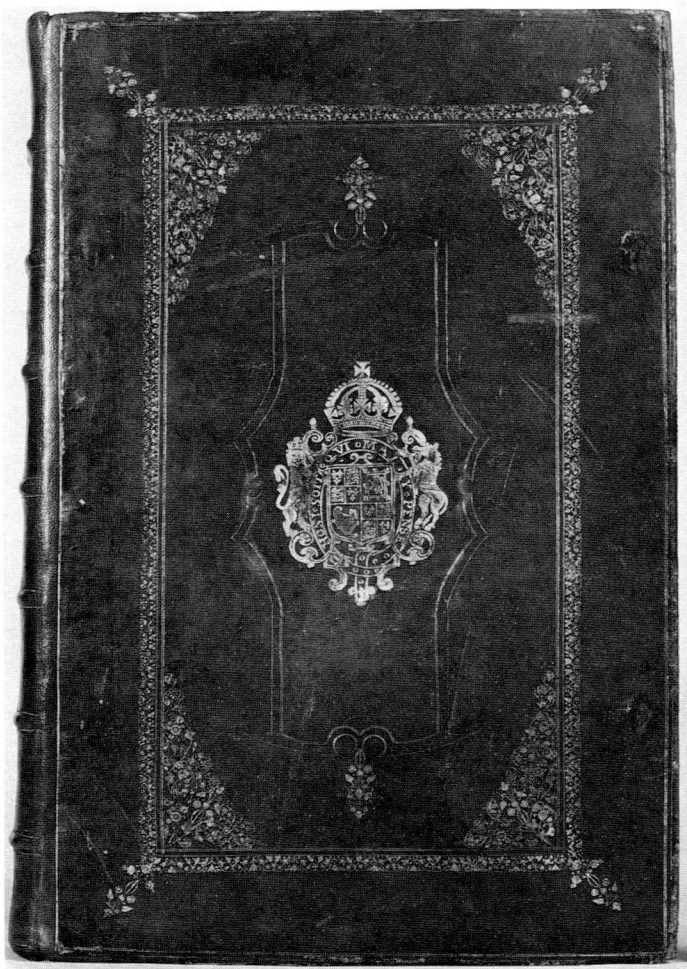

48. J. Foxe, *The Third Volume of the Ecclesiastical Historie*, London, 1641. Red goatskin, gold tooled, with the arms of Charles II.
BL 201. h. 7. 422 × 275 × 72 mm.

48a. J. Foxe, *The Third Volume of the Ecclesiastical Historie*, London, 1641. Fore-edge painted underneath the gold with a portrait of Charles II, signed FLETCHER COMPINXIT.
BL 201. h. 7. Closed edge: 414 × 60 mm.

49. J. C. Bulenger, *Historiarum sui temporis libri XIII*, Lyons, 1619. Red goatskin, gold tooled, with the arms of Charles II.
BL C. 74. i. 5. 380 × 240 × 33 mm.

50. M. Z. Boxhornius, *Historia obsidionis Bredae*, Leiden, 1640. Red goatskin, gold tooled, with the cypher of Charles II on the spine.
BL C. 79. f. 15. 328 × 208 × 22 mm.

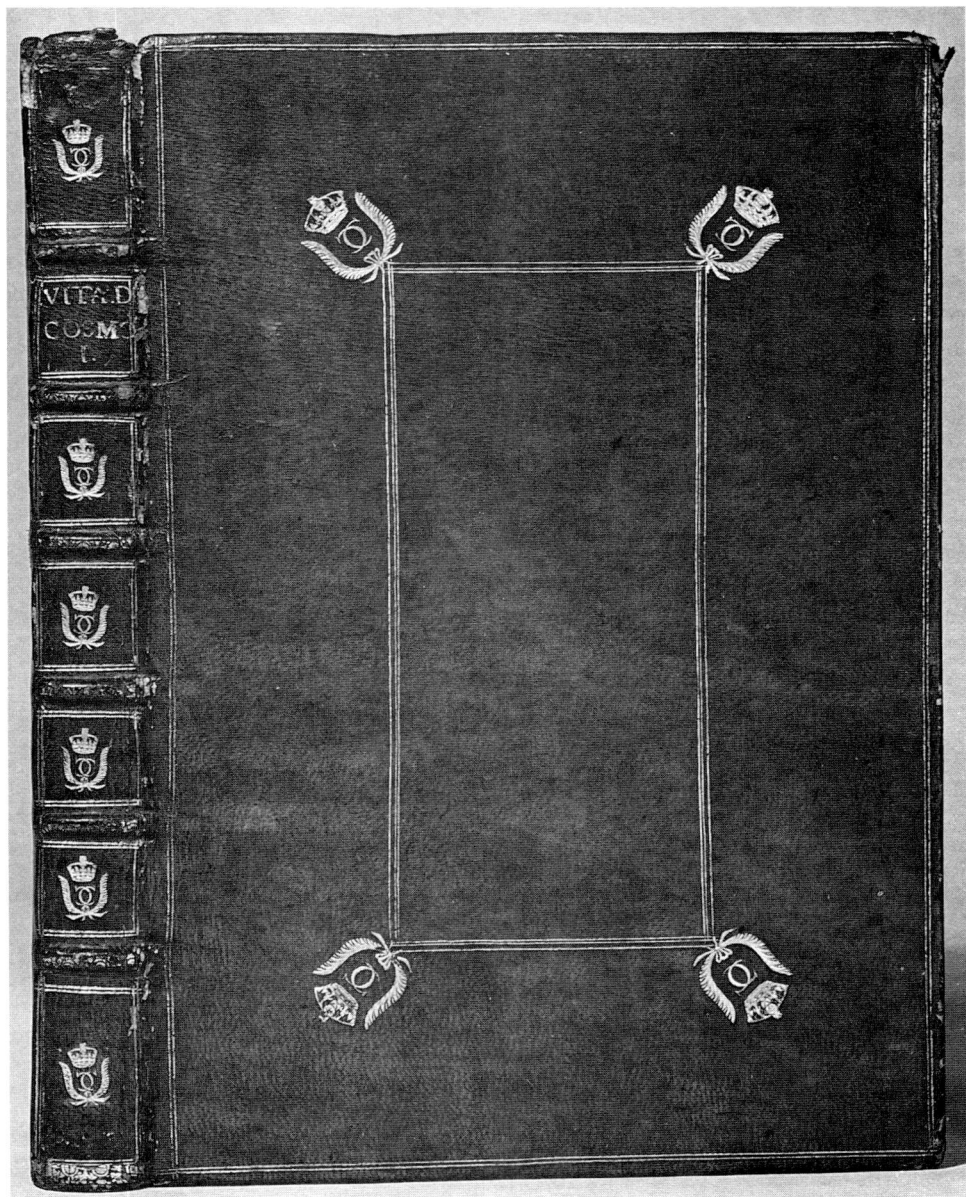

51. B. Baldini, *Vita di Cosimo Medici*, Florence, 1578. Red goatskin, gold tooled, with the cypher of Charles II.
BL C. 83. e. 6. 292 × 200 × 33 mm.

52. Katherine Philips, *Poems*, London, 1667. Black goatskin, gold tooled, with the cypher of Charles II. The arms of George III have been added later.
BL 83. l. 3. 330 × 207 × 27 mm.

53. *The Book of Common Prayer*, London, 1662. Red goatskin, gold tooled and decorated with black paint; with the cypher of Charles II.
University Library, Durham, SR. 5. F. 14 (Cosin, B. I. 12). 382 × 251 × 56 mm.

54. *Book of Common Prayer* [and] *Psalms of David*, London, 1669. Fore-edge painting underneath the gold, showing the crowned cypher of Charles II containing a Tudor rose.
BL 7. f. 13. Closed edge: 360 × 40 mm.

55. *Holy Bible*, Oxford, 1680. Red goatskin, gold tooled and decorated with black paint; with the cypher of William and Mary.
Huntington Library, 149044. 502 × 320 × 100 mm.

56. *Book of Common Prayer* [and] *Psalms of David*, London, 1662. Brown marbled calf, gold tooled, with the cypher of Charles II.
BL C. 83. e. 13. 302 × 190 × 28 mm.

57. *Book of Common Prayer*, London, n.d. [and] *Psalter*, London, 1669. Black goatskin, gold tooled.
Huntington Library, 325000. 375 × 245 × 51 mm.

58. *Book of Common Prayer*, London, 1662. Red goatskin, gold tooled, with the cypher and arms of Charles II and FOR THE CHANCERY.
Public Record Office, C. 95. 2. 415 × 275 × 60 mm.

59. 'Liber Carolinus', Register for the Order of the Garter, MS on vellum, 1638–88. Red goatskin, gold tooled, with the cypher of Charles II. Chapter Archives, St George's Chapel, Windsor Castle. 410 × 307 × 55 mm.

60. *The Statutes and Ordinances of the ... Garter*, MS 1682. Black goatskin, gold and blind tooled, with the cypher of Charles II.
Pierpont Morgan Library, MA 1760. 252 × 202 × 11 mm.

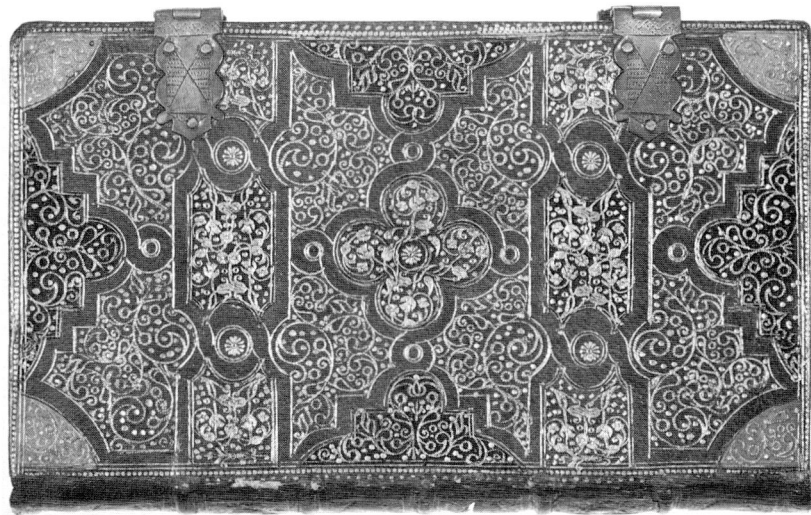

61 (left). *La liturgie*, London, 1678. Red goatskin, onlaid in black and pale brown, gold tooled. Pierpont Morgan Library. 160 × 95 × 25 mm.

62 (right). William Cockburn, *Oeconomia corporis animalis*, London, 1695. Black goatskin, gold tooled BL C. 183. c. 6 (lower cover). 193 × 120 × 22 mm.

63. T. Greenhill, *Nekrokedeia: or the art of imbalming*, London, 1705. Red goatskin, gold tooled.
BL C. 109. f. 12. 265 × 205 × 40 mm.

64. *The Full Anthems*, MS *c*.1665. Red goatskin, onlaid in beige and black, gold tooled. BL MS Harl. 6346. 368 × 239 × 50 mm.

65. D. Loggan, *Oxonia illustrata*, London, 1675. Red goatskin, gold tooled, with the arms of Charles II.
BL 128. h. 10. 443 × 307 × 28 mm.

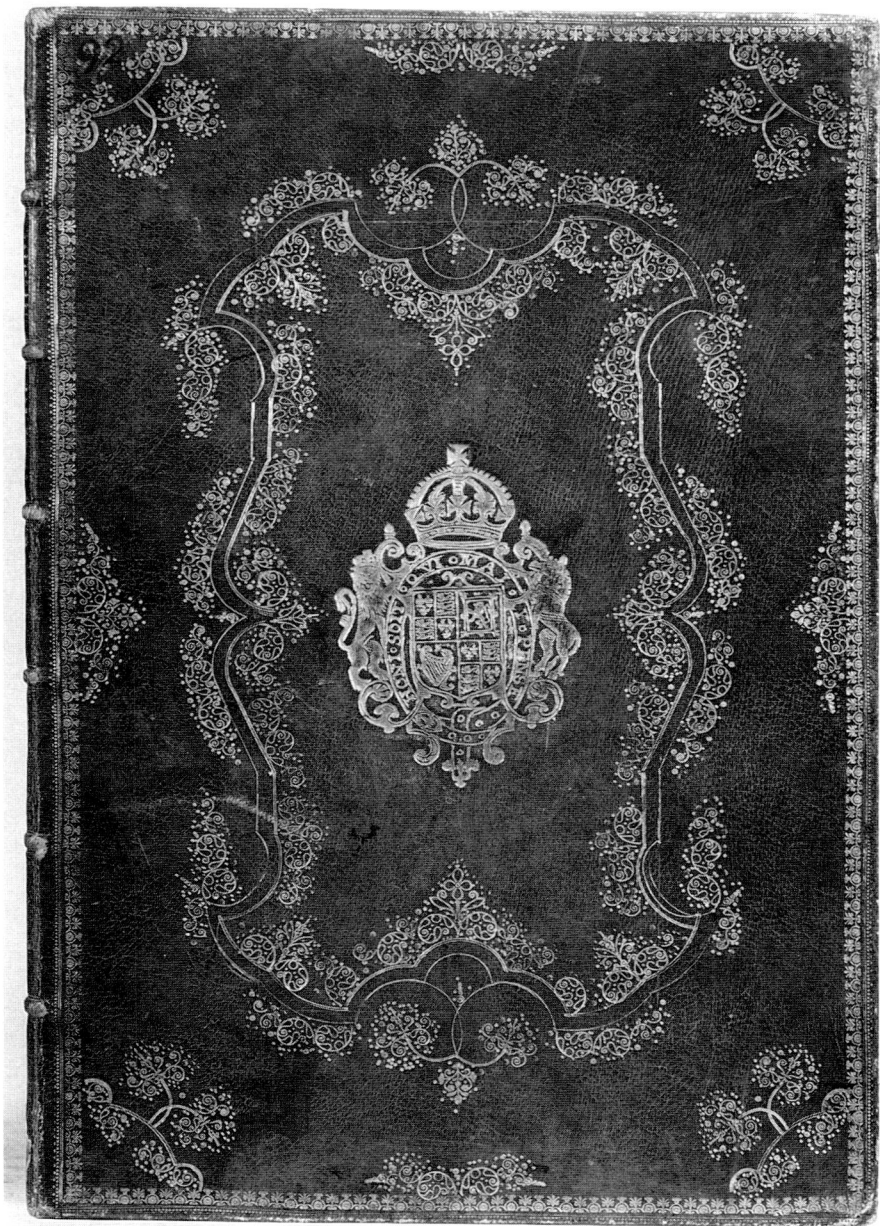

66. *Regulations 'To Establish good Government and Order in our Court'*, MS *c*.1675. Red goatskin, gold tooled, with the arms of Charles II.
BL Stowe MS 562. 375 × 260 × 15 mm.

67. *Octateuch* MS on vellum, *c.*1430. Red goatskin, tooled in gold and decorated with black and silver paint.
Magdalene College, Cambridge, Pepys, 1603. 212 × 144 × 75 mm.

68. *Book of Common Prayer*, Cambridge, 1666 [and] *Holy Bible*, Cambridge, 1668. Red goatskin, gold tooled.
BL 6. e. 3. 235 × 180 × 53 mm.

69 (left). E. Waller, *Poems*, London, 1668. Blue goatskin, gold tooled, with the arms of Mary d'Este, Duchess of York (later Queen Consort of James II). BL C. 28. e. 7. 176 × 115 × 20 mm.

70 (right). [R. Allestree], *The Government of the Tongue*, Oxford, 1667. Red goatskin, gold tooled, decorated with black and silver paint. BL C. 108. d. 32. 189 × 118 × 15 mm.

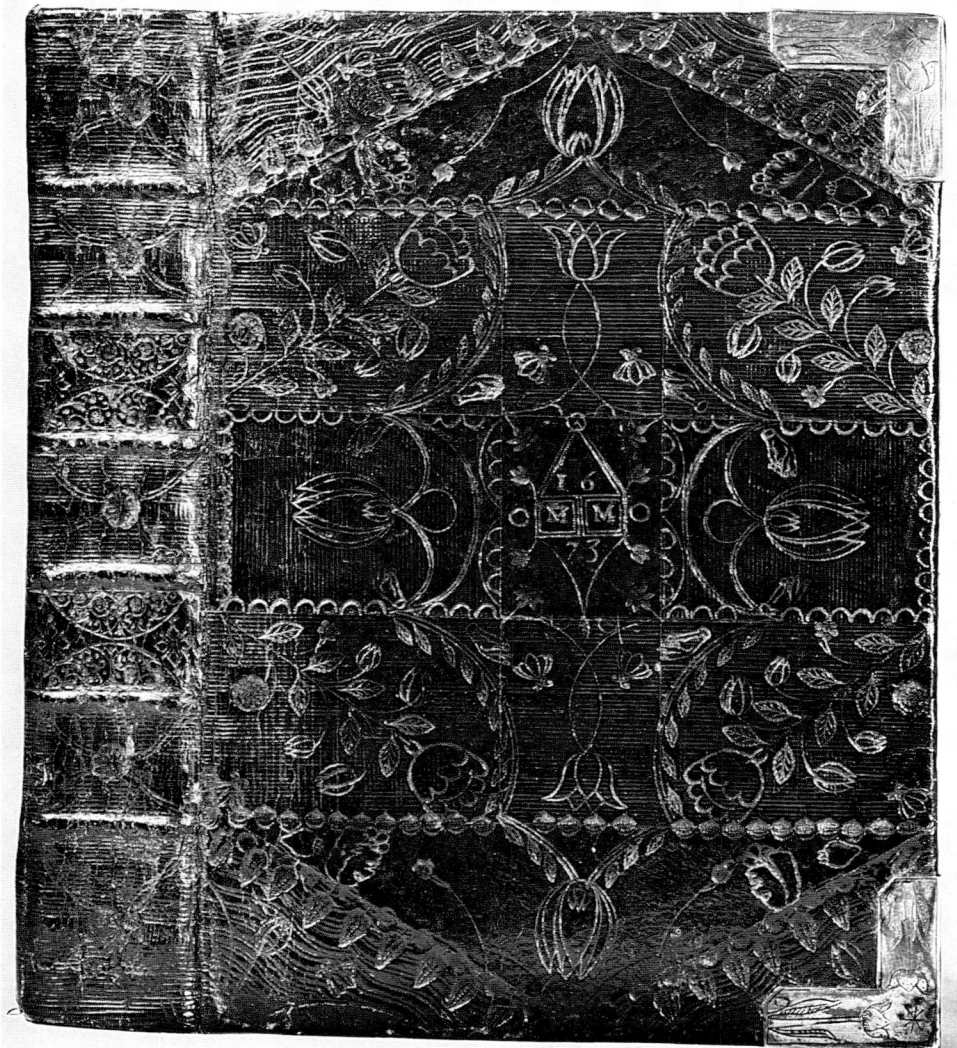

71. *Holy Bible*, London, 1660 [and] *Whole Book of Psalmes*, London, 1661. Black goatskin, blind tooled, with 'MM 1673'.
BL Henry Davis Gift. 168 × 115 × 36 mm.

72. G. J. Grelot, *Relation nouvelle d'un voyage de Constantinople*, Paris, 1680. Red goatskin, gold tooled.
BL 150. g. 16. 260 × 198 × 30 mm.

73. A. Cowley, *Works*, London, 1674. Dark-blue goatskin, onlaid in red, gold tooled. BL C. 69. h. 8. 302 × 198 × 32 mm.

74. *Book of Common Prayer* [and] *Holy Bible* [and] *Whole Book of Psalmes*, Cambridge, 1683. Black goatskin, onlaid in cream and red, gold tooled.
Pierpont Morgan Library, 55183. 238 × 185 × 84 mm.

75. E. Scarburgh, *The English Euclid*, Oxford, 1705. Red goatskin, gold tooled.
BL 59. f. 2. 450 × 293 × 32 mm.

76 (left). [R. Allestree], *The Ladies Calling*, Oxford, 1677. Red goatskin, gold tooled. Eton College. 188 × 123 × 20 mm.

77 (right). *Book of Common Prayer* [Greek], Cambridge, 1665, [and] *Whole Book of Psalmes*, London, 1663. Red goatskin, gold tooled. BL C. 69. ff. 9 (lower cover). 169 × 109 × 23 mm.

78. *A Declaration of the Royal Navy of England composed by Anthony Anthony . . . and by him presented to K. Hen[ry] 8 . . . 1546*, MS on vellum. Red goatskin, gold tooled. Magdalene College, Cambridge, Pepys, 2991. 567 × 375 × 50 mm.

79. J. Wallis, *Opera mathematica*, vol. 3, Oxford, 1699. Blue goatskin, gold tooled; the arms of George III have been added later.
BL 48. g. 3. 383 × 270 × 80 mm.

80. Edward, Earl of Clarendon, *The History of the Rebellion and Civil Wars in England*, Oxford, 1703–4 (vol. 3). Red goatskin, gold tooled.
BL 202. i. 4. 452 × 295 × 60 mm.

81. Joseph Gander, *The Glory of Her Sacred Majesty Queen Anne in the Royal Navy*, London, 1703. Red goatskin, onlaid in black, gold tooled. The central onlay with the cypher of George III has been added later.
BL 88. g. 19 (lower cover). 217 × 167 × 27 mm.

82. E. Settle, *Virtuti Sacellum. A funeral poem to the memory of . . . John Earl of Dundonald*, London, 1720. Black goatskin, gold tooled, with the arms of the Earl of Dundonald. BL C. 66. f. 16. 295 × 194 × 10 mm.

83. Marcus Annaeus Lucanus, *Pharsalia*, [Rome], 1469. Red goatskin, gold tooled. The arms of George III have been added later.
BL 167. i. 15. 329 × 229 × 33 mm.

84. Enea Silvio Piccolomini [*Pope Pius II*], *Cosmographiae liber*, MS 15th c. Red goatskin, gold tooled. Signed on the spine.
BL MS Harl. 3976 (lower cover). 327 × 225 × 57 mm.

85. Firmianus Lactantius, *Divinarum Institutionum adversus gentes libri 7*, MS 15th c. Red goatskin, gold tooled.
BL MS Harl. 3110. 346 × 235 × 62 mm.

86. R. Holland, *Observations on the Small Pox*, London, 1728. Red goatskin, gold tooled. Black goatskin doublures, gold tooled, with the cypher and motto of Queen Caroline.
BL 43. f. 16 (doublure lower cover). 202 × 129 × 20 mm.

87. *Carmina ad Nobilissimum Thomam Holles Ducem de Newcastle*, Cambridge, 1755.
Dark-blue goatskin, gold tooled.
BL C. 66. k. 11 (lower cover). 420 × 260 × 12 mm.

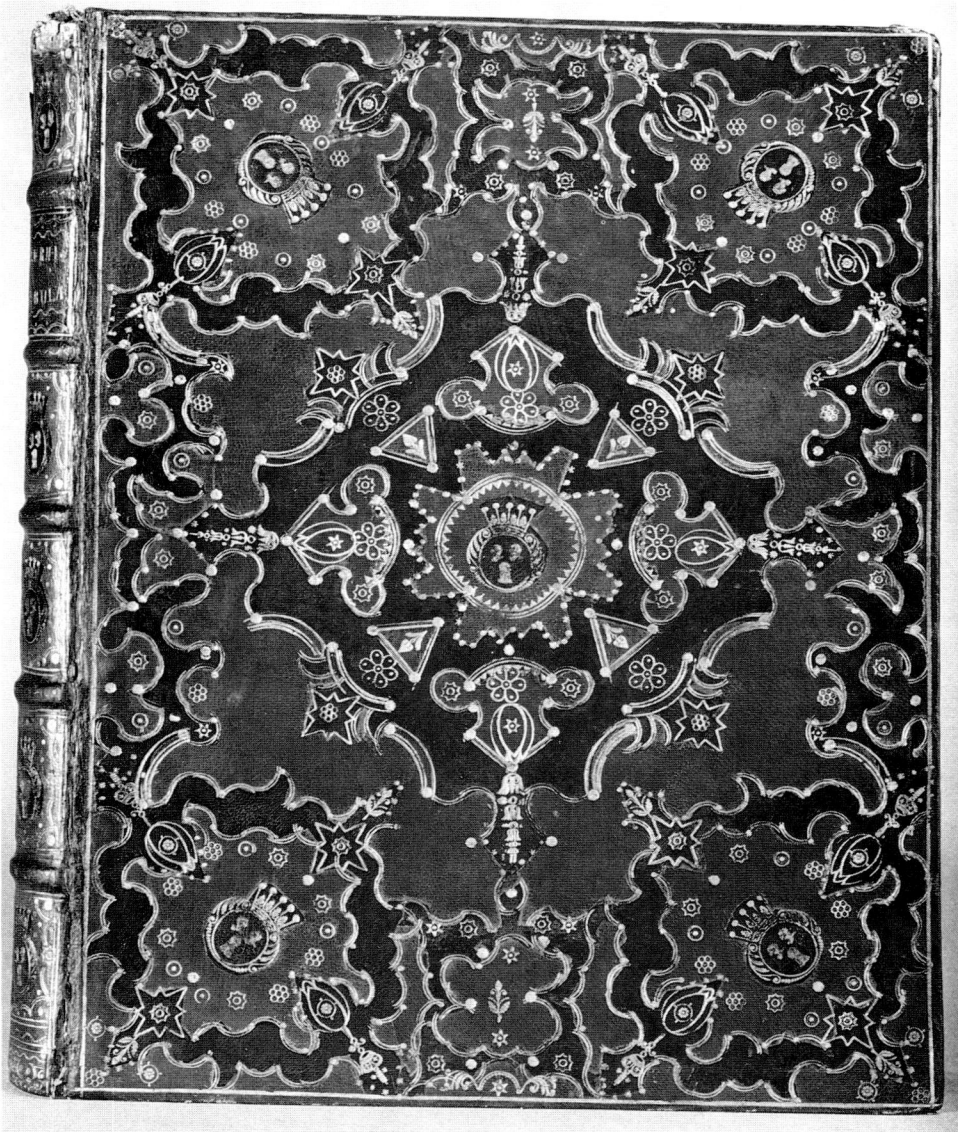

88. G. Faerno, *Fabulae Centum*, London, 1743. Red goatskin, onlaid in black, gold tooled, with the arms of George, 3rd Earl of Cholmondeley.
BL C. 67. f. 21. 302 × 235 × 40 mm.

89. Sir David Dalrymple, *Memorials and Letters relating to the History of Britain in the Reign of James I*, Glasgow, 1762. Red goatskin, gold tooled; the arms of H. Walpole may have been added later.
BL C. 108. ppp. 4. 184 × 120 × 20 mm.

90. M. Akenside and R. Glover, *Works*, London, 1737–58. Green goatskin, gold tooled. Gold-tooled brown calf doublures.
BL C. 108, g. 22. 271 × 205 × 54 mm.

91 (left). J. Toland, *The Life of John Milton*, London, 1761. Red sheep, gold tooled.
BL C. 66. e. 4 (lower cover). 206 × 130 × 27 mm.

92 (right). *A Letter from a Member of the Marine Society*, London, 1757. Red sheep, gold tooled.
BL 288. c. 29 (lower cover). 210 × 131 × 20 mm.

93. James Stuart and Nicholas Revett, *The Antiquities of Athens*, vol. 2, London, 1787. Red goatskin, gold tooled, with a paper onlay showing Pallas Athene. Collection A. G. Thomas (lower cover). 552 × 380 × 38 mm.

94. R. Adam, *Ruins of the Palace of the Emperor Diocletian, at Spalatro*, London, 1764.
Red goatskin, gold tooled, with the arms of George III.
BL 137. h. 10. 534 × 385 × 55 mm.

95. Lucius Apuleius, *The XI Bookes of the Golden Asse*, London, 1566. Red goatskin onlaid in brown calf and citron goatskin, gold tooled.
Huntington Library, 12926. 200 × 145 × 20 mm.

96. *Holy Bible*, Oxford, 1808. Black goatskin, gold tooled.
BL C. 155. a. 8 (lower cover). 305 × 239 × 74 mm.

97 (left). C. Lascaris, *Erotemata*, Venice, 1494/5. Olive-green goatskin, gold tooled, with the arms of C. M. Cracherode.
BL 1A. 24382. 210 × 152 × 25 mm.

98 (right). *Der gantze Psalter Königs und Propheten Davids*, London, 1751. Red goatskin, onlaid in black, citron, and green, gold tooled, with the arms, motto, and initials of George, Prince of Wales.
BL 218. d. 3. 173 × 103 × 19 mm.

99. James Beattie, *An Essay on the Nature and Immutability of Truth*, London, 1774. Red goatskin, gold tooled, with the cypher of George III and the initials J.B. BL 30. b. 17. 231 × 132 × 59 mm.

100. William Caslon, *A Specimen of Printing Types*, London, 1785. Red goatskin, gold tooled. Dedication copy to George III with his cypher.
BL 60. e. 18. 248 × 158 × 15 mm.

101. S. Butler, *Hudibras*, 3 vols., London, 1793 (vol. 1). Red straight-grain goatskin, gold tooled.
BL C. 155. c. 3. 300 × 235 × 42 mm.

102. Missal, MS *c*.1384 (vol. 2). Rebound in 2 volumes in brown, diamond-grained calf, gold and blind tooled.
Westminster Abbey, MS 37. 550 × 380 × 92 mm.

103. Bible [German], 2 vols., Nuremberg, 1483 (vol. 1). Maroon goatskin, sunk centre panel, gold and blind tooled, with the crowned cypher of George III. BL C. 11. d. 4–5. 420 × 285 × 57 mm.

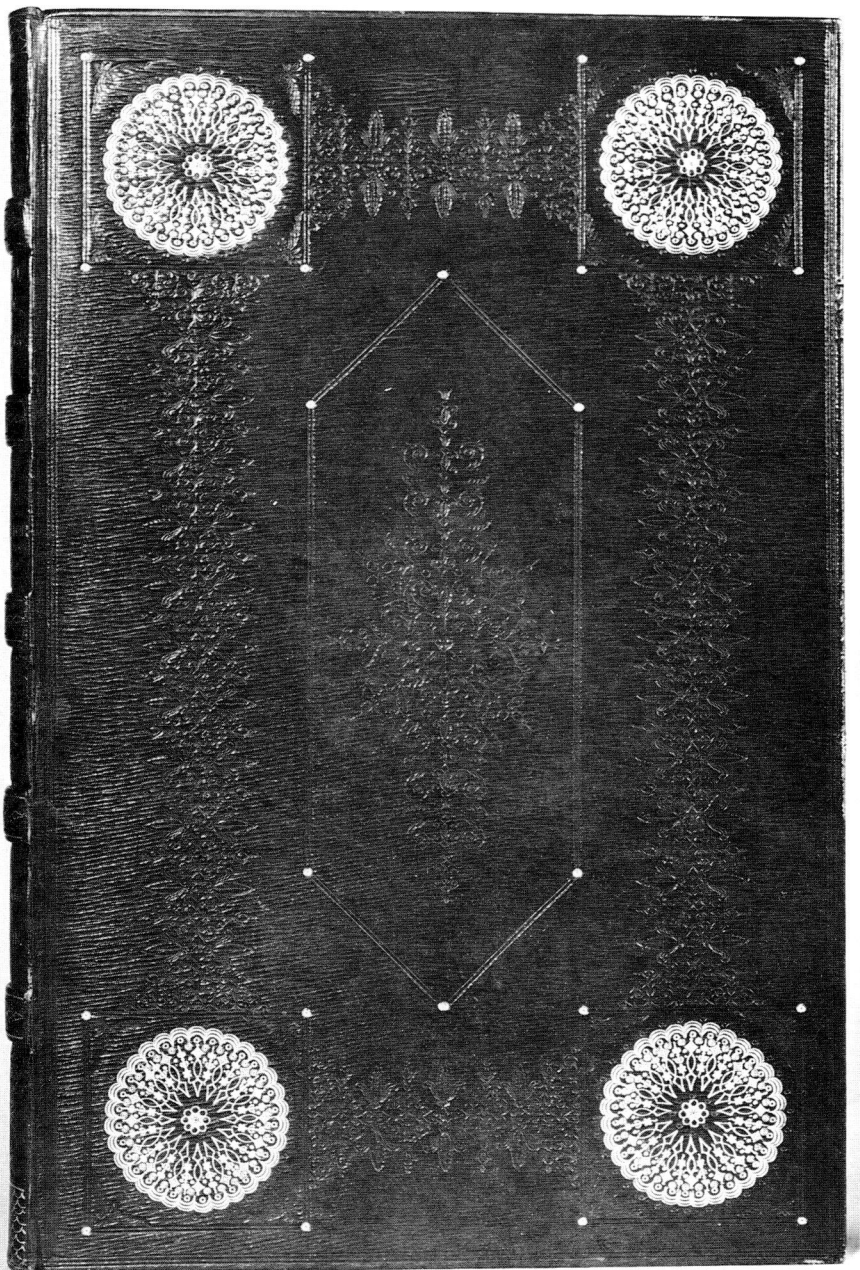

104. Sir William Dugdale, *The Antient Usage in Bearing ... Arms*, Oxford, 1682. Dark-blue, straight-grain goatskin, gold and blind tooled.
BL G. 11802. 357 × 225 × 29 mm.

105. Valerius Maximus, *Factorum et dictorum memorabilium libri*, Mainz, 1471. Blue straight-grain goatskin, gold tooled. The arms of Thomas Grenville have been added to the doublures.
BL G. 9153 (doublure lower cover). 284 × 195 × 69 mm.

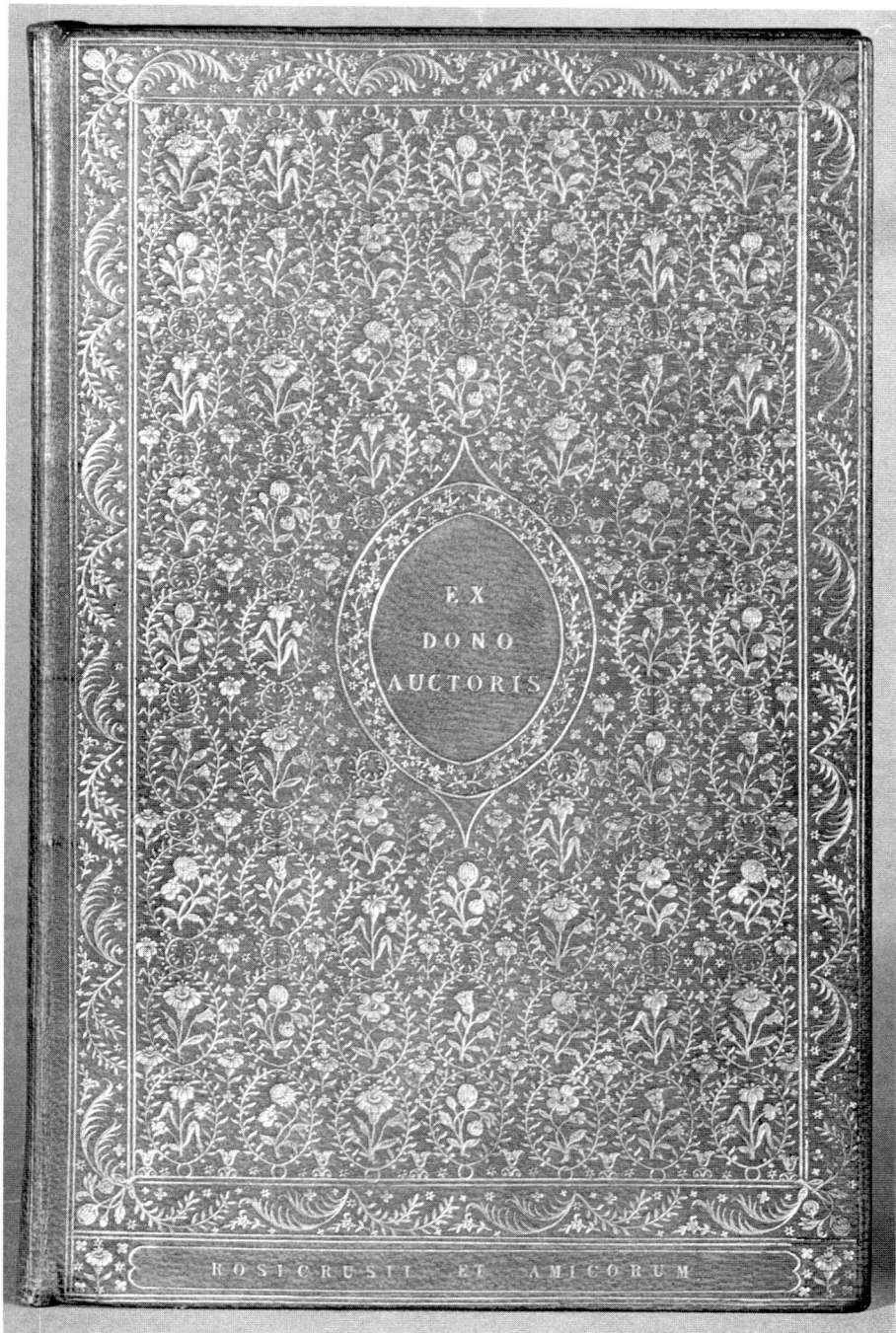

106. J. C. Brunet, *Manuel du libraire*, 4 vols., Paris, 1814 (vol. 1). Citron goatskin, gold tooled.
BL C. 151. f. 3. 232 × 149 × 39 mm.

107. H. Moses, *Vases from the Collection of Sir Henry Englefield, Bart.*, London, [1820]. Olive-green straight-grain goatskin, gold tooled, with the arms of the Hon. William Ponsonby.

BL C. 154. i. 13. 300 × 240 × 25 mm.

108. Shute Barrington, Bishop of Durham, *Sermons, Charges and Tracts*, London, 1811. Blue straight-grain goatskin, gold and blind tooled.
BL C. 151. g. 3. 231 × 140 × 35 mm.

109. I. Walton and C. Cotton, *The Complete Angler*, London, 1825. Green goatskin, gold tooled, with bronze medals of Walton and Cotton inserted. BL C. 151. d. 7. 200 × 130 × 55 mm.

110. *Jones' Views of the Seats, Mansions, Castles etc. of Noblemen and Gentlemen in England, Wales, Scotland and Ireland*, London, 1829. Red calf, embossed in blind.
BL C. 155. b. 11 (lower cover). 278 × 215 × 54 mm.

111 (left). Michael William Balfe, *The Bohemian Girl … the words by Alfred Bunn*, London, 1843. White vellum, gold tooled, decorated with coloured paint; with the royal arms. BL RM 5. d. 1. 217 × 140 × 8 mm.

112 (right). *The Good Shunammite*, London, 1847. Black *papier maché*. BL C. 30. b. 2. 167 × 115 × 13 mm.

113. A. Pitcairne., *Babell, a Satirical Poem*, Edinburgh, 1830. Dark-blue goatskin, onlaid in orange, red, green, blue, and white, gold tooled. Huntington Library, 109596. 260 × 206 × 22 mm.

114. Sir Thomas More, *The History of King Richard the Third*, Chiswick, 1821. Brown goatskin, gold tooled.
BL C. 72. c. 4. 255 × 158 × 18 mm.

115. F. Mistral, *Mireille*, Paris, 1884. Orange goatskin, onlaid in green and purple, gold tooled.
BL. C. 68. k. 2. 438 × 294 × 45 mm.

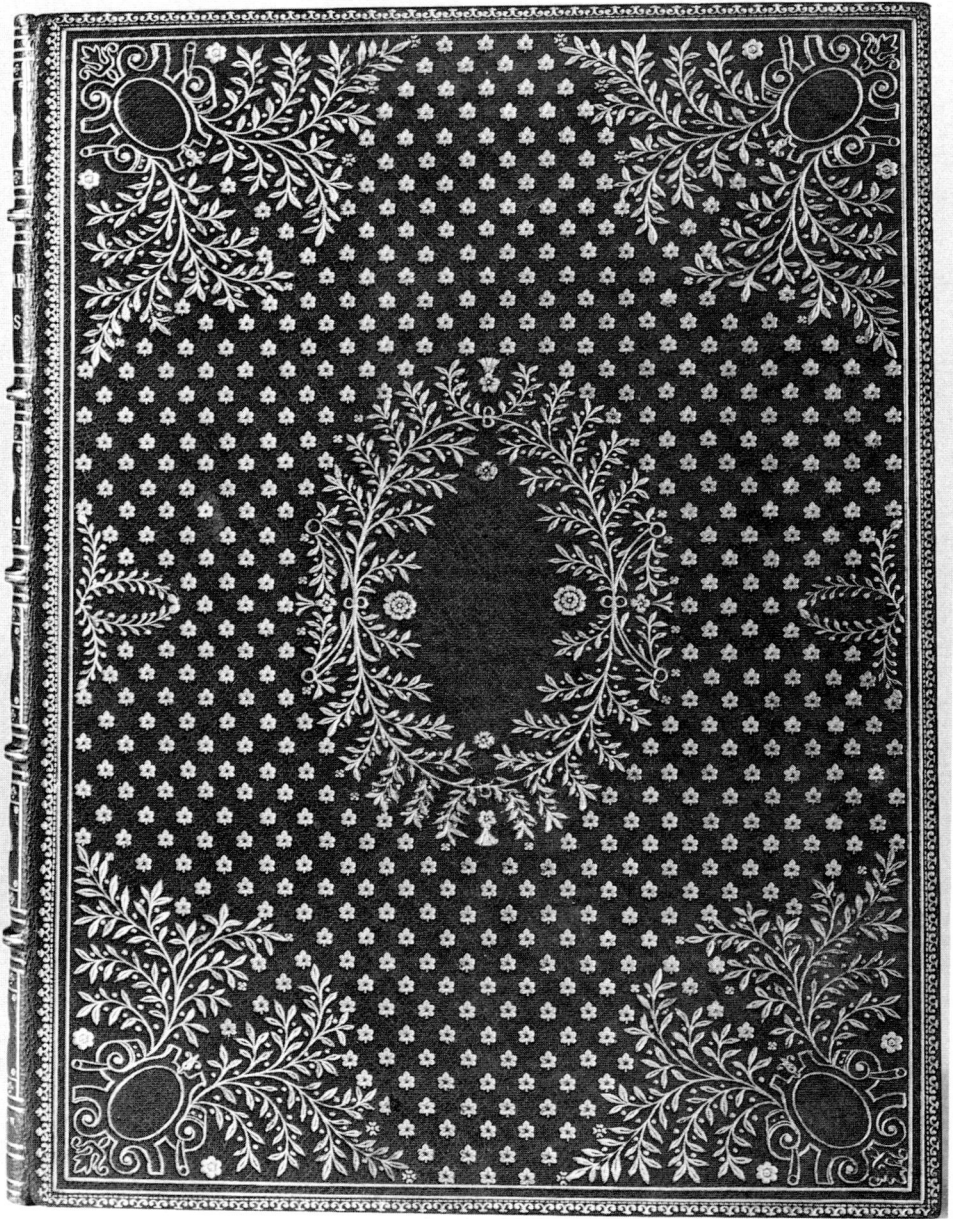

116. Tyell Eulenspiegel, *Howleglas*, London, 1867. Brown goatskin, gold tooled. BL C. 68. g. 1. 216 × 160 × 11 mm.

117. O. Uzanne, *La reliure moderne*, Paris, 1887. Green goatskin, onlaid in red, brown and orange, gold tooled.
BL C. 68. i. 18 (lower cover). 264 × 180 × 38 mm.

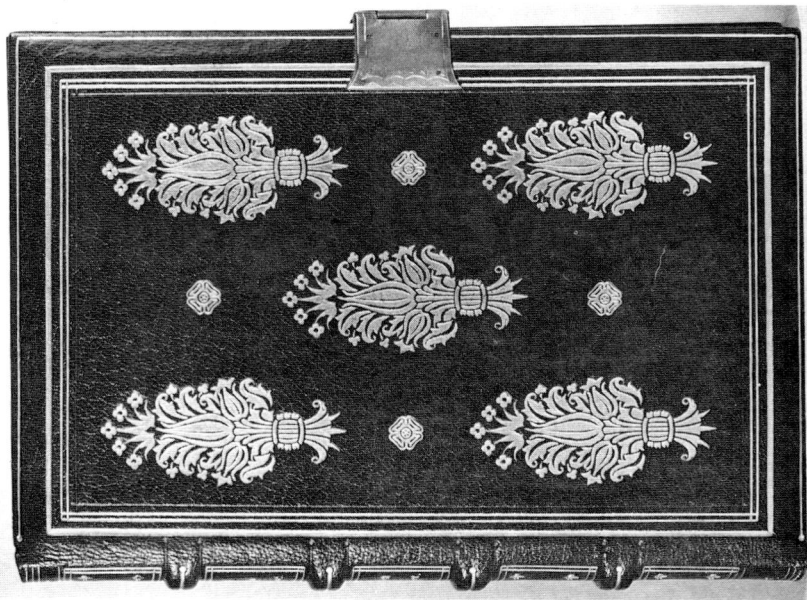

118 (left). S. Brant, *The Shyppe of Fooles*, London, 1517. Brown goatskin, gold tooled. BL C. 57. e. 12. 182 × 130 × 25 mm.

119 (right). Currer, Ellis, and Acton Bell (pseud.), *Poems*, London, 1846. Green goatskin, onlaid in red and fawn, gold tooled. BL C. 69. c. 6. 167 × 105 × 13 mm.

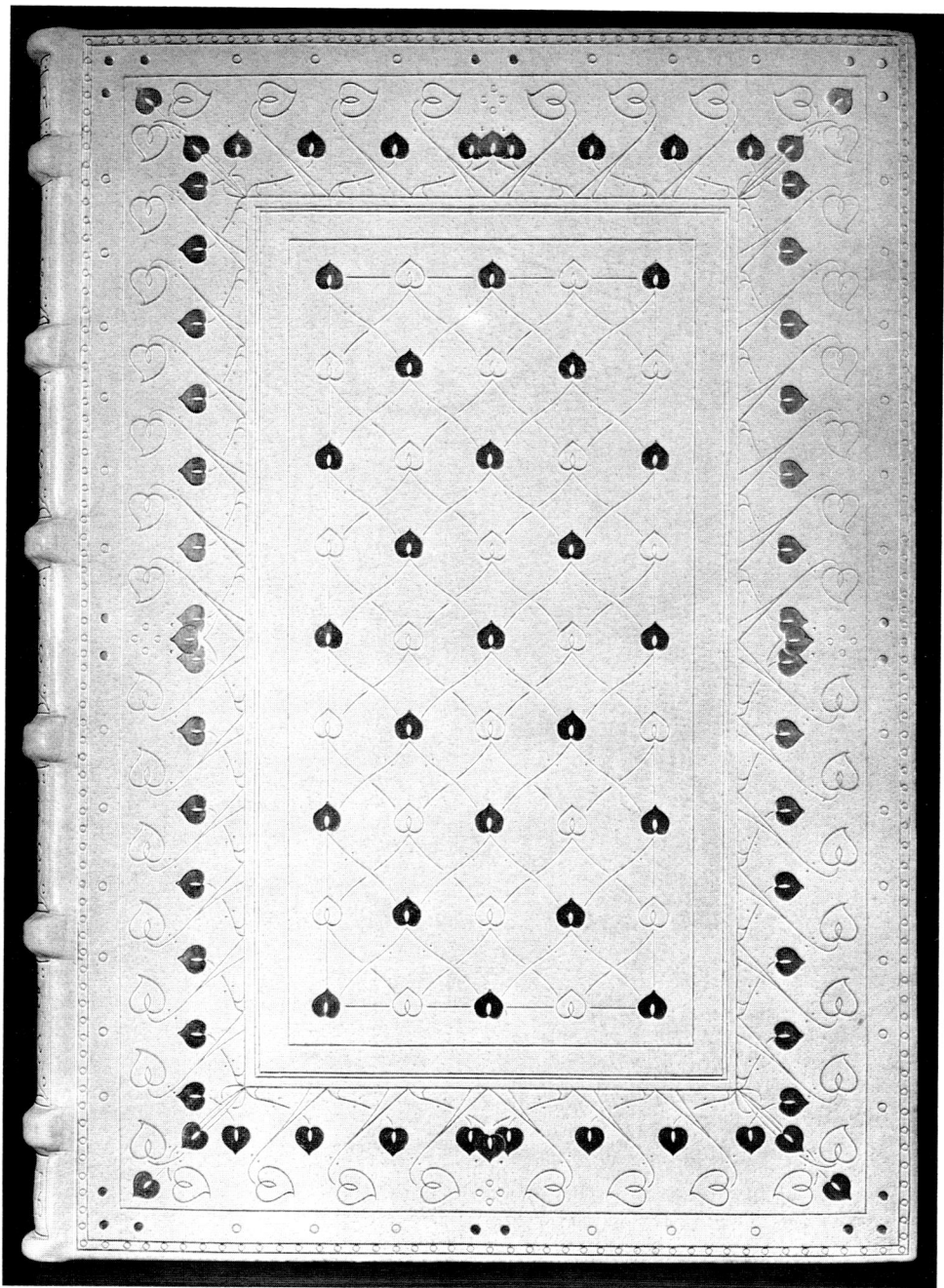

120. G. Chaucer, *Works*, Hammersmith (Kelmscott Press), 1896. White pigskin, gold tooled.
BL Ashley 5170. 431 × 295 × 65 mm.

121. J. A. Symonds, *Walt Whitman*, London, 1893. Dark-green goatskin, gold tooled. BL C. 143. b. 9. 230 × 167 × 27 mm.

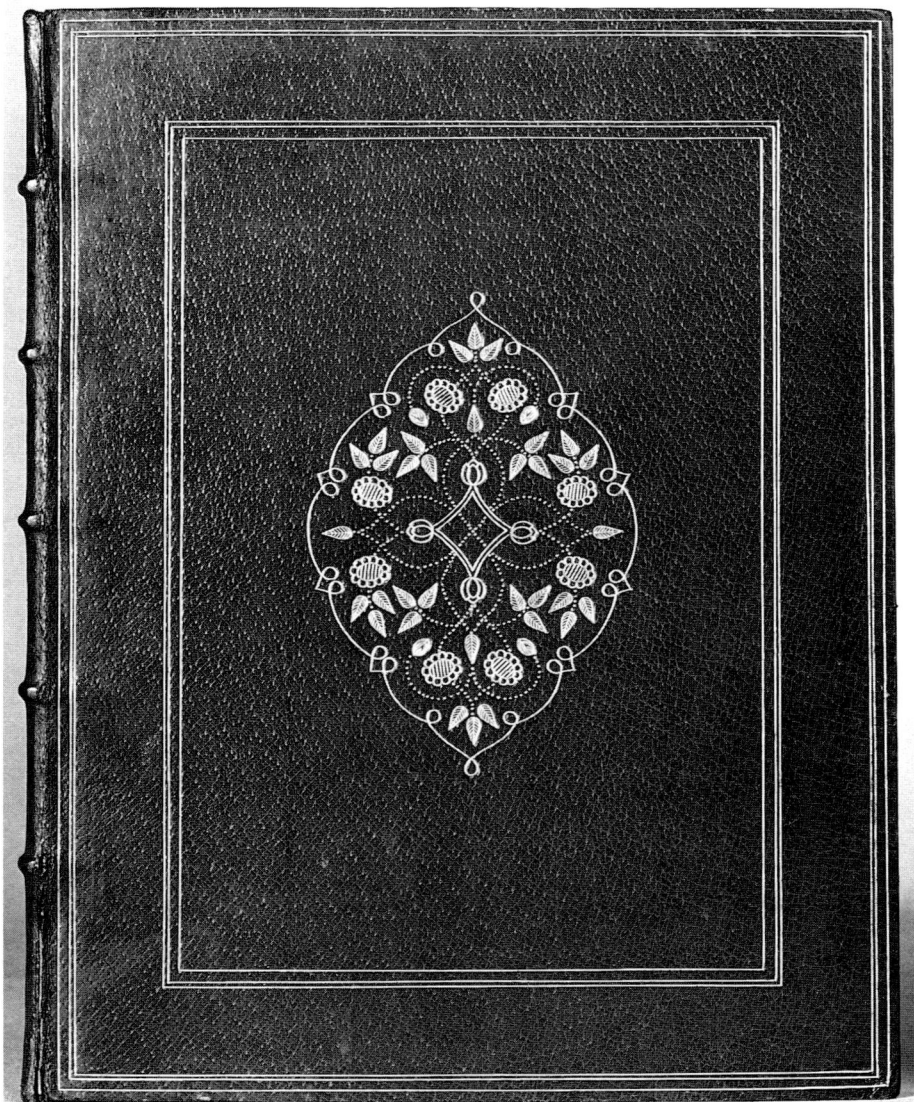

122. B. Thomas and H. G. Barker, *Our Visitor to 'Work-a-Day'*, typescript, [1899]. Red-brown pigskin, gold tooled.
BL C. 108. f. 4. 260 × 200 × 13 mm.

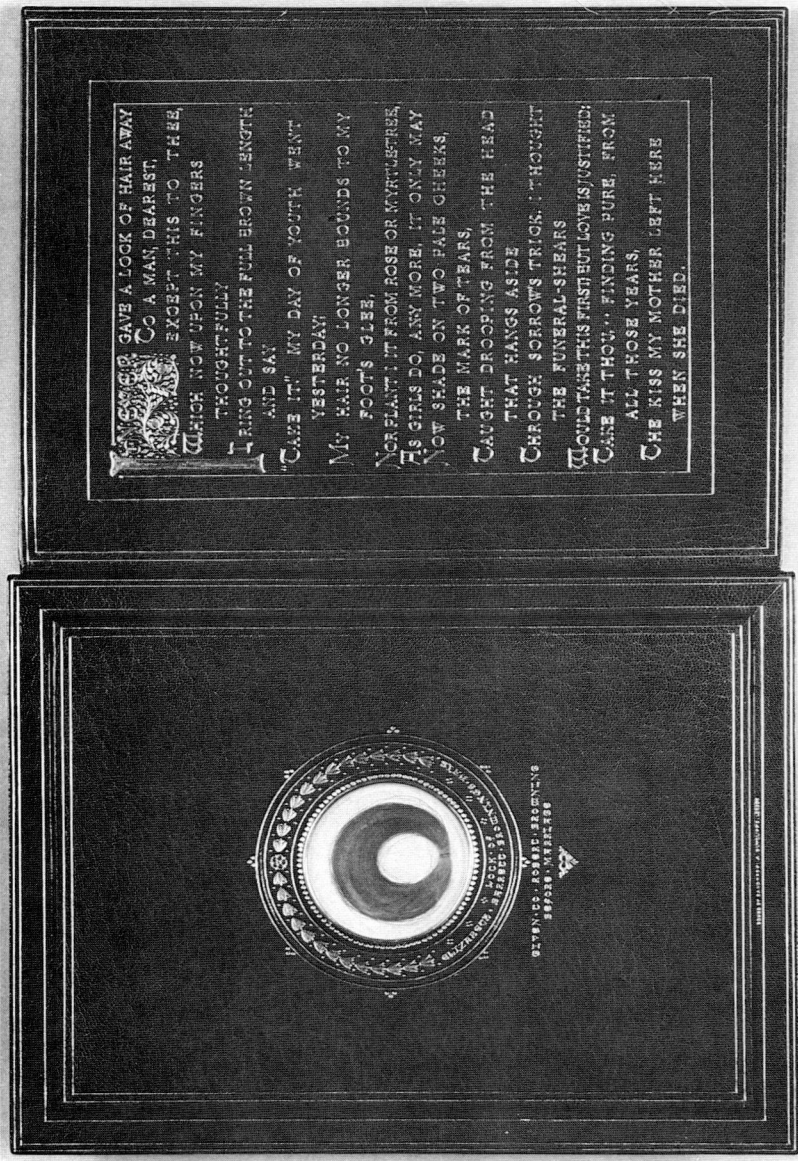

123. Elizabeth Barrett Browning, *Sonnets*. Reading, 1847. Red goatskin, gold and blind tooled. Doublures and fly-leaves of gold-tooled green goatskin. The doublure of the upper cover has a circular compartment containing a lock of Elizabeth Barrett Browning's hair. BL Ashley 4715 (doublure). 266 × 405 × 20 mm.

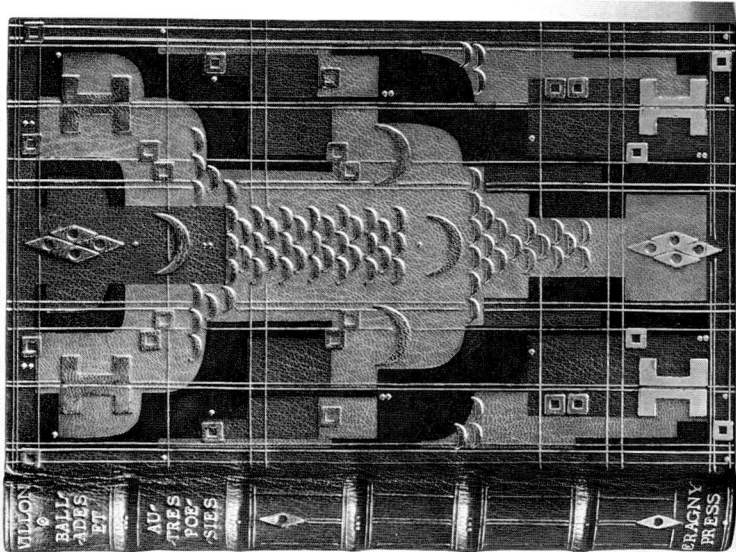

124 (left). Robert Burns, *Poems, chiefly in the Scottish Dialect*, Glasgow, 1927. Green goatskin, gold tooled, with inlaid painted medallions.
BL C. 108. e. 17. 233 × 146 × 23 mm.

125 (right). François Villon, *Les Ballades*, London, 1900. Orange goatskin, inlaid in green and fawn, gold tooled.
BL C. 108. bbb. 6. 200 × 130 × 23 mm.

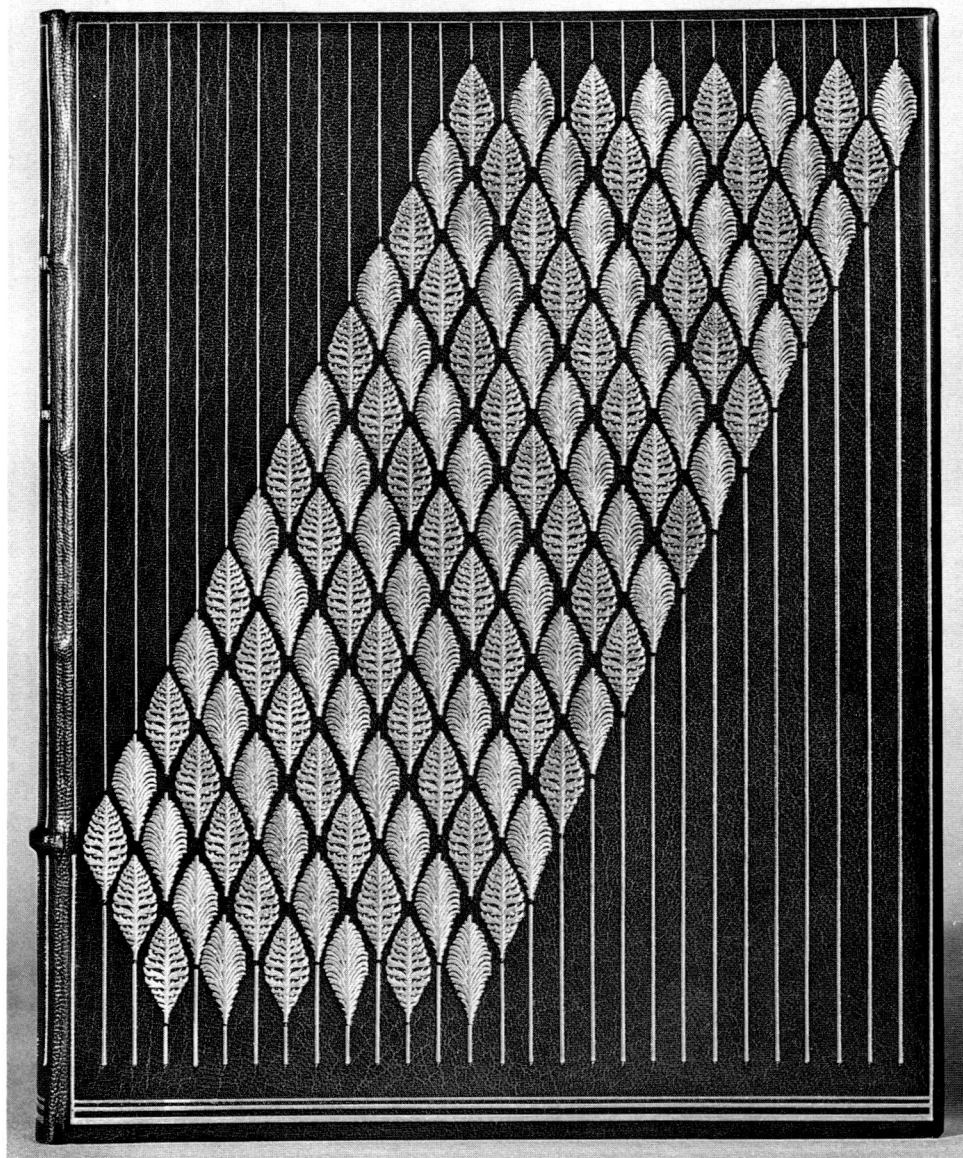

126. J. W. Fortescue, *The Story of a Red-Deer*, Newton, 1935. Brown goatskin, gold tooled..
BL C. 108. g. 2. 250 × 190 × 28 mm.

127. John Donne, *X Sermons*, London, 1923. Black goatskin, gold tooled.
BL C. 144. d. 8. 302 × 200 × 25 mm.

128. H. E. Bates, *Through the Woods*, London, 1936. Yellow goatskin, blind tooled.
BL C. 128. f. 10. 265 × 198 × 22 mm.